STREAMLINED
PROCESS
IMPROVEMENT

STREAMLINED PROCESS IMPROVEMENT

The Breakthrough Strategy to Reduce Costs, Improve Quality, Increase Customer Satisfaction, and Boost Profits

H. JAMES HARRINGTON

New York   Chicago   San Francisco   Lisbon
London   Madrid   Mexico City   Milan   New Delhi
San Juan   Seoul   Singapore   Sydney   Toronto

This publication is designed to provide accurate and authoritative information in regard to the subject matter covered. It is sold with the understanding that neither the author nor the publisher is engaged in rendering legal, accounting, securities trading, or other professional services. If legal advice or other expert assistance is required, the services of a competent professional person should be sought.

—From a Declaration of Principles Jointly Adopted by a Committee of the American Bar Association and a Committee of Publishers and Associations

McGraw-Hill books are available at special quantity discounts to use as premiums and sales promotions or for use in corporate training programs. To contact a representative, please e-mail us at bulksales@mcgraw-hill.com.

This book is printed on acid-free paper.

I dedicate this book to everyone with whom I have come in contact over the years. I am not me—I am the parts of the input I have received from all of you. As I grow older, I realize that as much as I would like to be the best, the real happiness is in the journey I am taking and the people with whom I come in contact along the way. I have been blessed far more than I deserve with true friendship that all of you have given so freely to me. I am sorry for some of the things I have done and even sorrier for some of the things I haven't done. My close friends have helped me develop some of my ideas, and my foes have shown me that there are always two sides to every situation and we all live in a complex world where right and wrong differ based upon where we stand and what we see. I have learned that even if I failed today, God gives me another day to do it right, but if I am wrong and God doesn't give me tomorrow as some time He will not, you should all know that your help, friendship, and love has made my life easier over the hard times and more enjoyable during the good times.

Finally, this book is dedicated to all those business leaders who wish to explore this brave new world of organizational excellence with the help of experienced guides and counselors in order to discover what works and what doesn't and to apply the lessons learned to their own organizational and business networks.

Thanks for all you have given me over the years.

Contents

Acknowledgments

I want to acknowledge Candy Rogers, who converted and edited endless hours of dictation and corrected misspelled words to turn out the finished product. I couldn't have done it without her dedication, help, and proofreading.

I also would like to acknowledge the many organizations whose senior management and boards of directors I have worked with over the past four decades who have helped to form the frameworks, concepts, ideas, and methods outlined in this book. And I would like to thank the many sponsors that helped me drive the research forward by participating in meetings, audio and video conferences, and roundtables.

In addition, I would like to thank the American Society for Quality (ASQ) and the International Academy for Quality for their unfailing support for advancing many of these concepts at the national and international level.

I would like to give special recognition to Alla Zusman, Boris Zlotin, Zion Bar-El, and Ron Fulbright, who helped me prepare the attachment on HU Diagrams. Alla and Boris provided key input in the development of this new methodology.

I would be remiss not to recognize all the inputs and constructive ideas that I received from Chuck Mignosa. He is always there to debate any subject and provide me with another point of view that helps to clarify my thinking.

I would also like to thank Frank Voehl and his Process Improvement Team at Nova Southeastern University for their insights and contributions to this book and to the Streamlined Improvement Process companion workbook that will be used to teach classes on using the SPI methodology.

STREAMLINED
PROCESS
IMPROVEMENT

Introduction to Streamlined Process Improvement (SPI)

Business Process Improvement (methodology) investigated and established by Dr. H. James Harrington and his group [represents] some of the new strategies which bring revolutionary improvement not only in [the] quality of products and services, but also [in] the business processes which yield the excellent quality of the output.

—Professor Yoshio Kondo,
the leading Japanese quality authority

Introduction

We have more opportunities to improve our processes than we have problems to solve.

—H. James Harrington

This book is designed to help you *streamline* your processes, making them more efficient and effective. This will allow you to sell your products and services at a lower price and still make more profit than your competitors. In car design, streamlining reduces an auto's air resistance, making it operate more effectively and making it more attractive to customers. On the other hand, a lean car has only the essentials.

When you streamline your processes, they operate at lower cost and cycle time and at increased efficiency and effectiveness. (See Figure 1.1.) In addition, the resulting changes are implemented with much less resistance and greater acceptance by the management team and the employees than processes redesigned using reengineering, DMADV, or Design for Six Sigma methodologies.

Today we hear a lot about Lean Six Sigma—it is the removal of all waste from the organization. Currently, most organizations could be represented by the overweight person in Figure 1.2.

Our processes are full of bureaucracy and waste. As we run into a problem, we just add more and more bureaucracy so that the problem will not reoccur. This just wastes time and money. A Lean Six Sigma organization could be represented by the person in Figure 1.3.

As you can see, the person in the figure is very lean; all fat has been removed. People who are that thin have often gone to extremes to lose the fat and keep it off, but in doing so, they have thrown their body's meaningful checks and balances out of kilter. They have often lost their natural protection from disease (problems) and are susceptible to any and all of the diseases that come along. Toyota got into its quality and recall problems because it got too lean. The streamlined organization can be represented by the figure in Figure 1.4.

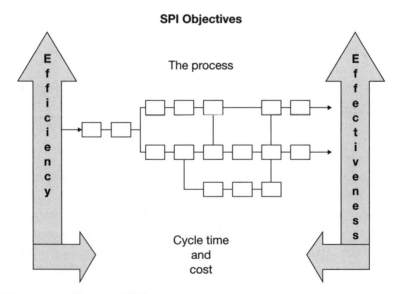

Figure I.I   Impact of SPI activities on processes

Figure 1.2   A very fat person

Figure 1.3   An extremely skinny person

Figure 1.4 Streamlined body

With streamlining you may start out as the person depicted in Figure 1.2, but after beginning an exercise program, you lose (remove) the waste and transform fat into muscle. You feel better, are healthier, and are more creative. You streamlined not only the processes, but also the way you think and go about doing business.

Streamlining Fundamentals

The following are the key fundamentals that must be considered when you undertake to streamline a process:

1. The process to be streamlined should be chosen based on how valuable it is to the organization, how badly the process is broken, and what the impact upon the organization would be if the process were improved.
2. It is a mistake to try to improve too many processes at the same time. Do only three or four at a time.
3. A good database that measures performance of the current process should be in place before you make changes to the process. This is

necessary so that you will be able to accurately measure the impact that the future-state solution has on the organization.

4. The way to begin is to ask the question, Is the process essential to the organization?
5. Simplification is better than computerization.
6. The real value of a process is how well it interacts with the other processes.
7. The best-designed process is worthless if it is not accepted by the people who will be using it.
8. Excellent communication and trust are key elements in making the streamlined process methodology a success.
9. The executive team needs to understand and fully support the SPI methodology and the output from the Process Improvement Team (PIT).
10. The external customer is the one who defines what the output from the process needs to be.
11. The combination of the process and the internal customer requirements must provide the organization with the best overall value. Internal customers' desires may not be honored unless they add value to the organization.
12. The white-collar processes have potential for quantum improvement.
13. The processes that service the external customers should be optimized, and the others should be designed to support them.
14. The total process key measurements need to be improved, not the measurements that are related to subprocesses within the major process.
15. The key process improvement indicators are increased external customer satisfaction, reduced output costs, reduced cycle time, and increased employee morale.
16. The people who will be key players in using the process should be included in the SPI projects.
17. The risks have to be understood before any changes are made to the process.
18. Streamlining requires resources; it can't be accomplished without a budget and people assigned to it. The employees assigned to the PIT should have their workload in other areas reduced by 20 to 40 percent.
19. The variation in the cycle time and output quality should be minimized.

Technology Warning

All too often, organizations jump to automate their processes without evaluating how effective the processes can function without being automated. This is usually a major error, as technology should serve the processes, not the other way around. Frequently, technology will speed up your processes so that you are able to make more errors faster than ever before. In other words, if the process is bad, automating it just causes an automated mess. Since technology is an enabler, rather than a process driver, it should only be applied after the process is streamlined. Far too often we automate a process or use technology to expedite the process when we should be simplifying the process. Carla Paonessa, a partner at Arthur Andersen Consulting, stated: "Just automating something that should not have been done manually won't get you to be more productive. What will work is eliminating bottlenecks, reducing mistakes, focusing on customer service, and then and only then, introducing new technologies" (Henkoff, 1991).

Employment Security

Employment security is one of the most critical and complex political and economic issues facing top management as a result of implementing SPI. An SPI project very often will reduce the workforce requirements by 30 to 60 percent. We have seen it reduce the number of people required to operate the process by as much as 80 percent. Not addressing this condition up front often results in the failure of an SPI project. Employees often look at a process improvement project as a way to reduce the number of employees. How can you expect your employees to give freely of their ideas to increase your productivity and minimize waste if it means that their job or a friend's job will be eliminated? If you start a continuous improvement process and then have layoffs, what you are going to end up with is employees who are continuously trying to sabotage your improvement process.

Corporate America has been on a downsizing kick since the late 1980s; its answer to business pressure is to slim down and lay off with the hope of raising stock prices, but that does not work. Three years after the downsizing, these organizations' stock values are negative on an average of 25 percent. Figure 1.5 shows stock prices going up right after

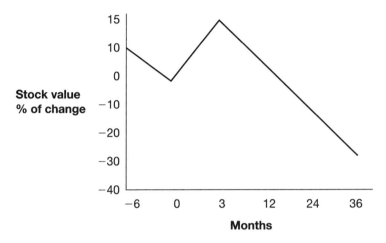

Figure 1.5   How the average stock price reacts to change

the downsizing because short-term profits were driven by the efforts expended before the downsizing. But soon the reduced resources and the loss of employee trust begin to be reflected in the organization's performance, and stock prices drop below the level before the downsizing. This stimulates another downsizing cycle.

SPI, on the other hand, attacks the same problem, the reduction of overhead costs, but does it without decreasing the ability of the organization to meet its external customer expectations. SPI allows the organization to "right-size" its processes, removing activities that are no-value-added from the external customer's standpoint. For example, Xerox was able to reduce its operating costs by $40 million per year by redesigning a few business processes. That's the equivalent of laying off over 1,000 employees.

> *We had done downsizing and old fashioned budget cutting, but we have never changed our business environment from the bottom up.*
> —Harry Beeth, Assistant Controller, IBM
> Corporate Headquarters (*CFO*, 1996)

Large layoffs produce sudden, substantial stock gains. These gains occur because the impact of the removed employees has not reached the customer and their compensation has been removed from the bottom line, making the organization appear to be more profitable than it really is. But in the long run, the downsizing has a negative impact. CEO Frank Poppoff of Dow Chemical put it this way, "Layoffs are horribly expensive and destructive of shareholder value."

The cost to lay off and replace is growing all the time. Dow Chemical estimates that it costs between $30,000 to $100,000 for technical and managerial-type personnel. Not only do layoffs cost the organization money and some of its best people, but when it comes time to hire, the best people do not trust the organization and will not come to work for it.

An alternative approach of a golden parachute or early retirement is equally bad. The people who leave are all the best performers who will not have a problem finding new jobs. The deadwood, who barely meet minimum performance, stay because they know it will be hard to find an equally good job in today's job market.

Employees can understand that the organization needs to cut back when demand for the product falls off, and they can accept that. The problem we face is what happens to the employees whose jobs have been eliminated due to performance improvement initiatives. We know that programs like SPI are designed to improve productivity, but if our share of the market does not keep pace with our productivity improvement, what will management do with the surplus employees? To cover this scenario and to alleviate employees' fears, top management should release a "no-layoff policy." A typical no-layoff policy would state: "No employee will be laid off because of improvements made as a result of the performance improvement initiative. People whose jobs are eliminated will be retrained for an equivalent or more responsible job." You will note that the policy does not guarantee that employees will not be laid off as a result of a downturn in your business. It only protects employees from being laid off as a result of the improvement process. These are people who would still be working if SPI had not been implemented.

Federal Express Corporation has a no-layoff philosophy. Its "guaranteed fair treatment procedure" for handling employee grievances is a model for firms around the world.

I know of one organization that was able to eliminate 200 jobs as a result of a performance improvement process. As the company started the improvement process, it put a freeze on new hires and used temporary employees to cover the workload peaks. This step was reviewed with the labor union leaders, and they concurred with the use of the temporary employees to protect regular employees' jobs. As a result, attrition took care of about 150 surplus jobs. The organization held a contest to select 50 employees who were sent to a local university to work toward an engineering degree. While at school, they received full pay, and their additional expenses were paid for by the organization. Results were phenomenal. All the employees within the organization started to look for ways to eliminate their jobs so they could go to school.

> *Organizations that believe that if it isn't broke don't fix it are slaves to the status quo.*

> —H. James Harrington

What Is Streamlined Process Improvement?

We have taken away the employee's God-given right to do error-free work by not providing them with processes that are capable of error-free performance.
—H. James Harrington

Introduction

Upper management provides the vision and direction, teams correct the problems, and individuals provide the creativity, but it is the processes within any organization that get things done. No matter how good your management and your employees are, your organization cannot be successful if it is using the same business processes it used in the 1990s.

The question in everyone's mind today is, To be more competitive, should the organization concentrate on continuous improvement or on breakthrough methodologies? In research and development, people argue whether to spend more of their R&D dollars on basic research or on applied research. The answer to both questions is that you must do both to survive.

Department improvement teams, natural work teams, task teams, self-managed work teams, Statistical Process Control, Quality Function Deployment, suggestion systems, etc., all have focused upon continuous improvement, and we do need continuous improvement. But some parts of our business need that "jump-start." Many of the processes that we are using to manage the organization need to have their associated costs and cycle time cut by 50 percent within the next 12 months. When you need a major reduction in cycle time or cost and an improvement in output quality in a specific business process, a methodology called *Business Process Improvement (BPI)* is used. It is also sometimes called *Business Process Management (BPM)*, and it combines methodologies like benchmarking, Streamlined Process Improvement (SPI), process reengineering, focused improvement, new process design, process innovation, activity-based costing, and new process specification into one logical way of initiating drastic, rapid change in a single business process. This book focuses on just one of these methodologies—SPI, which is sometimes called *process redesign* because about 80 percent of the BPI improvements are the result of this approach.

A two-year study of product organizations in Canada, Germany, and the United States asked the question, "What tools will be of primary importance in achieving future quality improvements?" A list of 10 choices was provided from which to select the most important. In Japan, Failure Mode and Effect Analysis was number 1, and BPI was number 2. In Germany, Pareto Analysis was number 1, and BPI was number 2. In the United States, Statistical Process Control was number 1, and BPI was number 2. Based upon these data, it is easy to see that in the coming years, BPI will be the most important approach used to improve organizations worldwide. Continuous improvement results in a 10 to 20 percent improvement in the total organization per year. BPI will give you a 30 to 90 percent reduction in cost, cycle time, and error rates in as short a time as six months for the single process to which it is applied. (See Figure 2.1.)

The primary difference between the BPI methodology and continuous improvement is that continuous improvement focuses on eliminating and preventing errors. Breakthrough improvement focuses on doing the right things right all the time. Let's look at a good example: An older-model electronic organ used 163 parts to simulate the sound that a violinist makes when rocking his or her finger on the violin string. The unit did an excellent job. But when the unit was streamlined (redesigned), the same function was produced with only 51 parts at 40 percent of the cost, with increased reliability and equally good sound quality.

The following are typical examples of the improvements that have been realized when SPI methodology was used to improve processes:

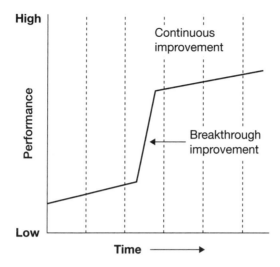

Figure 2.1 Continuous versus breakthrough improvement applied to a process

Environment	Industry	Results
Accounts payable	Semiconductor	65% reduction in cost
Accounts payable	Air carrier	35% reduction in departmental cost
Claims processing	Insurance	30 to 40% reduction in cost and cycle time
Administrative services	Insurance	60% reduction in per-transaction cost while volume of transactions was growing 350%
General accounting	Paper products	30 to 40% reduction in account closing cycle time

At the General Dynamics–Convair Division in San Diego, California, SPI was used to identify cost reduction opportunities totaling $250 million (from a total budget of $1 billion) and a cycle time reduction equaling 30 percent of the entire product cycle time.

IBM, by focusing on entertainment expense reporting, treasury, and information management, was able to realize $178 million in annual cost savings (*CFO*, 1996).

What Are Business Processes?

If people are the heart of the organization, then processes are the brain. The organization's processes define how activities are conducted and include both the production and support activities.

> **Definition:** A *process* is any activity or series of activities that takes an input, adds value to it, and provides an output to a customer.

Based upon this definition, everything we do is a process. The alarm goes off in the morning, and that starts our getting-dressed process. The phone shatters the tranquility of our office, and our communication process gets started. Our spouse calls out, "Dinner's on!" and that starts our nourishment process.

These examples are all very personal, but they make the point. In an organization, large processes involve many different functions and departments within functions existing and coexisting in order to manage the organization. The new product development process, for example, involves research and development, marketing, manufacturing, quality assurance, manufacturing engineering, sales, field services, production control, and other functions. The order entry process involves sales, scheduling, purchasing, production control, and information services. These are large cross-functional processes that determine how the organization functions. The success of the total organization depends largely upon how streamlined and responsive these processes are.

No matter how good your managers are, no matter how hard your employees try, if your critical business processes are outmoded and ineffective, all the stakeholders are going to lose. Unfortunately, too many managers feel that either they or their employees are the problem, when, in truth, it is the processes that are the problem. If anyone is at fault, it is management, because the managers have not recognized the crying need to improve the organization's business processes and have not assigned the required resources to improve them.

Typical improvement realized when SPI methodology is applied to a business process ranges between 300 to 1,500 percent in as short as a six-month period. Because SPI yields such drastic improvement, it is often one of the tools applied during the first year of a three-year performance improvement plan. I have also seen organizations that have started with SPI when upper management could not unanimously agree on implementing the total improvement process or did not have the resources. It's a wonderful methodology to save a few million dollars and free up some resources to help with the implementation of Total Improvement Management (TIM). (See Harrington, 1995, for more information on TIM.)

Compaq Computers provides a good example of the type of savings that can be realized by applying SPI-type approaches to a few critical business processes. Compaq focused on 10 sales, marketing, and logistic projects. As a result of the company's process improvement activities, it identified in excess of $100 million in potential savings. In addition:

- There was a 50 percent reduction in elapsed time to respond to fluctuations in demand mix.
- There was a 50 percent reduction in carrying costs necessary to meet a target level of market responsiveness.
- The average lead time was reduced by 10 to 20 percent on selected commodities.

A business process is a series of logically related activities that utilize resources to provide specific results required to achieve a basic business objective. SPI makes use of the people involved in the process to measure, analyze, document, streamline, benchmark, and improve these business processes.

There is a hierarchy to our business processes. At the top there are the systems processes. Typically the entire organization can be divided into 6 to 10 system processes, which can then logically be divided into major processes. Major processes are work flow that is required to conduct a major business objective. Major processes can be divided into subprocesses. A subprocess is a logically related sequence of work flow that makes up portions of the major processes. Subprocesses can be further

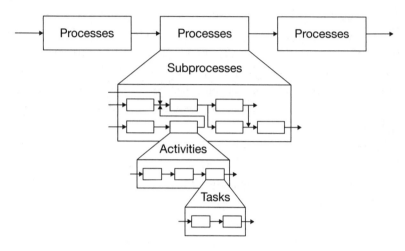

Figure 2.2 Process hierarchy

divided into activities. Activities take place within the process. They are usually performed by units of one (one person or one department). Activities can be divided into tasks, which are detailed steps to perform an individual activity. Most of the improvement comes as a result of changes at the activity level, although in some cases entire subprocesses are eliminated. (See Figure 2.2.)

Why Use SPI?

SPI is a systematic way of using interfunctional teams to analyze and improve the way the organization operates by improving the effectiveness, efficiency, and adaptability of the organization's processes. What will SPI do for your organization?

Improves	**Reduces**
Effectiveness	Costs
Efficiency	Cycle time
Customer satisfaction	Variation
Morale	Interdepartmental conflict
Adaptability	Bureaucracy

Why change? The following is a list of typical reasons why processes are streamlined. They are streamlined to:

- Address the lack of system flexibility
- Lower costs
- Move decision making closer to the customer
- Streamline our ability to meet customer satisfaction
- Shorten return on investment cycle
- Increase market share
- Improve productivity
- Increase access to and control of information
- Minimize the number of contacts that customers have
- Make the customers feel that they are getting customized service
- Get a competitive advantage or edge
- Grow profits
- Increase return on assets
- Make it easy for customers to do business with us
- Make use of technology that is out there but that we aren't yet using
- Keep up with our competition
- Improve employee morale
- Increase market share
- Minimize bureaucracy
- Meet customer delivery schedules
- Decrease backlog
- Introduce changes because the present process will not meet the strategic plan goals
- Reduce inventory
- Improve quality

The following are the kind of changes that occur when an organization streamlines its processes:

- Work units change—from functional departments to process teams
- Jobs change—from simple tasks to multidimensional work
- People's roles change—from controlled to empowered
- Job preparation changes—from training to education
- Focus of performance measures and compensation shifts—from activity to results
- Advancement criteria change—from performance to ability
- Values change—from protective to productive
- Managers change—from supervisors to coaches

- Organizational structures change—from hierarchical to flat
- Executives change—from scorekeepers to leaders

Typical examples of improvement that have been realized using SPI are:

- Output quality improved by 100 percent
- Overhead cost reduced by 30 to 50 percent
- Cycle time reduced by 40 to 60 percent
- Lead times reduced from weeks to hours
- Number of ideas the employees generated increased by 100 percent and quality of the ideas improved by 50 percent
- Capacity increased by 40 to 60 percent
- Inventory reduced by 50 to 70 percent

How Management Has Been Misled

After using a continuous improvement strategy for 10 years, Alcoa Corporation's CEO, Paul H. O'Mull, scrapped it, calling it a major mistake. He felt that Alcoa needed a quantum improvement to reach world-class standards.

All too often, management has compared these drastic breakthrough improvements to the 10 to 15 percent per year improvements that continuous improvement methodologies are realizing. Based upon this comparison, management has directed its efforts to the SPI methodology, expecting profits to increase 500 to 1,000 percent. Why, then, doesn't the SPI methodology improve the bottom line as management expects? Why does a continuous improvement effort of 15 percent per year provide better results than the SPI methodology? The answers lie in understanding the difference between the impact that breakthrough improvement and continuous improvement have on your bottom line.

Breakthrough versus Continuous Improvement

If you are not improving, you are not holding still; instead, you are slipping backward at a rate of about 5 to 10 percent per year compared with what your competitors are doing, because they are improving (see Figure 2.3). For the sake of discussion, let's assume that a typical organization has conservatively 500 business processes going on within the organization. Experience has proved that you should not attack all these business processes at the same time, because applying SPI to even one process has a major impact on and causes disruption in the entire organization. Applying SPI to more than three processes at the same time tends to make the organization go out of control. IBM tried applying SPI to 78 of its critical business processes at one time at its site in San Jose, California, and soon learned that it was having difficulty assimilating the changes because so many things were changing at once.

Let's assume that an organization works with 3 processes per year out of the 500 processes, and each of the 3 processes improves 1,000 percent. This would improve the total organization's performance by only 6 percent $[(3/500) \times 1,000\% = 6\%]$.

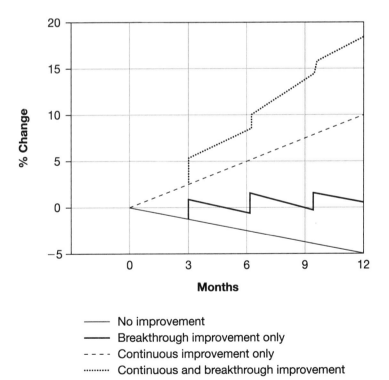

Figure 2.3 Comparative performance change with continuous and breakthrough improvement

Now consider that the other 497 processes degrade 5 percent over the year because they are not improving. The net result is only a 1 percent improvement (see Figure 2.3).

Let's compare these results with those obtained using a continuous improvement methodology applied to all 500 processes at a rate of 10 percent per year improvement (see Figure 2.3). You can see that the continuous improvement methodology results in a 9 percent per year advantage over the SPI methodology and a 15 percent advantage over competitors if they are not using continuous improvement or breakthrough methodologies. This advantage is achieved because the total workforce is working to improve all the business processes and the production processes.

When breakthrough improvement and continuous improvement are combined, the result is a 60 percent improvement per year over continuous improvement alone. It is for this reason that both continuous and breakthrough improvement must be used by organizations that truly want to be the very best.

The following table shows the difference in the ways an organization approaches continuous and breakthrough improvement.

		Continuous Improvement	SPI
1.	Target	Errors	Process
2.	Timing	Long term	Short term
3.	Change level	Gradual	Dramatic
4.	Magnitude of change	Small steps	Big steps
5.	Improvement impact	Continuous and incremental	Intermittent
6.	Type of change	Constant and gradual	Abrupt and violent
7.	Change agents	Everyone	Small groups
8.	Approach	Team building and problem solving using consensus to maintain and improve	Innovative team and individualism used to dissect and rebuild
9.	Effort	Easy to start; hard to maintain	Hard to start; little effort required to maintain
10.	Technology	Problem solving, common sense, and common knowledge	New inventions, streamlining, and information technology

	Continuous Improvement	SPI
11. Primary focus	People	Processes
12. Usage	Effective all the time	Most effective when behind or in a fast-growing economy
13. Magnitude of improvement	5 to 15% per year	30 to 60% per process

What SPI Is Not

SPI is not an experimental, theoretical model. It has been successfully implemented in companies such as Corning, Boeing, IBM, LTV, Nutrasweet, Florida Power & Light, and Compaq; it has been used in large companies like Ford and in small companies like AccuRate, which had only 85 employees. I have been using it for over 25 years. Early work started on the SPI methodology within IBM during 1982. Since that time, it has developed into a proven, exact methodology refined through years of experience under different organizational environments. During its evolution, parts of the methodology have been known by many names, including *process redesign, focused improvement, process innovation,* and *process streamlining.*

Why Improve Your Business Processes?

Our business processes were created to fulfill a specific need, but from that point on, most of them were neglected. They were not updated, not reviewed, not refined, not audited, and they did not keep pace with the changing business needs. When the process failed, management quickly intervened and put in a quick fix. Soon our business processes looked like patchwork quilts.

Over the years our business environment has changed, becoming more and more complex, but our business processes have not kept pace. In fact, they have changed very little. In the 1980s we could afford to make a major business blunder, come out with products six months late, and still have a profitable organization. Today, a six-month slip in a new product will cause a company to completely miss the product window.

The acceptable margin for error that was built into our business processes has now disappeared.

In our manufacturing processes we expect our employees to produce output at the parts-per-million level, but in our business processes, we accept a 20 percent error rate as acceptable, and often even consider this as outstanding performance. Over 30 percent of the people who request information by telephone from the IRS receive faulty information. The vice president of Saab's Research and Development Group reported that the group's poor-quality cost was running at 78 percent of the total R&D budget. Approximately 55 percent of the finance department's budget is poor-quality cost. In manufacturing the scrap goes out in scrap barrels. In the white-collar areas it goes out in the waste basket. Boeing, to impress upon its white-collar workers the importance of doing the right thing right every time, brought together all of its employees in a large hangar. Suddenly the hangar doors opened and truck after truck backed in and dumped piles and piles of paper on the floor. Soon the employees were standing knee-deep in paper. When the caravan of trucks stopped, management appeared on the balcony pointing out to the employees that this was the white-collar scrap for last week for which they were responsible.

How to Improve Your Business Processes

The complexity of our business environment and the many organizations involved in the critical business processes make it necessary to develop a very formal approach to SPI. This methodology is called PASIC, and it is conveniently divided into five subprocesses (phases) that consist of a total of 31 different activities. (See Figure 2.4.)

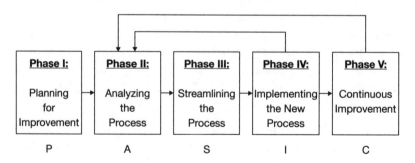

Figure 2.4 The five phases of the SPI methodology

Phase I: Planning for Improvement (eight activities)

Phase II: Analyzing the Process (eight activities)

Phase III: Streamlining the Process. Refining the process (six activities)

Phase IV: Implementing the New Process. Installing the new process (six activities)

Phase V: Continuous Improvement. Making small-step improvements (three activities)

In a personal letter dated July 14, 1990, Dr. W. Edwards Deming, one of the world's leading quality consultants, wrote, "I teach optimization of a system and the aim of the system. I do not associate my name with Total Quality, because I have no idea what people mean by these words."

Phase I: Planning for Improvement

> **Definition:** The *Process Improvement Team (PIT)* consists of a group of people who are responsible for creating a streamlined process over a two- to three-month period. The team is usually made up of 6 to 10 people who represent the key departments involved in the process being streamlined and some key technical experts. They will usually devote about 50 percent of their time to streamlining the assigned process.
>
> **Definition:** *Executive Improvement Team (EIT)* consists of a group of top managers who oversee the improvement efforts for the organization.

During Phase I the EIT is trained on the SPI methodology, selects the critical processes, and assigns process owners. The process owners organize a PIT that sets process boundaries, establishes total process measurements, identifies process improvement objectives, and develops a project plan. There are eight activities in this phase (also see Figure 2.5):

- Activity 1: Define Critical Business Processes
- Activity 2: Select Process Owners

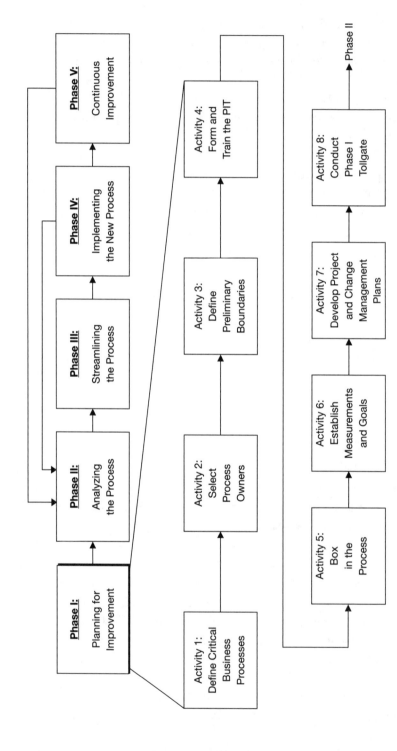

Figure 2.5 Activities in Phase I: Planning for Improvement

- Activity 3: Define Preliminary Boundaries
- Activity 4: Form and Train the PIT
- Activity 5: Box in the Process
- Activity 6: Establish Measurements and Goals
- Activity 7: Develop Project and Change Management Plans
- Activity 8: Conduct Phase I Tollgate

Phase II: Analyzing the Process

Unfortunately, most business processes are not documented, and often when they are documented, the processes are not followed. During this phase the PIT will draw a picture of the present process ("as-is" process), analyze compliance to present procedures, collect cost and cycle time data, and align the day-to-day activities with the procedures. The eight activities in this phase (also shown in Figure 2.6) are:

- Activity 1: Flowchart the Process
- Activity 2: Conduct a Benchmark Study
- Activity 3: Conduct a Process Walk-Through
- Activity 4: Perform a Process Cost, Cycle Time, and Output Analysis
- Activity 5: Prepare the Simulation Model
- Activity 6: Implement Quick Fixes
- Activity 7: Develop a Current Culture Model
- Activity 8: Conduct Phase II Tollgate

The purpose of Phase II is for the PIT to gain detailed knowledge of the process and its matrixes (cost, cycle time, processing time, error rates, etc.). The flowchart and simulation model of the present process (the as-is model of the process) will be used to improve the process during Phase III.

Phase III: Streamlining the Process

Don't streamline the process to get rid of people—use it to improve the process. The streamlining phase of SPI is the most critical and the most fun. It is during this phase of the SPI methodology that the creative

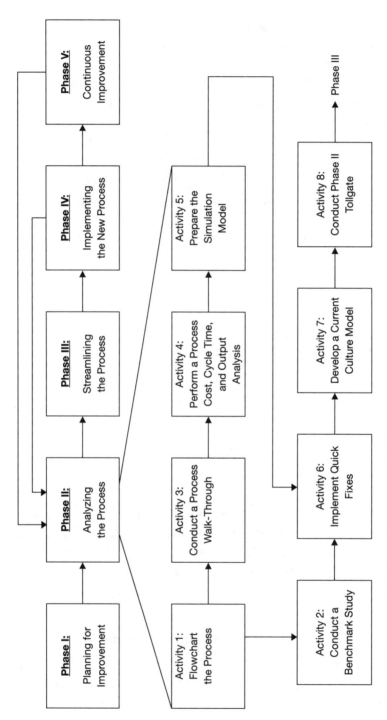

Figure 2.6 Activities in Phase II: Analyzing the Process

juices of the PIT members are really put into action. The streamlining phase consists of the following six activities (see also Figure 2.7):

- Activity 1: Apply Streamlining Approaches
- Activity 2: Conduct a Benchmarking Study
- Activity 3: Prepare an Improvement, Cost, and Risk Analysis
- Activity 4. Select a Preferred Process
- Activity 5: Prepare a Preliminary Implementation Plan
- Activity 6: Conduct Phase III Tollgate

Apply the Streamlining Approaches

A streamlining approach takes the present process and removes waste while reducing the cycle time and improving the process effectiveness. After the process flow is streamlined, automation and information technology (IT) are applied, maximizing the process's ability to improve its effectiveness, efficiency, and adaptability. SPI is sometimes called *focused improvement* or *process redesign* since it focuses its efforts on the present process. It results in decreasing cycle time, cost, and error rates between 30 and 60 percent. It takes about 80 to 100 days to develop the best-value future-state process. This is the correct approach for 70 to 80 percent of an organization's critical business processes.

Best-Value Future-State Solution

All too often, a PIT only develops one new process design. This can be a costly conservation of time. All processes do not have to be world class unless they drive the core capabilities and competencies of the organization. For example, the hiring process at Hewlett Packard (HP) can be 10 to 20 times longer than it is at Manpower without impacting Hewlett Packard's performance. Even if Hewlett Packard could reduce its hiring process cycle time to one day from its present cycle time, the improvement would have no measurable impact on HP's bottom line.

Organizations today should be selecting the new process that provides them with their best-value future-state solution (BVFSS), which may or may not represent today's best practices. When the PIT develops one solution, the team members try to minimize efficiency and effectiveness while maximizing adaptability. They present one answer with no options to the management team. Typically, they define the

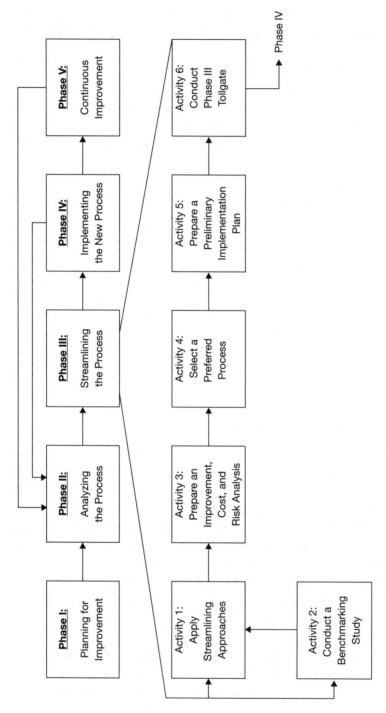

Figure 2.7 Activities for Phase III: Streamlining the Process

single new process and then develop estimates and data to prove that their solution is correct and that there is an attractive return on investment (ROI). This usually does not result in a BVFSS. To identify the BVFSS, the PIT must consider the interactions among efficiency, effectiveness, and adaptability. In addition, the PIT must consider implementation cost, implementation cycle time, potential risk, and the solution's impact on the organization's culture. The best way to define BVFSS is to develop one solution and then go back and develop two or more different solutions.

There are many different ways to develop alternative solutions. One approach would be to define different solution objectives for each alternative future-state solution. For example:

- *Solution #1.* Define the process that will give the best combination of efficiency, effectiveness, and adaptability measurements, ignoring the implementation cost and implementation cycle time.
- *Solution #2.* Define the process that will generate the best combination of efficiency, effectiveness, and adaptability that can be implemented within a 90-day period.
- *Solution #3.* Define the process that will deliver the best combination of efficiency, effectiveness, and adaptability that can be implemented at a cost of less than $100,000 and has minimum risks related to meeting the efficiency, effectiveness, and adaptability projections.
- *Solution #4.* Define the process that will improve output quality the most without increasing processing costs and that can be implemented within a six-month period.

It is easy to see that as different solution objectives are set for each of the process designs, future-state solutions will vary greatly. Often, generating alternative future-state solutions will generate new ideas that will alter previously developed future-state solutions.

Each time a future-state solution is developed, a simulation model should be created so that the new process design can be exercised and evaluated. Table 2.1 is a simple performance analysis database for three alternative future-state solutions designed for the same process.

By studying Table 2.1, it is easy to see that all the future-state solutions perform better than the original process. Future-State Solution #1

Table 2.1 Comparison of Three Future-State Solutions

	Performance Estimate			
	Original Process	**FSS #1**	**FSS #2**	**FSS #3**
Effectiveness (Quality)	.2	.002	.01	.006
Efficiency (Productivity)	12.9 hr/cycle	4.3 hr/cycle	6.3 hr/cycle	5.3 hr/cycle
Adaptability	25%	75%	80%	65%
Cycle Time	305 hr	105 hr	105 hr	85 hr
Cost/Cycle	$605	$308	$410	$380
Market Share Improvement	−2%	+3%	+2.5%	+2.7%

	Implementation Estimate		
	FSS #1	**FSS #2**	**FSS #3**
Cost	$1,300,000	$20,000	$280,000
Implementation Cycle Time	24 months	6 months	15 months
Probability of Success	50%	95%	85%
Major Problem	New competitor	Training time	New org. structure

represents best practices, but it is very costly and has a long implementation cycle. It also has a high risk associated with it because the information systems department does not want to transfer its operations over to a new computer system.

Future-State Solution #2 can be implemented very quickly and inexpensively, but its performance is worse than the other two future-state solutions. Future-State Solution #3 provides a middle-range option.

The selection of the BVFSS will vary from organization to organization and will depend on the stability of the process enablers that are used in the future-state solutions. For example, if the customer effectiveness requirement is .05, probably Solution #2 would be dropped from consideration. Another factor to consider would be the number of items that go through the process, as this affects the total cost of operating the process. If information technology is an important part of the future-state solution, implementation cycles become a very important factor because IT solutions that take more than 12 months to implement often are obsolete before they are implemented. Frequently, the savings related to quick implementation far outweigh the savings related to better performance of the future-state solution.

For example, suppose the process in Table 2.1 is obsolete five years after the future-state solution is defined. Using this as an assumption, our savings will be based on a five-year cycle. Table 2.2 defines the total cost of implementing the present system over a five-year period compared with the three future-state solutions. The calculations are based on processing 100 units per month through the process.

By analyzing the data in Table 2.2, we see that Future-State Solution #1 (FSS #1) should not be implemented even if it is best practices if the only consideration is cost, because it has a negative impact on the bottom line. Frequently, the results of reengineering and benchmarking

Table 2.2 Five-Year Analysis of FSS Process Cost for the Original Process and Three Different Future-State Solutions

Original process	$CT = (60 \text{ months} \times \$605 \times 100) + 0 + 0$ $CT = \$3,630,000$
FSS #1	$CT = (24 \text{ months} \times \$605 \times 100) + (36 \text{ months} \times \$308 \times 100) + \$1,300,000$ $CT = \$1,452,000 + \$1,108,000 + \$1,300,000$ $CT = \$3,860,800$
FSS #2	$CT = (6 \text{ months} \times \$605 \times 100) + (54 \text{ months} \times \$410 \times 100) + \$20,000$ $CT = \$363,000 + \$2,214,000 + \$20,000$ $CT = \$2,597,000$
FSS #3	$CT = (15 \text{ months} \times \$605 \times 100) + (45 \text{ months} \times \$380 \times 100) + \$280,000$ $CT = \$907,500 + \$1,710,000 + \$280,000$ $CT = \$2,897,500$

$T1$ = Time in months that the original process is used
$T2$ = Time in months that the FSS is in place
  I = Items processed per month = 100
$C1$ = Cost per cycle original process = $605
$C2$ = Cost per cycle of the FSS
$C3$ = Cost to implement the FSS
CT = Total cost to operate the process for 5 years
$CT = (T1 \times C1 \times I) + (T2 \times C2 \times I) + C3$

projects are unsatisfactory when this type of analysis is not conducted. It is very easy for the PIT and management to get excited about the future-state solution projected performance improvement and charge ahead without realizing what impact the future-state solution has on the bottom line.

The ROI for FSS #2 is 207 to 1 compared with FSS #3, whose ROI is 2.6 to 1. In this case, if cost is the only consideration, FSS #2 is the BVFSS. Unfortunately, efficiency is only one of the three parameters that need to be considered to define the BVFSS. In addition, the PIT must also consider effectiveness and adaptability. This makes the analysis more than three times more complicated than the example presented. More information on BVFSS can be found in *The Complete Benchmarking Implementation Guide* (Harrington, 1996).

Phase IV: Implementing the New Process

During this phase, an implementation team is pulled together to install the selected process, measurement systems, and control systems. The new in-process measurement and control systems will be designed to ensure that there is immediate feedback to the employees, enabling them to contain the gains that have been made and to improve the process further. This phase consists of six activities (see also Figure 2.8):

- Activity 1: Prepare a Final Implementation Plan
- Activity 2: Implement New Process
- Activity 3: Install In-Process Measurement Systems
- Activity 4: Install Feedback Data Systems
- Activity 5: Transfer Project
- Activity 6: Conduct the Phase IV Tollgate

Phase V: Continuous Improvement

Now that the process has undergone a major breakthrough in performance, you cannot stop improving. This is not the end of the improvement activities; it is just the beginning. Now the process must continue to improve, usually at a much slower rate (5 to 15 percent per year), but it must continue to improve. During this portion of the cycle,

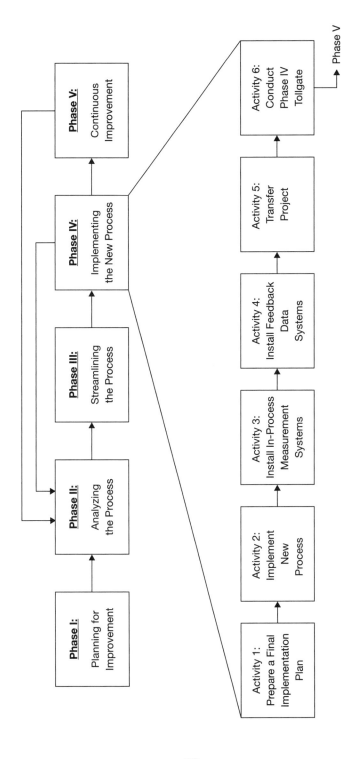

Figure 2.8   Activities for Phase IV: Implementing the New Process

the process owner will continue to monitor the effectiveness, efficiency, and adaptability of the total process. Department improvement teams (natural work groups) in each area will continually work on improving their portion of the process by setting their own personal improvement objectives. This is an acceptable approach because the process owner continues to monitor total performance to ensure that suboptimization does not occur. This phase consists of three activities (also see Figure 2.9):

- Activity 1: Maintain the Gains
- Activity 2: Implement Area Activity Analysis
- Activity 3: Qualify the Process

Summary

SPI is the most effective way to bring about meaningful and positive changes to your major processes. It will set the stage for a culture change that questions the status quo and looks for that better way to do everything. SPI is designed to upgrade your major processes. It is much more effective at improving processes than methodologies like Six Sigma or Plan-Do-Check-Act, which are designed for problem solving.

You need to be better today than you were yesterday and be much better tomorrow than you are today.

—H. James Harrington

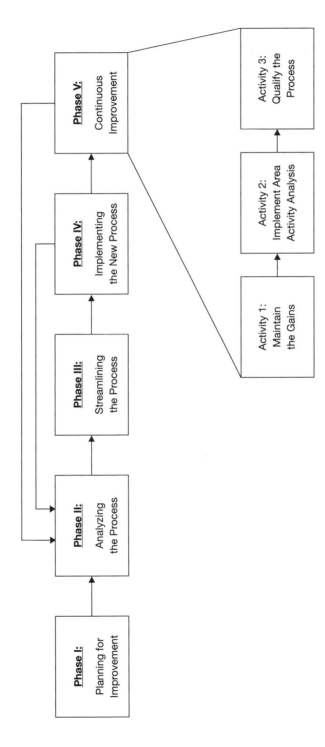

Figure 2.9 Activities for Phase V: Continuous Improvement

Phase I: Planning for Improvement

A good start is the best way to get outstanding results.
—H. James Harrington

Introduction

This is one of the most critical phases in the total methodology, and it is usually the one that is done the poorest. Too many organizations want to start flowcharting and skip through the planning phase without selecting the right process, defining the results that they need, training the Process Improvement Team (PIT), or preparing a comprehensive project that is supported by the PIT and management.

Objective of the planning phase: To ensure success by building leadership, understanding, and commitment and by selecting the correct PIT and processes.

Key Outputs

- Establish an Executive Improvement Team (EIT).
- Appoint a Process Improvement champion.
- Provide executive training.
- Develop an improvement model.
- Communicate goals to employees.
- Review business strategy and customer requirements.
- Select the critical processes.
- Appoint process owners.

- Select the PIT.
- Define key measurements.
- Define project objectives.
- Develop a project plan.

The planning phase is divided into eight activities. (See Figure 3.1.)

- Activity 1: Define Critical Business Processes
- Activity 2: Select Process Owners
- Activity 3: Define Preliminary Boundaries
- Activity 4: Form and Train the PIT
- Activity 5: Box in the Process
- Activity 6: Establish Measurements and Goals
- Activity 7: Develop Project and Change Management Plans
- Activity 8: Conduct Phase I Tollgate

Planning Phase

This is one of the most important phases, and it is often rushed through. This is a big mistake, since Phase I sets the direction for the rest of the phases. It is during this phase that the EIT gets to understand the Streamlined Process Improvement (SPI) methodology and when the major processes are defined and prioritized. The organization can waste a lot of time if the wrong processes are selected to be improved. Also during this phase the PIT is assigned. If the team make-up is wrong and they are not trained well, there is a very good chance that the project will fail. It is also the phase where the problem and scope of the project is defined.

Activity I: Define Critical Business Processes

The EIT is responsible for ensuring that the processes used within the organization are accomplishing the desired results. One of the primary responsibilities of the EIT is to provide processes that are less expensive and of higher quality than those an external supplier could offer and to provide the employees with the equipment, training, and processes that will allow them to excel. As a result, managers should be

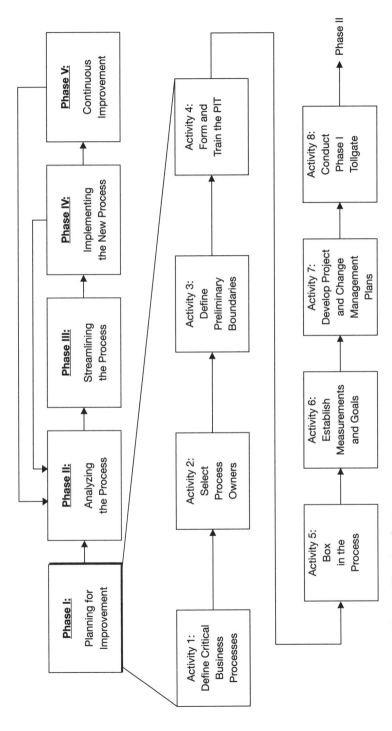

Figure 3.1 Phase I: Planning for Improvement

involved early in the SPI methodology. Not only should they understand this methodology, but they should be involved in each project. The EIT needs to:

- Be trained on what the SPI methodology is.
- Define what the critical processes are.
- Assign people to work on the SPI projects.
- Assign an SPI coordinator.
- Assign processes' owner.
- Review and approve project plans.
- Review and approve the future-state solutions.
- Assign implementation teams.
- Track results.
- Reward the PIT members who excel.
- Communicate the needs for SPI to the entire organization.
- Release required supporting documentation (for example, directives).
- Measure the success of the improvement effort.

Typically there is someone in the organization who believes that SPI is the correct approach to improving the organization's performance. He or she will champion the SPI methodology and obtain a commitment from the EIT to try to apply it to the organization. This person is often selected to be the organization's focal point for the SPI activities. He or she is sometimes called the *Process Improvement Czar.* We believe that it is advisable to appoint someone to this position for a period of one to two years. By that time, SPI activities will become part of the management system and will no longer require the efforts of a special person to maintain the momentum.

EIT Education

The EIT's key task is to become educated about SPI so that the team can lead the SPI concepts and coach its managers and employees. The champion, frequently assisted by an expert consultant, should design the education program to do the following:

- Familiarize the EIT with the specific purpose and activities of the SPI efforts.
- Build and reinforce the EIT's commitment to SPI.

- Involve the EIT in analyzing and improving critical business processes so that the team members can have a working knowledge of the concept.
- Motivate the EIT in launching and structuring the SPI effort.
- Teach the EIT how to select the right processes to apply SPI to.

This educational process can best be accomplished through a one-day workshop, which should be scheduled very early in the SPI process. Most of the EIT will not be familiar with the SPI concepts, and as a result, they will need to gain understanding of why it is the correct approach for the organization. A typical agenda for this meeting would be:

- An explanation of the workshop schedule and objectives
- An overview of the major SPI steps
- A review of the process for launching an SPI effort
- A review of other major steps required to get the SPI project operational
- A closer look at how to use SPI tools
- A definition of the major process

During this meeting, the following topics may be addressed:

- The critical business processes
- Outside case studies
- Education and training for the PIT
- Ways to measure success
- Key people to lead the individual projects

The group should end the discussion with a very personal commitment related to each member's readiness to support the entire SPI strategy. Depending upon the executive committee members' interaction and the detail related to the SPI tools that are presented, a second day may be required to get through the agenda.

Identify Critical Processes

The EIT is responsible for identifying the organization's major existing business processes. In short, it should answer the question, What do we do in our business, and how do we do it?

Many approaches have been used over the years to accomplish this. Some organizations asked us to interview each executive and his or her key support people to identify the critical processes. They also asked us to collect the data related to the quality of their output and the cost to produce that output. Other organizations just relied on the EIT's knowledge of its groups' activities and its judgment. (We believe that the members of the EIT should have a good enough understanding of their processes to make a first cut at defining the processes that need to be improved without collecting additional data and incurring related costs.)

We find that a good way to start to define the organization's critical processes is to define 5 to 10 major groupings and then make a list of the processes that support each grouping. (See Figure 3.2.)

It is important that the process name indicate that something is being accomplished. It should not be the name of a department. For example, HR is the name of a department; a process in HR is the hiring process. Similarly, the purchasing department (department name) uses order processing to perform some of its activities. Our experience indicates that you will end up with a list of between 60 and 120 different processes as a result of this exercise. Appendix A lists typical processes for an organization. Reviewing this list may help you to define your major processes.

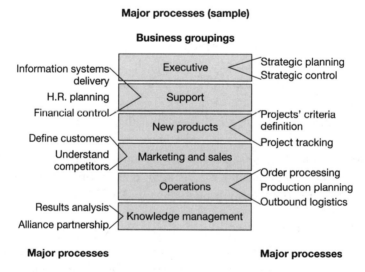

Figure 3.2   Process definition

To narrow this long list down, there are many things that you could consider. For example, how do the customers or consumers—the end users—feel about the value of the outputs from the processes? How do the processes impact the needs of all the stakeholders of the organization? Or consider the outside pressure from competition and government regulations. Then there are the inputs that are required to make the process work. You might consider how easy they will be to change. A current example of an input that may be considered is the price of gasoline. Figure 3.3 shows these considerations as they relate to the processes.

A simple way to narrow the list is to select two or three parameters and evaluate the impact of these parameters on each of the processes. Typical parameters that might be used are "How many problems are the processes creating?" (1 = little, 2 = some, 3 = many) and "How much resources each month are required to perform the activities that make up these processes?" (1 = 1 to 10 employee person months, 2 = 11 to 30 employee person months, 3 = over 31 employee person months).

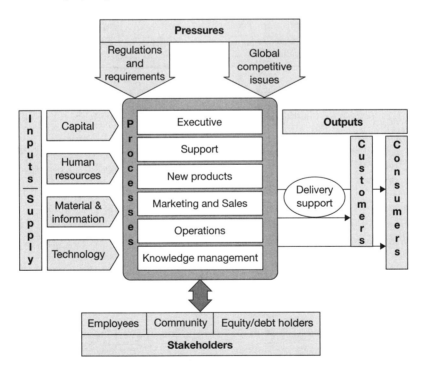

Figure 3.3 Process selection consideration

These figures are then multiplied together to get a weighted figure for the process. (See Table 3.1.)

Based upon Table 3.1, the processes rated 9 and 6 would be the first-cut candidates for SPI. This approach typically will reduce the list to 20 to 30 processes. A second cut to reduce the list further could use "Customer Impact" and "Improvement Opportunity." (See Figure 3.4.)

Table 3.1   Sample of Simple Process Prioritization Analysis

Process Name	Problem Status	Resources Required	Rating
Records management	1	1	2
Component qualification	3	3	9 X
Accounts receivable	3	3	9 X
Budget control	2	2	4
Applications development	3	3	9 X
Customer order	2	2	4
Suggestions	1	1	2
Personnel assessment	3	3	9 X
Supplier selection	3	2	6 X
Service cost estimating	2	2	4
Market survey	1	3	3

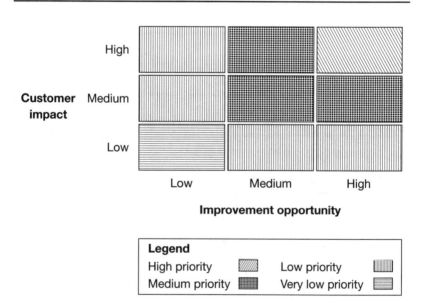

Figure 3.4   Process prioritization matrix

In Figure 3.4 the processes that are rated high in both parameters are the top-priority processes. The ones that are rated high in one parameter and medium in the other parameter are the next priority.

Engineered Approach to Selecting the Processes for SPI

Many approaches can be used to select projects. They range all the way from management intuition to complex analyses of how the processes affect the business opportunities. We will now show you a weighted-selection approach that is effective, using a health-care example.

In this approach each opportunity is evaluated on a number of parameters. For example:

- Changeability = 2 points
- Reduce cost = 2 points
- Decrease mortality = 5 points
- Improve patient care = 4 points
- Improve staff morale = 3 points
- Reduce wait time = 1 point

Each of these parameters is weighted by a point score from 1 to 5. A rating of 1 indicates that it is a low priority and a 5 that it is a very high priority. In Table 3.2, four typical improvement opportunities are listed with the six parameters. Although only four improvement opportunities are listed; in reality the list should contain dozens. Some of the typical opportunities for a health-care program include:

- Reducing inpatient wait time
- Reducing billing errors
- Reducing pharmacy errors
- Reducing response time to bed calls
- Improving information sharing
- Reducing record errors
- Offering better customer parking
- Increasing inventory turns
- Reducing tobacco consumption
- Improving risk management
- Reducing medication administration
- Recording medication administration records errors

Table 3.2 Typical Improvement Opportunities

Opportunities	A = 2	B = 2	C = 5	D = 4	E = 3	F = 1	Total
1. Reduce billing errors.	2 × 2	1 × 2	1 × 5	1 = 4	2 × 3	1 = 1	
	4	2	5	4	6	1	22
2. Improve on present bell response time.	4 × 2	1 × 2	2 × 5	5 × 4	2 × 3	5 × 1	
	8	2	10	20	6	5	51
3. Improve coronary artery bypass graft process.	3 × 2	4 × 2	5 × 5	4 × 4	2 × 3	1 × 1	
	6	8	25	16	6	1	62
4. Record medication administration records errors.	1 × 2	4 × 2	5 × 5	5 × 4	4 × 3	2 × 1	
	2	8	25	20	12	2	69

- Reducing critical-care recovery time
- Standardizing procedures for different treatments
- Reducing outpatient processing cycle

The six evaluation parameters are listed as A through F in the top of Table 3.2 along with the related weighting factors. Each of the improvement opportunities is evaluated on a scale of 1 to 5 for each evaluation parameter. A rating of 5 indicates that the opportunity will be easy to take advantage of or that it will have a big impact on the health-care profession. This rating is then multiplied by the weighted factor for the parameters being evaluated to define a score for the opportunity-evaluation parameter combination.

For example, "Reduce billing errors" was evaluated at weighting factor level 2, which means that it is rather difficult to change. Column A—"changeability"—has a weighting factor of 2. The total score for the "Reduce billing errors–changeability" combination is 4 (2 × 2 = 4). By summing up the individual scores for each parameter for an opportunity, the total weight for that opportunity can be calculated.

Based upon the analysis in Table 3.2, "Record medication administration records errors" is the most important improvement opportunity. Prescription errors are estimated to kill up to 25,000 people a year, according to Dirk Dusharme (2006) in his article "Federal Agency Requires Health Quality Reporting." You might think that physicians care more about their money than the health of their patients. When they write a check, they write out the dollar amount and then double-check it by spelling out the amount. The same physicians scribble out almost illegible instructions on prescription forms. Errors are very common; for example, a carelessly written prescription for 1.0 mg might be misread as calling for 10 mg.

Consideration should be given to balancing the workload within the organization and ensuring that all functions are participating. This approach concentrates attention on critical issues, sets priorities for resources, and ensures that the effort is manageable. Although it is a relatively simple and useful way to select business opportunities, this approach has a number of drawbacks. For example:

- "Pet projects" commonly are identified.
- Management perspectives may not be supported by hard facts.
- Top management may sway the decision.

As you finalize your selection of the business processes that will be improved, remember the "four Rs."

- *Resources.* There is a limited amount of resources available, and the present processes must continue to operate while we are improving them. Often, this means that a new process will be operating in parallel with the old process while the new process is being verified. Don't overextend yourself.
- *Returns.* Look closely at the potential payback to the business. Will the process reduce costs? Will it make you more competitive? Will it give you a marketing advantage?
- *Risks.* Normally, the greater the change required, the greater the risk of failure. Major changes always are accompanied by resistance to change. Breakthrough activities have the biggest payback, but they also have the biggest chance of failure.
- *Rewards.* What are the rewards for the employees and PIT members working to improve the process? How much will their quality of work life be improved? Will the assignment be challenging and provide them with growth opportunities?

At IBM San Jose, 86 of 250 business processes were selected initially as targets for the SPI approach, an unusually high number to work on at one time. We recommend that even a large organization address no more than 25 business processes and during the initial phase, only 2 to 3 processes. When these are completed, start another 2 to 3 SPI projects.

Preliminary Objectives

Once the EIT has selected the processes to which SPI will be applied, it should develop a set of preliminary objectives for the processes that will be active. This input will be used to provide vision and direction to the PIT. These preliminary objectives will ensure that an initial common understanding exists between the PIT and the executive team. Depending on the amount of knowledge and the data that the executive team has about the selected processes, these objectives will be more or less quantified. In some cases, the objectives may only set the direction for the PIT (*example:* reduce cycle time). In other cases, improvement objectives may be provided (*example:* reduce cycle time by 20 percent). The preliminary objectives should address effectiveness, efficiency, adaptability, and cycle time. In all cases, the objectives should be focused on meeting or exceeding customer expectations and can drive incremental or breakthrough improvement, depending on the degree of improvement desired.

It is very important not to blindly accept the preliminary objectives as the goals for the PIT. Normally, these objectives are set without detailed data or understanding of the present process. Letting the PIT set its own goals provides needed ownership. These goals often are more aggressive than the EIT-set objectives.

Employee Security

There is no doubt about it. Usually an SPI project will result in a number of jobs being eliminated, typically between 30 and 40 percent of the jobs in the process. Management should start planning for what it is going to do with this surplus staff. Layoffs are not the best answer, although it is the usual approach.

Your employees want the process to work better; they don't like to do work that is wasted effort or just adding to the bureaucracy of the organization. On the other hand, they need their jobs. You can't expect your employees to define how to improve the processes if it means that they will be put out of work. If you want your employees to contribute their ideas on how to improve the processes they are involved in, it is absolutely imperative that the EIT defines how it will take care of the employees whose jobs are eliminated as a result of the improvement process. We like to see a formal improvement policy that states that employees whose jobs are eliminated due to the improvement program will be assigned to an equal or better job and will not be laid off.

Operating Assumptions

Besides developing objectives, the executive team sometimes develops operating assumptions to help guide the PIT. These operating assumptions define the constraints (*example:* employee resources), specific opportunities (*example:* evaluate replacing the present phone system), or expectations (*example:* all changes will be implemented within the next 12 months). Often, the executive team will develop a set of general assumptions that will apply to all PITs and additional assumptions to provide direction to individual PITs. It is recommended that the EIT-generated assumptions be kept to a minimum, since they may restrict the creativity of the PIT. The process owner and the PIT will further develop the operating assumption list as the process develops.

The following is a list of the processes that are most often streamlined (Tennant & Wu, 2005):

- Sales and order entry, 9 percent
- Invoicing and billing, 11 percent
- Purchasing, 8 percent
- Advertising and promotion, 3 percent
- Product design and development, 5 percent
- Business planning, 9 percent
- Inventory management, 9 percent
- Production scheduling, 9 percent
- Distribution, 6 percent
- Technology, 7 percent
- Personnel management, 4 percent

Activity 2: Select Process Owners

Definition: *Process owner* refers to the individual(s) responsible for process design and performance. The process owner is also responsible for sustaining the gains and identifying future improvement opportunities within the process.

To get economy of scale, most organizations organize themselves into vertical functional groups, with experts of similar backgrounds grouped together to provide a pool of knowledge and skills, capable of completing any task in that discipline. This creates an effective, strong, and confident organization that functions well as a team, eager to support its own mission. Unfortunately, however, most processes do not flow vertically; they flow horizontally across the organization. (See Figure 3.5.)

The horizontal work flow, combined with the vertical organization, results in many voids and overlaps, and it encourages suboptimization, having a negative impact upon the efficiency and effectiveness of the total process. Often many problems are caused at the handoffs between the functional groups. How many times have we heard, "Engineering just threw the design over the wall to production"? We need to stop thinking about the functional organizations and start looking at the process we are trying to improve. We are always surprised when we sit down with a group of managers who are involved in a critical business process, such as the hiring process, and ask them, "Who owns the process?" Usually we encounter eight different managers all "sitting on their hands." No one owns these critical processes; everyone is doing a good job, and that is the problem. The managers are looking out for themselves, and no one makes sure that the activities are interrelated. A critical part of SPI is assigning a process owner to own each critical process.

A process owner may be selected for a number of reasons:

- He or she has the most resources in the process.
- He or she has the most to gain from the process working well.

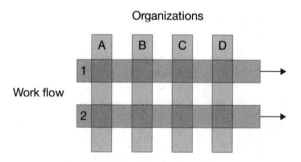

Figure 3.5 Horizontal work flow versus vertical organizations

- He or she is the customer of the output from the process.
- He or she has the technical knowledge to improve the process.
- He or she has a high degree of respect from the people working within the process.

The process owner's job description should include the following:

- Establish measurements and set targets to improve process efficiency, effectiveness, and adaptability.
- Keep the PIT informed about business changes that may affect the process.
- Ensure that the overall goals of the process are met and that the improvements made within the process do not negatively affect other processes or other parts of the organization (suboptimization).
- Define the preliminary boundaries and scope of the process.
- Form a PIT by:
  - Meeting with involved department heads to gain their commitment
  - Obtaining the names of potential members
  - Selecting team members
- Ensure that the PIT members are trained in SPI techniques and that they use basic improvement principles.
- Launch the PIT's activities by helping to:
  - Define process boundaries
  - Establish the team's mission
  - Register the team
- Organize the PIT's regular activities by:
  - Planning meetings
  - Preparing meeting agendas
  - Conducting meetings
  - Following up on PIT activities
  - Resolving or escalating differences between PIT members
- Safeguard the integrity of measurement data.
- Identify process-critical success factors and key dependencies.
- Define subprocesses and their owners (usually line managers).
- Direct the various SPI stages.
- Prepare documents of understanding.
- Monitor process qualification and process benchmarking activities.

- Identify and implement process changes required to meet business and customer needs.
- Maintain contact with the SPI champion and the EIT regarding:
  - The PIT's progress
  - Process qualification
  - Requests for special investments
  - Automation and mechanization issues
- Overcome obstacles to improvement by:
  - Ensuring that proper resources are available to the PIT
  - Settling interdepartmental conflicts
- Establish the appropriate mechanisms for continuously updating procedures and improving the effectiveness and efficiency of the overall process.
- Maintain contact with the customers of the process to ensure that their expectations are understood and met.

As soon as the process owners are identified, the SPI champion and their managers should sit down with them to review their job description, the improvement preliminary objectives set by the executive team, and the operating assumptions. Very soon after this meeting, they need to be trained in their new role so that they understand the SPI methodology and their role in improving the assigned process. A one-day overview will serve this purpose and allow the new process owners to function with a great deal of confidence. The process owners will receive much more detailed training after the team has been assigned.

At Xerox, process owners were assigned to all the key processes. This resulted in a cost savings of $200 million per year (Tomasko, 1993).

Activity 3: Define Preliminary Boundaries

One of the first jobs a process owner does is to define the process starting and ending boundaries. The starting boundary needs to have a measurable input that triggers the start of the process cycle. The ending boundary has to have a deliverable that goes to a customer. We find that different people define the beginning and ending boundaries of the same process in a very different manner. The development engineer sees the new product cycle process very differently from the way

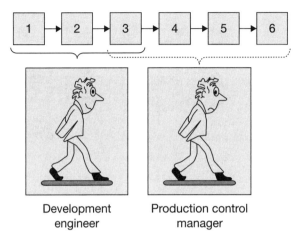

Development engineer

Production control manager

Figure 3.6   Two views of the same process

the production control manager views it. The development engineer considers the process over when he or she releases the prints to manufacturing. The production control manager considers the release of the engineering specification as the starting point of the process and the process is not complete until the new parts have been ordered and are in stock. (See Figure 3.6.)

Management has entrusted this decision of defining the preliminary boundaries to the process owner, as his or her judgment is usually good enough as a starting point.

Activity 4: Form and Train the PIT

The best way for the process owner to define who should be a member of the PIT and to get the SPI project started is to develop a block diagram that shows the flow of the process through the different departments within the organization. (See Figure 3.7.)

The process owner should then meet with the managers of all the departments involved in the process to:

- Discuss the purpose and objective of the SPI project.
- Review the block diagram.
- Determine how much resources the department expends on the process being studied.

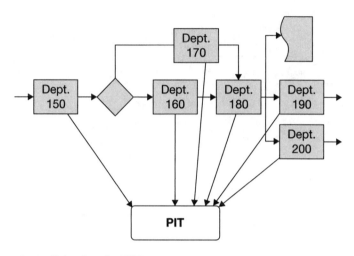

Figure 3.7 Selecting the PIT

- Define what inputs the manager needs to do his or her part of the process.
- Determine what process outputs leave from the department and whom they go to.
- Identify what problems his or her department is having with the process.
- Obtain any improvement suggestions the department manager may have.
- Define the PIT members' role.
- Determine whether the department should have someone on the PIT and, if one is needed, define who that individual will be.

The process owner should point out to the managers that their departments' representatives to the PIT should be experts in their knowledge and understanding of the detailed activities performed in their individual areas of the process. It is extremely important that the very best person in each department be assigned. The selected department representative should have the following:

- The authority to commit the department's resources
- The time to participate on the PIT

- Regard for the viewpoints, abilities, and skills of the other team members
- The time to follow up on the PIT assignments given during the PIT meetings
- Practical and actual process knowledge
- Credibility with other PIT members
- A desire to be part of the improvement initiative
- A belief that the process can be improved
- A willingness to embrace and lead change
- A vested interest in the process
- An innovative mind
- An understanding of the organization's mission and infrastructure
- An ability to think creatively

IBM used teams of 2 to 10 members, including experts in the area under review and other financial people who were well regarded by their peers. Harry Beeth, assistant controller at IBM corporate headquarters, stated, "If these teams came up with radical ideas, we didn't want others to think this was something crazy from the top. We wanted them to know that the idea came from people they respected" (*CFO*, 1996).

Training in Basic Problem-Solving Tools

The PIT members will need to have knowledge in the following 12 basic problem-solving tools:

- Team process
- Brainstorming
- Check sheets
- Graphs
- Histograms (frequency distribution)
- Pareto diagrams
- Scatter diagrams
- Nominal group techniques
- Delphi narrowing techniques
- Force-field analysis
- Cause-and-effect diagrams
- Statistical Process Control (SPC)

If for some reason the PIT members don't have this basic problem-solving knowledge, these tools need to be taught at the very beginning of the SPI cycle.

> *It became quite clear after we began operations that many of the participants did not have the conceptual and personal skills needed to make them effective ... It lays bare the bones of group activities. There was simply no slack to cover up a team's glitches or weak points.*
> —John Young, past president of Hewlett-Packard

Don't underestimate the importance of these meetings with the department managers. If these meetings are well managed, they will provide the process owner with important information about the process that he or she will find extremely valuable as the improvement effort progresses. Frequently as a result of these meetings, the process owner will need to establish new process boundaries.

Training in the 12 Fundamental SPI Tools

In addition to the basic team dynamics and problem-solving training that the PIT members should already be familiar with, the team members require special training in 12 fundamental SPI tools to prepare for streamlining the business processes. These tools include:

- SPI concepts
- Flowcharting and value stream mapping
- Interviewing techniques
- SPI measurement methods (cost, cycle time, effectiveness, efficiency, and adaptability)
- Lean and no-value-added activities' elimination methods
- Bureaucracy elimination methods
- Paper and process simplification techniques
- Simple language analysis and methods
- Process walk-through methods
- Cycle and cost time analysis
- Design of experiments and Statistical Process Control
- Workplace organization and work flow

Training in the 12 Sophisticated SPI Tools

It is seldom that all 12 sophisticated tools will be used on any given project, but often 1, 2, or even 3 of them may be essential for defining the best possible future-state solution. The 12 sophisticated tools that may be used are:

- Quality Function Deployment (QFD)
- Program Evaluation and Review Techniques Charting (PERT)
- Business Systems Planning (BSP)
- Process Analysis Technique (PAT)
- Structured Analysis/Structural Design (SA/SD)
- Value Analysis and Control
- Simulation modeling
- Information engineering
- Benchmarking
- Poor-quality cost
- Activity-Based Costing (ABC)
- Supply Chain Management

In his *Handbook on Teaching Undergraduate Science Courses*, Gordon Uno (1999) reported that students learn and retain information as follows:

- 10 percent of what they read
- 20 percent of what they hear
- 30 percent of what they see
- 50 percent of what they see and hear
- 60 percent of what they write
- 70 percent of what they discuss
- 80 percent of what they experience

Keeping this in mind, education and training are very important, but without experience in using the tools soon after the PIT training, the tools will be forgotten and the effort will have been wasted.

PIT First Meeting

At the very first meeting of the PIT, it is important that everyone have a common, agreed-to understanding of what the project is and what role he or she will play on the PIT. This involves:

- Understanding and defining the SPI process
- Understanding and defining the project objective
- Understanding and defining the boundaries

- Preparing the PIT mission statement
- Defining a PIT name
- Reviewing PIT members' job descriptions
- Agreeing on a PIT code of conduct
- Confirming time commitments
- Upgrading the current process so that it meets or exceeds the improvement goals and objectives.

Mission Statement

A good mission statement:

- Should be short (never more than five sentences)
- Define the scope of the activities
- Define what will be accomplished
- Include performance improvement targets and completion dates, in some cases

It is very important that you take time to establish a mission statement that all the PIT members agree with and feel can be done. A typical example could be "To understand and apply process SPI methodologies to the total budgeting process to make it more efficient, effective, and readily adaptable to the ever-changing business needs. The results will reduce the costs and cycle time required to prepare the annual budget. The future-state solution will be well documented and approved by the executive team within 60 working days."

As soon as the PIT develops a mission statement, it should also develop a name for the team. The PIT name should reflect the mission statement and include the names of the products and services provided by the process.

PIT Code of Conduct

It is important that the team agree on how the team will function (code of conduct). People who show up late for a meeting waste everyone's time and show no respect for the other members of the team. As a result, the PIT members should develop operating guidelines that include the following:

- How late is it acceptable to come to a PIT meeting? (We suggest five minutes maximum.)
- How late is it acceptable to come back from a PIT break? (We suggest two minutes.)
- No one should interrupt anyone else.
- No one should monopolize the conversation, i.e., talk for more than five minutes without turning the conversation over to someone else.
- Everyone should express an opinion at every meeting.
- Everyone should stay until the end of the meeting or for the scheduled time, whichever comes first.
- Always have an agenda for each meeting.
- Define how long after the meeting the minutes will be published.

Finalize the Process Boundaries

Earlier in the cycle the process owner had defined the preliminary process starting and ending boundaries. It is now time to get the view of the total PIT in regard to where these boundaries should be, as they may be too big or too small, which could impact the makeup of the PIT. As we have indicated before, there is a big difference between individual views of where the starting and ending boundaries should be. Let's take, for example, the process of having a barbeque.

Husband's Viewpoint

- Start point is when the first guest arrives.
- End point is when the last guest leaves.

Wife's Viewpoint

- Start point is preparing the guest list because it defines what she needs to buy.
- End point is when the last dish is washed and put away.

Son's Viewpoint

- Start point is when he sets up the tables and chairs the day of the party.
- End point is when he takes the garbage out.

The boundaries should be big enough to provide lots of improvement opportunities, but not so big that they will require too large a PIT to address the opportunities. Keeping this in mind, the process owner should lead the PIT in a discussion when the agreed-to starting and ending boundaries are set. He or she should then review the makeup of the PIT to be sure that the right areas are represented.

Activity 5: Box in the Process

The PIT has agreed on what the starting and ending boundaries are to be, but that is not enough. The team members need to define:

- What is included in the process?
- What is not included in the process?
- What are the outputs from the process?
- What are the inputs into the process?
- What departments are involved in the process?

To accomplish this, a technique called *Boxing in the Process* is used. This technique requires the PIT to add upper and lower boundaries to the starting and ending boundaries. The upper boundaries define things that come into the process at different points in the process other than at the starting boundary. The lower boundaries define things that leave the process at different points within the process, but not at the end of the process. In both cases, these are things that are outside the scope of the process being improved. Figure 3.8 is a barbeque process that has been boxed in.

You will note that in this case, the process begins with removing the steak from the refrigerator. The second step is to unwrap the steak, but at that same time when you removed the steak from the refrigerator, you also got from the cupboard the salt and pepper, the garlic powder, and a knife. These are things that are coming into the process from the upper boundary, but we did not include "acquiring the salt/pepper/garlic powder/knife/buying them from the store" as part of this process. We made the basic assumption that these items were available and that we could just pick them up and go forward with them.

Coming out of the "unwrap process" is the paper that we put in the garbage. We made the basic assumption that we did not have to define,

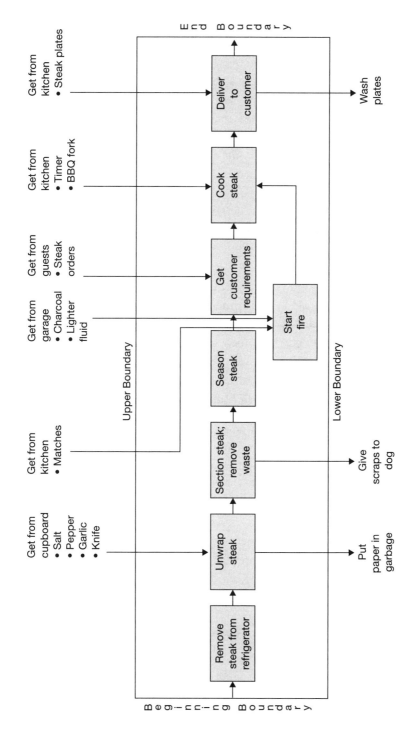

Figure 3.8 Boxing in the steak BBQ process

as part of this process, how we were going to dispose of the garbage. This is a lower boundary, where the paper left the process, but the disposal of the paper itself is not covered as part of the process.

To create a boxed-in process, the PIT will first develop a high-level block diagram of the process. At each block in the diagram, the team will define what is needed to complete that activity. If an input is required and doesn't come from a block within the present diagram, the PIT must decide if the creation of that input needs to be included in the project. If not, it is an output that comes in through the upper boundaries. (For example, money may be required to buy something, but the scope of the project doesn't include raising the funds for the organization.)

Often one of the outputs from a process step may go to an activity that you don't want to include in the process under study. As a result, this output leaves the process through the lower boundary. For example, data may be collected and sent to the information systems department for processing. In this case, the information systems processing of the data may be outside the scope of the project, even though the process data may reenter the process through the upper boundaries at a later point in the process.

Activity 6: Establish Measurements and Goals

Once the process has been boxed in, the PIT needs to define what key measurements are related to the process. It is important at this point to look at the total process, not individual department measurements that reflect only part of the process. This means that we will look at the process from the outside of the boxed-in process. (See Figure 3.9.)

There are three major kinds of process measurements. They are effectiveness measurement, efficiency measurement, and adaptability measurement. All three are very important and relate to different objectives.

Effectiveness Measurement

> **Definition:** *Effectiveness measurement* is the extent to which the output of a process or subprocess meets the needs and expectations of its customers. Quality is often thought of as a synonym for effectiveness, but effectiveness is a lot more.

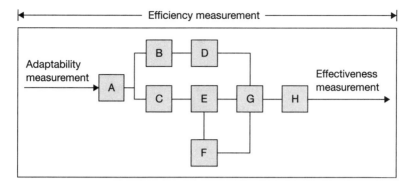

Figure 3.9 The three key kinds of process measurements

Effectiveness is having the right output at the right place at the right time at the right price. Effectiveness impacts the customer. Customer needs and expectations reflect the product and the service. For example, the following are all effectiveness measurements:

- Appearance
- Timeliness
- Accuracy
- Performance
- Reliability
- Usability
- Serviceability
- Durability
- Cost
- Responsiveness
- Dependability

To define the effectiveness of the process, the PIT should meet with the primary customer to determine what the customer's requirements are for the process. Customers always know what they want (the voice of the customer), but frequently they have a hard time expressing their desires in terms that can be used to measure effectiveness. Often we hear the voice of the customer in general terms, such as "I want quick service," or "I want error-free reports," or "I want things that work," or

"I want easy-to-use output." What the process needs is measurable characteristics that can be:

- Evaluated before the output is delivered to the customers
- Documented in a specification so employees have a standard
- Agreed to by both the supplier and the customer

Efficiency Measurement

> **Definition:** *Efficiency measurement* is the extent to which a resource is minimized and waste is eliminated in the pursuit of effectiveness. Productivity is a measurement of efficiency.

The lack of effectiveness is easy to see and measure, but poor efficiency, on the other hand, is hard to recognize; we learn to live with it, and it slowly gets worse. We add more checks and balances when we have a problem, or more people are added to the process and we never remove them. Requirements for efficiency focus on the use of money, time, and other resources. Typical efficiency measurements are:

- Processing time
- Resources expended per unit of output
- Value-added cost per unit of output
- Percentage of value-added time
- Poor-quality cost
- Wait time per unit
- Cycle time
- Processing cost

The major focus of upper management is on efficiency measurements. As efficiency goes up, cost goes down. To date, the major measurement of a Six Sigma program's success is efficiency measurement (cost reduction), not customer satisfaction or reduced variation. Reducing cycle time in some processes also provides the organization with a very significant competitive advantage. We know of one case where by cutting cycle time in half, it doubled sales.

Adaptability Measurement

> **Definition:** *Adaptability measurement* is the adaptability of a process to handle future, changing, customer expectation, and today's individual special customer requirements. It is managing the process to meet today's special needs and future requirements.

Adaptability is an area largely ignored, but it is crucial for gaining a competitive edge in the marketplace. Customers always remember how you handle or don't handle their special needs. Basically adaptability is a measure of how much you can adjust the input to the process and still get the desired outputs from the process. For example, an insurance company can normally process a claim within three days, but in an emergency a claim can be processed within one hour. That is a sign of adaptability to the claim processing process.

Of our three key process requirements—efficiency, effectiveness, and adaptability—adaptability is by far the most difficult to measure, but it is one of the first ones that the customers will complain about. There are a number of ways to measure process adaptability:

- The average time it takes to get a special request processed compared with the average time it takes to process a standard request.
- The percentage of special requests that are turned down.
- The percentage of time that special requests are escalated. (In the service industry, the more people that a customer has to talk to in order to get an issue resolved, the less chance there is that person will be satisfied with the organization even if his or her issue has been resolved satisfactorily.)

Adaptability requirements should be established at the beginning of the SPI cycle so that the improvement activities can consider these parameters and the data system can be established to measure improvement. Adaptability is often overlooked in the measurement system. For example, one power supply manufacturing company that we worked with was firm that it didn't need adaptability measurements in its order cycle. The company's order cycle was 15 working days. We asked our clients if they ever had a customer who needed a power supply faster. Their answer was yes—this often happens, they replied, and we put priority on these special requests and get them right out. We asked our clients if it would be acceptable to reduce the standard cycle down to 8 days but have no ability to react to these special requirements. After thinking about it, they agreed that they needed adaptability measurements.

> *Be very careful in defining any of the measurements to be sure it is measurable. Specifications that aren't measurable are purely wish lists.*
> —H. James Harrington

Rule #1. Know Your Customer

It is important for the PIT to remember that the process can have internal and external customers. Both are important. External customers are easy to define, but it is often hard to define the impact of the process on all the internal customers. For example, few accounting departments treat the department managers as their customers; they treat them as suppliers. They prepare monthly reports in a format that is meaningful for them, not for the manager who is trying to control his or her spending and cost.

Every person has at least three different types of customer. All three need to be considered when the PIT is defining the process measurement system:

- *Primary customer.* The individual or group that receives the processes' output. This is usually the next activity in the process or everyone in the cc list. This customer is primarily interested in effectiveness measurements (quality).
- *Secondary customer.* The individual or group that has authorized them to perform the tasks. This is usually their manager. This customer is primarily interested in efficiency measurements (cost and processing time.)
- *End customer.* The individual or group that uses the end product that the organization provides. This customer is primarily interested in price and effectiveness measurements.

Jacques Nasser, former CEO of Ford Motor Company, is very customer focused, and he wants all managers and employees to also be customer focused. As a result, teams of Ford employees went out to customer-insight centers for a course on how to listen and how to talk to customers. They then went out on an eight-week assignment to talk to Ford customers; they discussed subjects like design, safety, comfort, ease of use, even down to types of coffee holders. This is one of the functions that made Ford by 1999 the world's most profitable automotive maker—over a two-year period, stock prices increased 130 percent. It is one of the reasons that Ford was the only one of the Big Three automakers in the United States that didn't need bailout money from the government.

The process design must consider the customer's present and future needs and desires. All types of processes have only one purpose—to satisfy the internal customer's and external customer's requirements as fast as possible and at minimum cost to the organization. These requirements may be documented, verbal, or even unknown by the customer himself or herself. The process design needs to consider what the customer will want 2, 5, or even 10 years from now. This means that you will need to get into your time machine and advance your thinking by 3 to 10 years. One of the biggest mistakes you can make is to believe that the customer knows your technology well enough to predict what types of services or products it will be creating in the future. We like to classify customers' requirements in the following five ways:

- Articulated requirements—what they tell you they require
- Observed requirements—what you see that they require
- Hidden requirements—needs that the customer has but has a hard time defining
- Latent requirements—requirements that are not needed now but will be needed in the future
- Technology-driven requirements—needs that new technology developments will trigger

The problem, which many PIT members encounter, is that they only recognize the articulated requirements, and as a result, they are unable to predict future customer requirements. These organizations live in a reactive mode—always trying to catch up, always running behind the leaders in the industry, picking up the leftovers from the really successful organizations.

Dr. Noriaki Kano in the 1980s developed a model that depicts customer preferences. (See Figure 3.10.) The Kano Model depicts three ways that customers perceive the different features/parts of a service or product that they receive:

1. *Basic needs.* These are features that are expected by the customers even if they are not stated or specified. For example, when you go into a restaurant and ask for a glass of water, you expect the glass to not be cracked. If it is cracked, you are dissatisfied. If it isn't cracked, you are neither satisfied nor dissatisfied; it has just met your basic needs. In looking at the Kano Model, you may think that a customer would be satisfied even if all the basic needs were met. I believe that all the basic needs must be fulfilled in order to have a satisfied customer. But once these needs are met, doing a better job at fulfilling additional needs does nothing to make the customer more satisfied.
2. *Performance requirements.* These are the needs that the customer articulates either in writing or verbally. The better you execute these needs, the more satisfied the customer will be. For example, if you went to a hotel and got a cot to sleep on, you probably would be dissatisfied. But if you got a king-size bed with a feather mattress on it, you would probably be very satisfied.
3. *Unexpected features.* These are things that the customer didn't require and were not specified; these are things that surprise the customers.

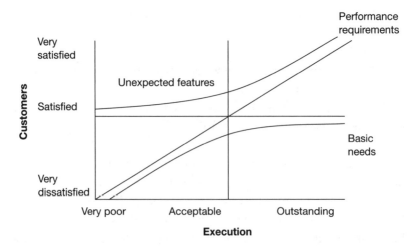

Figure 3.10   The Kano Model

These are features that delight the customer and make him or her more satisfied with the product and/or service delivered. Not having the feature doesn't dissatisfy the customer, because he or she didn't expect to receive the feature. For example, a customer would be delighted to find fresh free cookies in the hotel room or a basket of fruit.

There are two other views that the customer will have about the products or services that were not covered in the Kano Model. They are:

1. *Indifference.* This is a feature that the customer doesn't care if it is there or not as long as it doesn't cost more money. It usually is a feature that won't be used. For example, there are many features in my Microsoft Office software that I will never use.
2. *Dislike.* These are features that the customer doesn't want to have in the product or service. They result in dissatisfying the customer. For example, sending out a newsletter by e-mail instead of mail would result in reduced customer satisfaction for people who don't like to read long e-mails or those who don't use computers. Another example would be the caller ID feature on the telephone; this feature is viewed as a "dislike" feature by some people.

You can understand why it is very important that each of the output measurements needs to reflect its customer perspective of the measurement and or features. In conducting a survey or in a discussion with the customer, it is good to ask the question in two ways—one is a functional way and the second is a dysfunctional way. For example, if the phone had caller ID on it, how would you feel? Then ask the question, If the phone didn't have caller ID on it, how would you feel?

It is important to remember that customer perception is weighted by still another factor—the price customers will pay for the feature. Price is a performance requirement, and if an unexpected feature drives the performance price up too much, it could cause decreased customer satisfaction.

It is also important to realize that there is a difference in the need to meet external and internal customer requirements. For example, if an external customer wants a product or service on Monday, you should do everything possible to provide it. But if an internal customer wants something delivered on Monday and that means someone will have to come in and work on Saturday, it now becomes a business decision. Management needs to evaluate what impact it would have on the organization if the internal customer doesn't get the output until Tuesday. In many cases internal requirements are preferences, not requirements, and as such, these can be negotiated to come up with the optimum business performance.

How to Get Customer Requirements

There are six main ways of getting customer requirements:

- Focus groups
- In-depth interviews
- Observational interviews
- Projective testing
- Leading-edge groups
- And, of course, the most basic—surveys

Each of these has advantages and disadvantages.

Focus Groups

Focus groups are small gatherings of 8 to 10 people who discuss a specific set of topics to define the situation.

Advantages
- Cost effective.
- Interactive.
- Productive.
- Open atmosphere.

Disadvantages
- May not be factual.
- Can be biased.
- Can get misdirected.
- Strong individuals can lead the group to their point of view.

In-Depth Interviews

These are one-on-one interviews using a prepared set of questions designed to obtain in-depth insight into the customer's culture and requirements.

Advantages

- No group pressure.
- Confidential.
- Open discussion.
- In-depth discussion.

Disadvantages

- Costly.
- Time consuming.
- Lack of group dynamics.

Observational Interviews

These are observations of the customer's characteristics and activities when they are using the product or service.

Advantages

- You see what they do.
- Little bias.
- Hidden requirements are identified.

Disadvantages

- Costly.
- Time consuming.
- Individual customer dependent.

Projective Testing

This is used to define hidden and latent requirements. It uses approaches like word association and fill-in-the-blank exercises.

Advantages

- One-on-one discussions.
- In-depth insight into customer feelings.
- You can discuss something or someone else.

Disadvantages

- Very subjective.
- Expensive.
- Time consuming.

Leading-Edge Groups

These consist of workshops or focus groups with customers who are ahead of the average or mainstream customers. These are technology discussions that are designed to define how the future technology will drive future customer needs (typically two to three days per session).

Advantages

- Identify emerging requirements.
- Define breakthrough ideas and concepts.

Disadvantages

- Hard to set up.
- Very costly.
- Time consuming.
- Difficult to interpret the results.

Surveys

Surveys can be conducted by direct interface with the individual or by indirect contact (for example, by mail or the Internet). The survey design plays a critical part in the accuracy of the results. The sample selection also can cause the results to be inaccurate. Both these factors need to be considered when designing and conducting the survey.

Advantages

- Cost effective.
- No group pressure.
- Confidential.
- Large sample size.
- Productive.

Disadvantages

- Individual customers dependent.
- Can get misdirected.
- Important things may not be identified.

Understanding Your Customer's Interface

The following 10 questions will help you understand your customers and potential customers better than you have ever understood them before.

1. Why do customers need your product or service?
2. How do they find your or your competitor's products or services?
3. What do the customers use to select the products or services they buy?
4. How do they buy the products or services?
5. What is the delivery process?
6. How is the product put to use?
7. How is the product or service actually used on a day-to-day basis?
8. What problems are the customers having in using your or your competitor's products or services?
9. What are the problems with repairing or maintaining the products?
10. How does the customer dispose of the product?

Setting Goals and Objectives

Now the PIT should go back and review the objectives set by the EIT for their projects and develop a set of initial goals. These goals should define specific levels of improvement that will be accomplished by specific dates. For example, cycle time will be reduced to 30 days by

August 16, 2010, without having a negative impact upon any of the effectiveness measurements. Take time and do a good job in setting goals for the project, as the project's success will be measured against the project team's ability to meet these goals. The PIT should consider the amount of the investment that the company will be making in the PIT and be sure that the targeted improvement justifies the investment. A 3-to-1 return on investment (ROI) should be the minimum, with a target of 8 to 1 as average. If the PIT feels that it can't meet these requirements on ROI, it should alert management to the situation. Often ROI is not as important as increased customer satisfaction, particularly when we are not meeting customer requirements. In all cases, external customer satisfaction and requirements should be the driving force behind any improvement process; secondary is reducing costs, especially if those reduced costs decrease the product or service price.

> *Americans want and deserve a federal government that is fair, effective, efficient, and, above all, productive.*
> —Ronald Reagan, White House announcement, July 31, 1985

Activity 7: Develop Project and Change Management Plans

It is now time for the PIT to pull all the loose ends together into a formal project plan. An SPI project should be treated like any other project, and it should have a project plan developed for it. At a minimum the project plan should include (see Figure 3.11):

- Mission statement
- Staffing requirements
- Work breakdown structure (WBS)
- Key process measurements
- Goals
- Value proposition
- Change management plan
- Risk and mitigation plan
- Budget

The individual who is leading the PIT and the person maintaining the project plan should have training in project management. We find that Microsoft Project is a satisfactory software package to use to prepare and update the WBS.

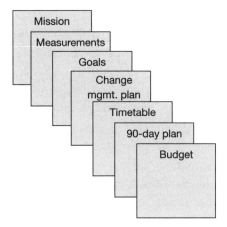

Figure 3.11   SPI project plan

Preparing a Value Proposition

Definition: *Value proposition* is an analysis and quantified "review …
of the benefits, costs, and value that an organization can deliver
to customers and other constituent groups within and outside of
the organization. It is also a positioning of value, where Value =
Benefits – Cost (cost includes risk)" (Wikipedia, 2011).

The PIT should prepare a value proposition using the goals it has
set for the project. The value proposition document should include formulas on how the impact of the streamlining process will be measured.
This is just a rough estimate of the improvement impact, but the PIT
members should take time to make it as close to accurate as possible
based upon their knowledge of the process and the key measurements
related to the process. For example, consider a process where the processing time to approve a new project is 400 employee hours and the
goal is to reduce this processing time to only 280 hours. The cost per
hour is $30/per employee. If the goal is reached, the savings would be
$3,600 per project. On average the organization approves 30 projects
per year, so the yearly savings from meeting this goal is estimated to be
$108,000/per year.

Because the figures are estimates, the accuracy of the numbers may be questioned. I like to have someone from accounting helping the PIT members to develop the value proposition, as the person from accounting often can get hold of the relevant data and frequently can provide the PIT with additional areas that the change will have an impact on. Take time to do a good job in preparing a value proposition since it is a key input to the members of the executive team in their decision related to continuing or dropping the project. The value proposition also is the PIT's commitment to the organization on the impact that the new process will have on the organization. But don't be afraid to be aggressive in these estimates in order to challenge the PIT members to be more creative in their approach to streamlining the process.

At this point, only Phases II and III need to be included in the WBS. One of the biggest mistakes that the PIT makes is to ignore the change management part of the process plan. The radical changes that an SPI project brings about in the organization cause a great deal of stress on the people that need to change. There are different degrees of complexity that the individual and the organization realize during the change process.

Depending on the type of change, one or more of the following things become involved—tasks, technology, people, and structure. A change that has the least impact upon the organization is a *level one magnitude impact* change; this is a technology change that impacts just the tasks that are performed. A *level two magnitude impact* occurs when you add people to the equation. Adding structure to the equation creates a *level three magnitude impact*, which is the most complex. (See Figure 3.12.)

The level one magnitude impact is a two-way interface between technology and the task. In the level three magnitude impact there are 6 two-way interfaces, increasing the complexity of the change by a factor of 3. Unfortunately most of the SPI projects are at a level three magnitude impact.

It is extremely important that you start your change management activities early in the cycle, because the word quickly gets out to the people who are working in the process that something is taking place, and the rumor mill will exaggerate the impact that your project will have on them. Typically the rumor starts that SPI and process reengineering will be eliminating 90 percent of the jobs, and so 90 percent of the people working in the process will be gone. That quickly kills any cooperation that you will have from the people within the process.

Level one magnitude impact—Task only—One level of complexity

- Structure—none
- People—none
- Technology ⟷ Task

Level two magnitude impact—People added to equation—Three levels of complexity

- Structure—none
- People ⟷ Task
- Task ⟷ Technology
- Technology ⟷ People

Level three magnitude impact—Structure added to equation—Six levels of complexity

- Structure ⟷ Technology
- Structure ⟷ People
- Structure ⟷ Task
- People ⟷ Task
- People ⟷ Technology
- Technology ⟷ Task

Figure 3.12 Effect change has on an organization

Key activities in organizational change management are:

- Assess human and organizational impact related to a specific change.
- Identify deficits in teamwork among key people affected by the change.
- Identify critical implementation problems that must be addressed for change to be successful.
- Determine readiness of key individuals to perform their roles.
- Improve effectiveness of resource allocation by directing resources to areas that contribute to risk of implementation.
- Measure strength of resistance, potential causes, and effective treatment.
- Identify barriers created by past experience that block new effort.
- Incorporate change management components into the transition plan.

Organizational Change Management

Organizational Change Management (OCM) objectives are:

- Develop a sound change management plan that supports process implementation.
- Maximize the degree of sponsor commitment.
- Minimize the degree of resistance.
- Minimize the risk related to implementation.
- Maximize the level of the effectiveness of the implementation team.
- Get people to make the trip.

Note: OCM is a methodology unto itself, so we will just skim over it in this book. We recommend that you read the book *Change Management Excellence: The Art of Excelling in Change Management* (Harrington, 2006) to obtain the best practices related to change management and to understand how to transform your organization from one that is resistant to change to a resilient organization.

> *You can manage change or it will manage you. The choice is yours.*
> —H. James Harrington, *Change Management Excellence: The Art of Excelling in Change Management*

Definition: *Organizational Change Management (OCM)* is a comprehensive set of structured procedures for the decision-making, planning, execution, and evaluation phases of the change process.

> *Managing change has an art and science all of its own.*
> —Ellen Florian, author

OCM should be used whenever any one of these conditions exists:

- When the change can have a major impact on the organization's performance
- When there's a high cost if the change isn't carried out successfully

- When there is high risk that certain human factors could result in implementation failure
- When a project must be completed in a much shorter time than usually is required

You could have the greatest system in the world, but if people don't believe in it, it is worthless.

—Tom Brown, former Vice President of
Purchasing at AETNA (*CFO*, 1996)

Change Is a Process

We can think of change as a real process, just like any of the processes that go on within the organization. It's the process of moving from a present state, or as-is state, through a transitional period that's extremely disruptive to the organization, to a future desired state that someone believes is better than the current state (present state). (See Figure 3.13.) This process is driven by:

- Motivation to get things moving
- A clear vision that inspires the people that need to change
- An implementation architecture that makes the change occur in the most effective and least disruptive way

We have to be aggressive about changing. The status quo is our enemy.
—Marie Eckstein, Executive Director, Dow Corning

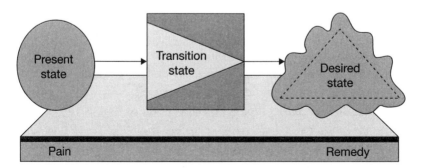

Figure 3.13 Change is a process

> **Definition:** *Change* is a condition that disrupts the current state. Change activities disrupt the current state.
>
> **Definition:** *Present state, current state, as-is state,* and *status quo* are all terms that indicate a state in which individual expectations are being fulfilled. It's a predictable state—the normal routine.
>
> **Definition:** *Transition state* is the point in the change process at which people break away from the status quo. They no longer behave as they've done in the past; yet they still haven't thoroughly established the "new way" of operating. The transition state begins when the solutions disrupt individuals' expectations and they must start to change the way they work.
>
> **Definition:** *Future state* is the point at which change initiatives are in place and integrated with the behavior patterns that are required by the change. The change goals and objectives have been achieved.

It is necessary the people understand the reason for the transformation that is necessary for survival.

—W. Edwards Deming

People are very control oriented. They're the happiest and most comfortable when they know what's going to happen and their expectations are fulfilled. Keep this in mind.

For example, if I came home from a long trip at 11:30 p.m. and found all the doors unlocked and the lights on, but my wife wasn't home, that would be a change for me. It's customary for her to greet me at the door with a kiss. My expectations would've been disrupted. People resist change because they're more disturbed about the disruption of the current state than they are afraid of the change itself. How would I react to this disruption in expectations? I'd call my son to find out if he knew where his mother was. I would wake up her friends to see if they knew anything regarding her whereabouts. I would call the local hospitals. I would be upset, worried, and unhappy. When change occurs and expectations aren't met, the four Cs come into play:

- Competence
- Comfort
- Confidence
- Control

Change makes people feel that they're not competent enough to handle the unknown that comes with change. Change makes people feel uncomfortable because they're entering a world they haven't experienced before. Changes in a work environment cause people to lose their confidence. Before the change, they knew their jobs better than anyone else, but now they have to start learning all over again. Change causes people to feel that they have lost control over their lives and actions. From the individual's standpoint, the people who are making the change are controlling their destiny. The person has lost control over his or her own life.

When the four Cs are disrupted, emotions within the organization quickly head in a negative direction. Stress levels go up very quickly because people start to worry about what will happen to them and their friends. Productivity drops off as people take time to discuss what's going to happen and as they start to question whether they're doing the right thing. The organization becomes unstable as people start to react more slowly to the present process. People become afraid because they're uncertain about what's going to happen to them. This drives up the anxiety level of the total organization. Conflicts seem to break out everywhere. When people are worried and nervous, little things will send them over the edge. Little things that would've been ignored become the most important things in life. The slightest negative comment is blown way out of proportion.

Yes, change and the accompanying disruption of expectations cause the organization to tense up, to become high strung and explosive. The child in all of us takes over, and we become very emotional.

The focus of OCM implementation methods is on the transition from the present state to the future state. The journey of this transition can be long and perilous, and if not properly managed with appropriate strategies and tactics, disastrous. Each major improvement effort in the total performance improvement management plan will undertake this journey from present to future state. That's why OCM must be part of each of the total performance improvement management plans.

Pain Management

> *Change only occurs when individuals make a choice to change. We have to establish with people that there is less pain in moving forward.*
> —William Bridges, *Managing Transitions*

Best practice is to build the resolve and commitment necessary, not only to initiate an improvement project, but to also sustain that project all the way to completion. We've seen many organizations make the common mistake of strong, zealous initiation of improvement projects, only to have them flounder from lack of resolve to sustain the project to completion. Obviously, then, the best practice in this case is to build the necessary commitment to sustain the change with senior and middle management, thereby enabling the organization to manage the change process over time.

One of the main issues in any change project is achieving "informed commitment" at the beginning. You can apply a basic formula that addresses the perceived cost of change versus the perceived cost of maintaining the status quo. As long as people perceive the change as being more costly than maintaining the status quo, it's extremely unlikely that you've built the resolve to sustain the change process. The initiator of the change must move to increase people's perception of the high cost of maintaining the status quo and decrease their perception of the cost of the change, so that people recognize that even though the change may be expensive and frightening, maintaining the status quo is no longer viable and is, in fact, more costly. This process is called *pain management.*

Pain management is the process of consciously defining, orchestrating, and communicating certain information to generate the appropriate awareness of the pain associated with maintaining the status quo, compared with the pain that will result from making the change. The "pain" that the initiator is dealing with isn't actual physical pain. Rather, change-related pain refers to the level of dissatisfaction a person experiences when his or her goals aren't being met or aren't expected to be met because of the status quo. This pain occurs when people are paying or will pay the price for an unresolved problem or for a missed key opportunity. Change-related pain can fall into one of two categories: present-state pain (as-is pain) and anticipated pain (lost-opportunity pain).

When one door closes, another opens; but we often look so long and so regretfully upon the closed door that we do not see the one which has opened for us.

—Alexander Graham Bell

Present-state pain (as-is pain) revolves around an organization's reaction to an immediate crisis or present opportunity, while anticipated pain (lost-opportunity pain), or, in other words, the pain if the change isn't made, takes a look into the future, predicting probable problems or lost opportunities. It's very crucial that management understand where its organization sits on this continuum of present-state pain versus lost-opportunity pain (additional pain that occurs if the organization doesn't change). This understanding enables management to better time the "resolve to change." If you try to build resolve or commitment too early, it won't be sustained; if you try too late, it won't matter. Management has a wide variety of pain management techniques from which to choose. Some of the techniques being used by Fortune 500 companies include cost-benefit analysis, industry benchmarking, industry trend analysis, and force-field analysis, among many others. When senior and middle management have accepted the process of timing the resolve to change, a critical mass of pain associated with the status quo has been established, and the resolve to sustain the change process has also been established. It's only then that management can begin to manage change as a process instead of as an event.

When it comes to the employees who are affected by a change, they usually have a good understanding of the present-state pain in which they're involved. This may or may not be the true view of the present-state pain of the total process. In fact, it usually isn't. But even if the employees have a true view of the present-state pain of the process, they usually don't have any idea of its anticipated pain. For example, they may not realize that if they don't make a specific change, the organization will lose 50 percent of its customer base and the plant may be closed, and so everyone will be out of work. That's why management must communicate to all the affected employees the present-state and the anticipated pain related to what's being changed. It's not enough to do it one time. It must be repeated over and over again, thereby reinforcing the need for the change.

Any project that results from the performance improvement philosophy will, by necessity, cause change in an organization. Applying this best practice is critical in beginning to mobilize support and understanding for the reasons for change, to help the employees let go of the status quo and move forward to a very difficult state, known as the *transition state*. Managing people through the transition state to project completion requires resolve to not only initiate change but sustain it over time, with management continually communicating the necessity for change and supporting the actions required to bring it about.

It's important to remember that any type of disruption stimulates resistance. The individual's existing frame of reference provides unconscious psychological security. You can break this strong commitment to the current state only when the individual's perceived pain in the current state is greater than his or her perceived pain (fear) of the transitional and future states. (See Figure 3.14.)

Two factors determine the impact of the present-state pain. Each person has his or her existing frame of reference that defines his or her level of pain in the present state. In addition, each individual has a certain level of pain that he or she can stand before deciding to give up on the present state and embrace the change.

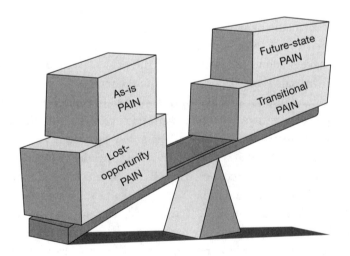

Figure 3.14   Pain management

The first part of the equation is to generate enough information about the pain related to the present state (as-is state) that the individual becomes open to making a change. Next, you minimize the individual's perception of the turmoil that he or she will go through during the transition state. You can accomplish this by providing information about the implementation plan, involving the employee in the planning, and providing education and training for the affected people early in the cycle.

The last part of the equation is to offer a realistic vision of the future state. Too often we make changes without considering the fabric or organizational context of the action. Contextual leadership is a key part of OCM. It's the ability to provide a specific frame of reference about the change and its impact upon the affected individuals. This ability gives people a view of the change so that they understand what's going to happen to them and why. To provide this level of understanding, you must prepare four key documents related to the future state:

- Vision statement
- Mission statement
- Operating plan
- Human attributes analysis

There's no such thing as the perfect solution. Every solution, no matter how good, creates new problems.
—H. James Harrington

A vision statement should be broad enough to define the future state, yet specific enough to be personal to the affected individuals. It should be progressive enough to open everyone's eyes to what can be accomplished, but at the same time, it must be realistic. Unrealistic vision statements will get ignored, as will "ho-hum" ones. A good vision statement stretches people beyond their current capabilities without setting up false hopes and dreams that they can't obtain. The vision statement should be the stimulus that unites people and motivates them to embrace the change.

Additionally, a good vision statement will instill enthusiasm and capture not only the individual's attention, but also his or her personal desires, logic, and objectives. It's designed to bridge the gap between the individuals who are affected by the change and the organization's need for the change. The vision statement should address:

- Why the organization is making the change
- How the change will affect the processes
- What's in it for the affected people and the organization
- What behavioral patterns will be affected

The vision statement should paint a picture of the future state to the degree that the individual can judge the amount of pain that he or she will encounter when the change is carried out. All employees realize that any change will cause future-state pain, no matter how good the intentions of the change team.

The mission statement also helps the individual to better understand the future-state environment and its pain. It provides an understanding of what must be accomplished if the future state is to be achieved. It will identify the human and technical objectives of the change.

The operating plan answers the question, What's going to change? It provides the work breakdown structure that defines how the change will be achieved.

The human attributes analysis completes the view of the future-state environment. It defines the personal attributes that will need to change for the change to be put into place. It will identify the need for changes in things such as:

- Values
- Beliefs
- Behaviors
- Attitudes
- Knowledge

With the completion and communication of these four key documents—vision statement, mission statement, operating plan, and human attributes analysis—the individuals affected by the change will be able to evaluate the degree of pain they'll be subjected to when the changes are carried out. Now, based upon their own experiences or management-supplied information, the affected employees should have developed in their own minds an opinion about the pain they're being or will be subjected to in these four conditions:

- Present-state (as-is state) pain
- Lost-opportunity pain
- Transitional pain
- Future-state pain

Based on their opinion about the pain they're experiencing and may be subjected to, they can decide to support the change, resist the change, or just wait to see how the change will affect them. If the combination of the present-state pain plus the lost-opportunity pain is greater than the combination of the transitional pain plus the future-state pain, they'll support the change. (See Figure 3.14.) If not, they'll resist it and do whatever they can to make the change project fail.

> *In the case of driving for excellence in these functional areas, you have to draw attention to the crisis to really make people take notice and say, "Yes, we want to do it differently here."*
> —Robert J. Herbold, former COO, Microsoft

Activity 8: Conduct Phase I Tollgate

Definition: *Tollgates* are process checkpoints where deliverables are reviewed and measured and where readiness to move forward is addressed.

Typically, if a total project has not completed all of its commitments that are due at the tollgate, the project doesn't progress to the next level until these commitments are met. Usually this is a management review to determine if the project should continue.

At each tollgate, the executive team and the project sponsor will review the status of the project to determine:

- If the project should continue to the next phase
- Whether the project should be dropped

- If part or all of the current phase or past phase should be redone
- What the impact of this project will be on other projects or other information that is now available

The approval of the project at each tollgate signifies that the reviewers agree that the:

- Phase activities have been successfully completed
- The goals as defined in the charter are acceptable
- The project is ready to progress to the next phase

The outputs that will be reviewed at the Phase I tollgate are:

- Mission statement
- Boxed-in process
- Key measurements
- Goals and objectives
- Project plan
- Change management plan
- Project budget

When the executive team accepts the inputs to the tollgate, the PIT has completed a major milestone and can start Phase II: Analyzing the Process.

Summary

Phase I is very important. Someone once said, "A problem defined is half-solved." We won't go that far, but it is well on its way to being attacked. What Phase I activities accomplish is laying the foundation for the follow-on activities.

One of the problems that the PIT faces is the fact that its members come from different departments. When they first come together, they often are very dysfunctional and defensive. They feel they are there to represent their department against all criticism. Typical statements that individual PIT members make are:

- "We need more people in our department."
- "No one gives us the inputs on time."
- "We get nothing but junk in. How can we do a good job?"

It is not a team working to improve the process; it is a group of combatants defending the way they are doing things now. As a result, a big part of Phase I activities is to transform the individual, fragmented thought patterns and get all the members willing to focus on the good of the total process, not just on the part they are working on. This is probably the biggest challenge that the process owner faces.

The biggest challenge that the Process Improvement Team faces is getting its members to put the good of the total ahead of the interest of their function.

—H. James Harrington

CHAPTER

Phase II: Analyzing the Process

You can't know how to get there unless you know where you are coming from.
—H. James Harrington

Introduction

Before you start wildly making changes, it is wise to understand what the current processes (good and bad points) are. Usually by this time, PIT members already have a number of changes they would like to make, but they need to be held back until they gain an understanding of the total process and the effects their ideas will have on the total process. Their ideas are important and may play an important part in the final process design, so you don't want to lose them. As a result, we recommend that the PIT establish a parking board where everyone and anyone's improvement ideas can be placed, if they can't be implemented or taken advantage of at the present time.

The best way we have found to develop this process understanding in the minds of the PIT members is by creating a flow diagram of the process.

Unfortunately most business processes are not documented, and often when they are documented, the processes are not followed. During this phase the PIT will draw a picture of the present process (as-is process), analyze compliance to present procedures, and collect cost, quality, processing time, and cycle time data.

There are eight activities in this phase. (See Figure 4.1.) They are:

- Activity 1: Flowchart the Process
- Activity 2: Conduct a Benchmark Study
- Activity 3: Conduct a Process Walk-Through
- Activity 4: Perform a Process Cost, Cycle Time, and Output Analysis
- Activity 5: Prepare the Simulation Model
- Activity 6: Implement Quick Fixes
- Activity 7: Develop a Current Culture Model
- Activity 8: Conduct Phase II Tollgate

The purpose of Phase II is for the PIT to gain detailed knowledge of the process and its matrixes (cost cycle time, processing time, error rates, etc.). The flowchart and simulation model of the present process (the as-is model of the process) will be used to improve the process during Phase III: Streamlining the Process. Without understanding the current process, it is impossible to project cost benefits and risks related to future-state solutions. All too often, organizations implement major changes that improve organizational performance, and as an afterthought, they try to measure the impact the change has on performance without a firm original database against which to compare the existing performance.

Analyze Phase

During this phase the PIT needs to establish a realistic, documented picture of the as-is process. This includes not only understanding the activities that take place within the process, but also determining the resources that are used at each activity and the problems encountered. During this phase every member of the PIT should gain a detailed understanding of the process and be able to identify opportunities for improvement.

Activity 1: Flowchart the Process

Many different types of flowcharting can be used to draw pictures of the business process. Some of the most common are:

- Block diagrams
- ANSI standards

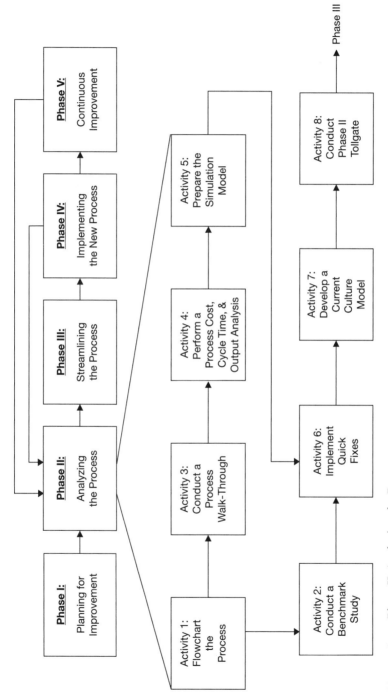

Figure 4.1 Phase II: Analyzing the Process

- Geographic
- Functional
- Data flow
- Communication flow
- Knowledge flow
- Value flow
- Value stream

Each of them can be broken down into more and more detail. (See Figure 4.2.)

It is not our intent to teach you how to flowchart at this time; that would take a book unto itself, and there are many approaches and many different configurations depending upon the type of process you are flowcharting. What we will do is provide you with some key thoughts that may help you during your flowcharting process.

Standard Flowchart Symbols

The most effective flowcharts use only widely known standard symbols. Think about how much easier it is to read a road map when you are familiar with the meaning of each symbol and what a nuisance it is to have some strange, unfamiliar shape in the area of the map you are using to make a decision about your travel plans.

The flowchart is one of the oldest of all the design aids available. For simplicity we will review only 10 of the most common symbols, most of which are published by ANSI. (See Figure 4.3.)

The 10 symbols listed are not meant to be a complete list of flow-chart symbols, but they are the minimum you will need to adequately flowchart your business process. As you learn more about flowcharting, you can expand the number of symbols you use to cover your specific field and needs.

Table 4.1 compares seven types of flowcharts. Figures 4.4 to 4.7 show examples of some of the different types.

Let's suppose the PIT chooses to use a typical block diagram like the one shown in Figure 4.5. The PIT members will now block-diagram the total process following the process flow. Once a block diagram of the process has been completed, the block diagram can be expanded into a detailed flowchart. The block diagram should start with the input into the

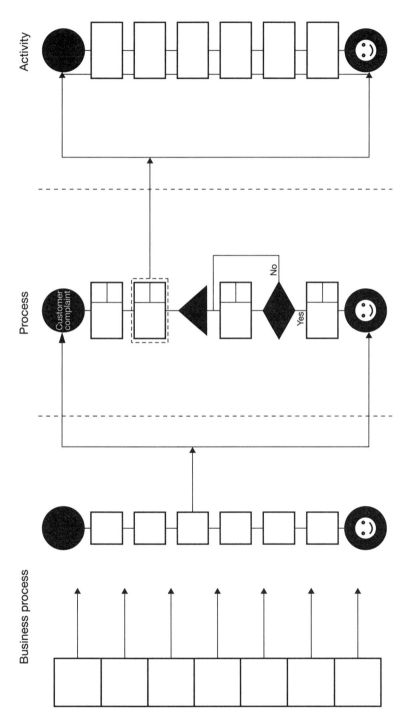

Figure 4.2 Flowchart structure

Activity

Process

Customer complaint

No

Yes

Business process

Symbol — Meaning

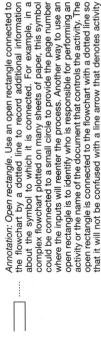

Operation: Rectangle. Use this symbol whenever a change in an item occurs. The change may result from the expenditure of labor, a machine activity, or a combination of both. It is used to denote activity of any kind, from drilling a hole to processing computer data. It is the correct symbol to use when no other one is appropriate. Normally, you should include a short description of the activity in the rectangle.

Movement/transportation: Fat arrow. Use a fat arrow to indicate movement of the output between locations (e.g., sending parts to stock, mailing a letter).

Decision point: Diamond. Put a diamond at the point in the process at which a decision must be made. The next series of activities will vary based on this decision. For example, "If the letter is correct, it will be signed. If it is incorrect, it will be retyped." Typically, the outputs from the diamond are marked with the options (e.g., yes-no, true-false).

Inspection: Square. Use to signify that the process flow has stopped so the quality of the output can be evaluated. It typically involves an inspection conducted by someone other than the person who performed the previous activity. It also can represent the point at which an approval signature is required.

Paper documents: Wiggle-bottomed rectangle. Use this symbol to show when the output from an activity included information recorded on paper (e.g., written reports, letters, or computer printouts).

Start/end: Circle. Use this symbol at the beginning and end points of a flowchart.

Symbol — Meaning

Delay: Blunted rectangle. Use this symbol, sometimes called a *bullet*, when an item or person must wait or when an item is placed in temporary storage before the next scheduled activity is performed (e.g., waiting for an airplane, waiting for a signature).

Storage: Triangle. Use a triangle when a controlled storage condition or when an order or requisition is required to remove the item for the next scheduled activity. This symbol is used most often to show that output is in storage waiting for a customer. The object of a continuous-flow process is to eliminate all the triangles and blunt rectangles from the process flowchart. In a business process, the triangle would be used to show the status of a purchase requisition being held by purchasing, waiting for finance to verify that the item was in the approved budget.

Annotation: Open rectangle. Use an open rectangle connected to the flowchart by a dotted line to record additional information about the symbol to which it is connected. For example, in a complex flowchart plotted on many sheets of paper, this symbol could be connected to a small circle to provide the page number where the inputs will reenter the process. Another way to use an open rectangle is to identify who is responsible for performing an activity or the name of the document that controls the activity. The open rectangle is connected to the flowchart with a dotted line so that it will not be confused with a line arrow that denotes activity flow.

Direction flow: Arrow. Use an arrow to denote the direction and order of process steps. An arrow is used for movement from one symbol to another. The arrow denotes direction—up, down, or sideways. ANSI indicates that the arrowhead is not necessary when the direction flow is from top to bottom or from left to right. However, to avoid misinterpretation by others who may not be as familiar with flowchart symbols, it is recommended that you always use arrowheads.

Figure 4.3 Standard flowchart symbols

Table 4.1 Comparison of Flowcharts

Types of Flowcharts	Level of Detail	What Is Charted	What It Includes
Process blocks	High	Activities	What
Process charts	Medium	Activities, Tasks, Decisions	What, how, where
Procedure charts	Detailed	Tasks, Material flow, Individual actions	How, where, who
Functional flowcharts	Medium	Activities, Tasks	What, who
Geographic flowcharts	Medium	Activities	What, where
Paperwork flowcharts	Detailed	Documents	How, where, who
Informational flowcharts	Medium	Information, Activities, Decisions	What, how, who, where

process and develop the flowchart so that all activities within the process under study are being charted. Normally flowcharts go down to the activity level only, but often some important activities are flowcharted down to the task level. Once you have completed the flowchart, look at each block on the flowchart and estimate the following:

- Processing time
- Cycle time
- Cost per activity
- Percentage of items that go through that activity
- Errors per activity

If you have any large cost or long processing time, it is often advisable to drill down to the next level so you can see how the costs and time are being spent.

Figure 4.8 is a form that the PIT can use to draw a simple flowchart, and Figure 4.9 is a sample flowchart using the simple flowchart form.

At this point, the processing time, cycle time, and cost are based upon best judgment of the PIT. Later on in this phase, actual data will be collected. (See Figure 4.10.)

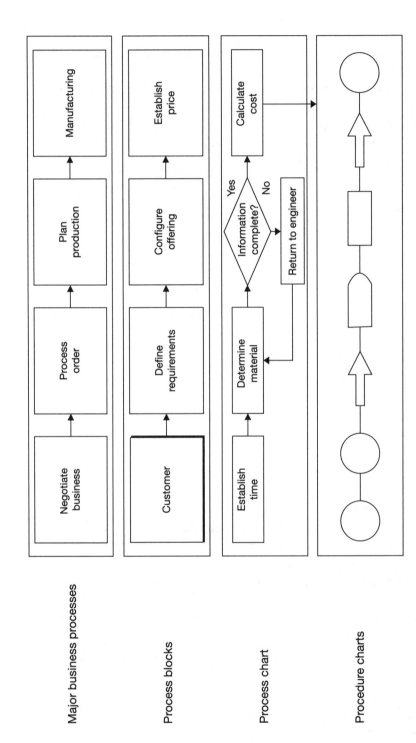

Figure 4.4   Relationships among flowcharting techniques

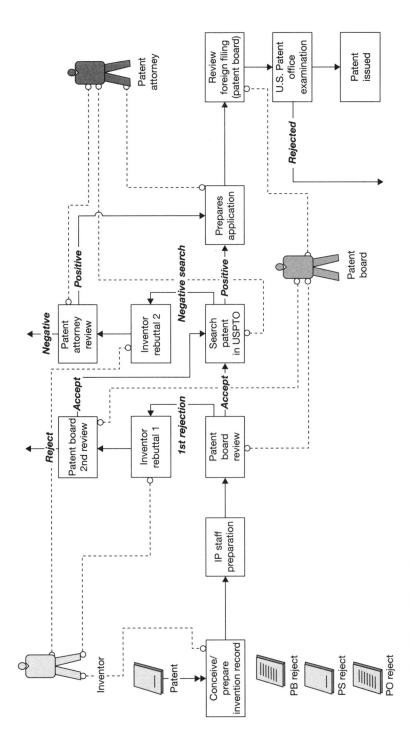

Figure 4.5 Typical block diagram

99

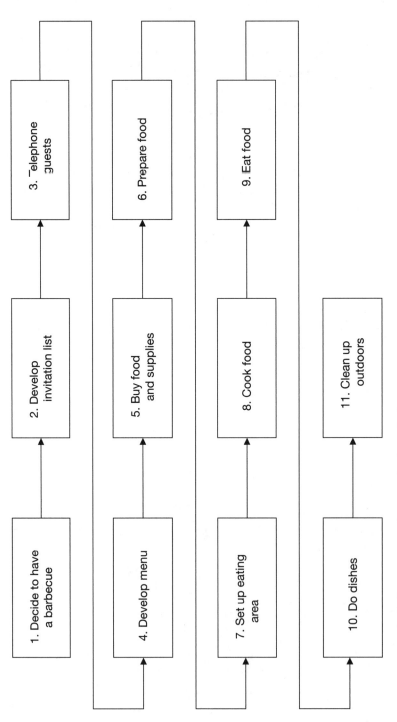

Figure 4.6 Block diagram example—conducting a barbeque

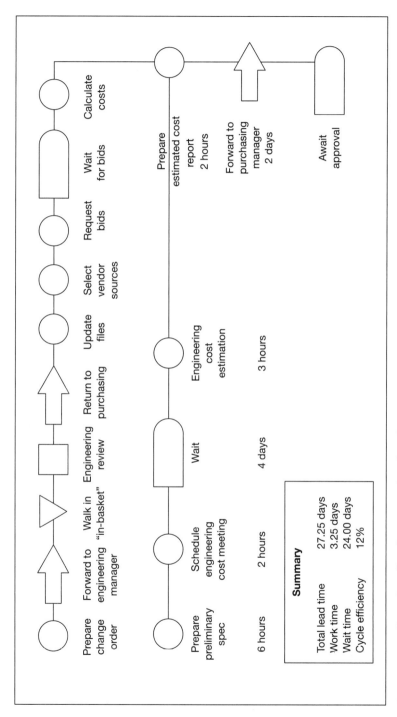

Figure 4.7 Procedure flowchart example—flowcharting a purchasing process

Prepare change order

Forward to engineering manager

Walk in "in-basket"

Engineering review

Return to purchasing

Update files

Select vendor sources

Request bids

Wait for bids

Calculate costs

Prepare preliminary spec

Schedule engineering cost meeting

Wait

Engineering cost estimation

6 hours

2 hours

4 days

3 hours

Prepare estimated cost report
2 hours

Forward to purchasing manager
2 days

Await approval

Summary

Total lead time	27.25 days
Work time	3.25 days
Wait time	24.00 days
Cycle efficiency	12%

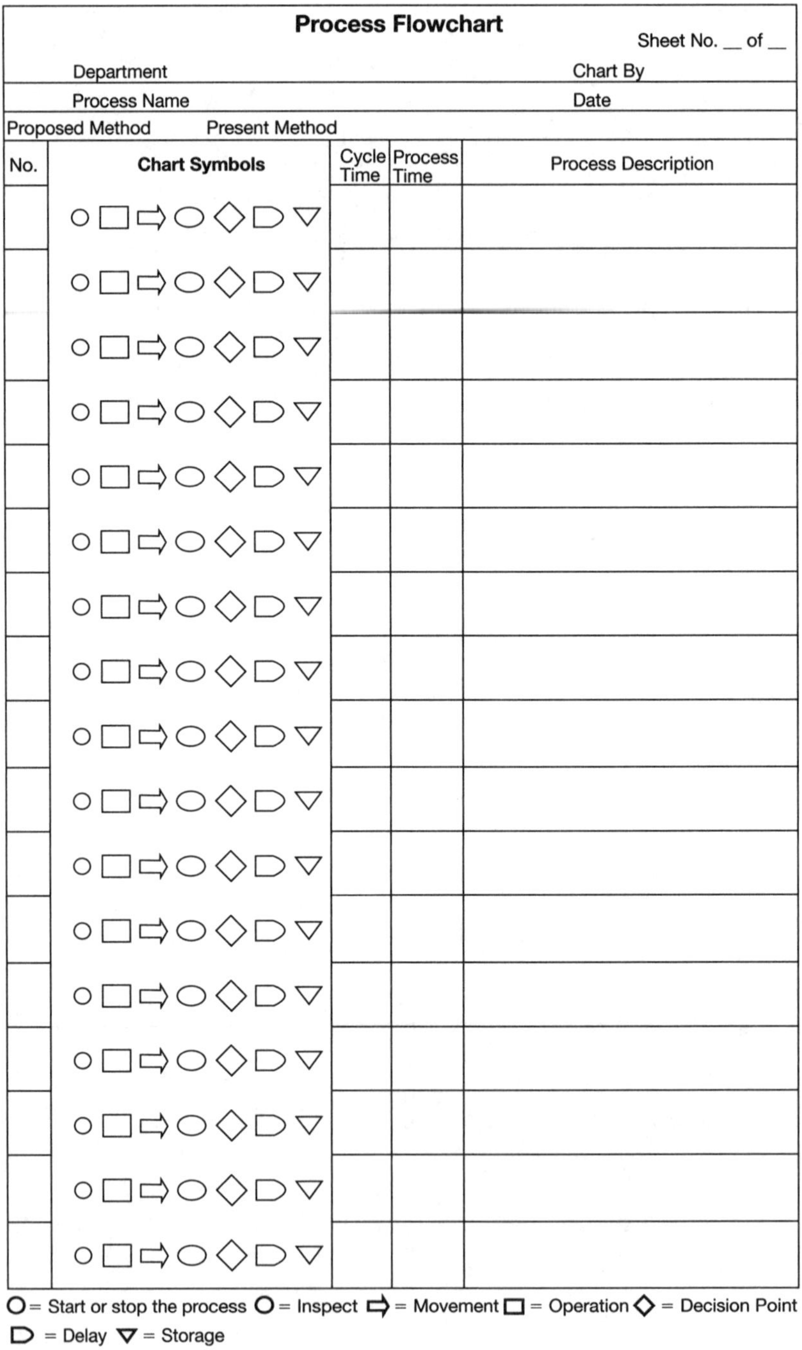

No.	Chart Symbols	Cycle Time	Process Time	Process Description
	○ □ ⇨ ○ ◇ D ▽			
	○ □ ⇨ ○ ◇ D ▽			
	○ □ ⇨ ○ ◇ D ▽			
	○ □ ⇨ ○ ◇ D ▽			
	○ □ ⇨ ○ ◇ D ▽			
	○ □ ⇨ ○ ◇ D ▽			
	○ □ ⇨ ○ ◇ D ▽			
	○ □ ⇨ ○ ◇ D ▽			
	○ □ ⇨ ○ ◇ D ▽			
	○ □ ⇨ ○ ◇ D ▽			
	○ □ ⇨ ○ ◇ D ▽			
	○ □ ⇨ ○ ◇ D ▽			
	○ □ ⇨ ○ ◇ D ▽			
	○ □ ⇨ ○ ◇ D ▽			
	○ □ ⇨ ○ ◇ D ▽			
	○ □ ⇨ ○ ◇ D ▽			
	○ □ ⇨ ○ ◇ D ▽			

Process Flowchart

Sheet No. __ of __

Department   Chart By

Process Name   Date

Proposed Method   Present Method

○ = Start or stop the process ○ = Inspect ⇨ = Movement □ = Operation ◇ = Decision Point
D = Delay ▽ = Storage

Figure 4.8 Sample form to use to draw a simple flowchart

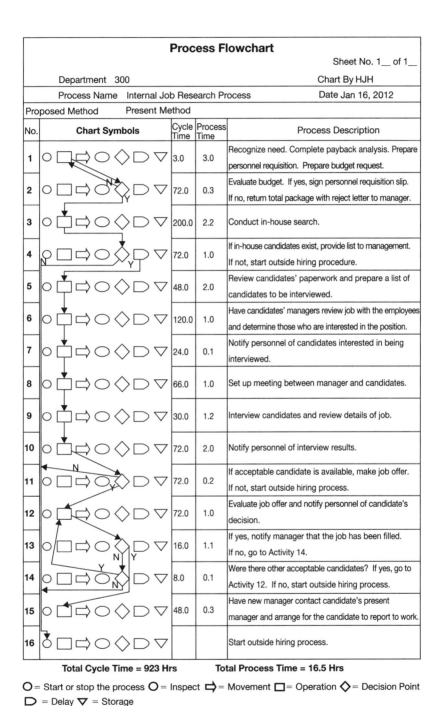

No.	Chart Symbols	Cycle Time	Process Time	Process Description
	Process Flowchart			Sheet No. 1__ of 1__
	Department 300			Chart By HJH
	Process Name Internal Job Research Process			Date Jan 16, 2012
	Proposed Method Present Method			
1		3.0	3.0	Recognize need. Complete payback analysis. Prepare personnel requisition. Prepare budget request.
2		72.0	0.3	Evaluate budget. If yes, sign personnel requisition slip. If no, return total package with reject letter to manager.
3		200.0	2.2	Conduct in-house search.
4		72.0	1.0	If in-house candidates exist, provide list to management. If not, start outside hiring procedure.
5		48.0	2.0	Review candidates' paperwork and prepare a list of candidates to be interviewed.
6		120.0	1.0	Have candidates' managers review job with the employees and determine those who are interested in the position.
7		24.0	0.1	Notify personnel of candidates interested in being interviewed.
8		66.0	1.0	Set up meeting between manager and candidates.
9		30.0	1.2	Interview candidates and review details of job.
10		72.0	2.0	Notify personnel of interview results.
11		72.0	0.2	If acceptable candidate is available, make job offer. If not, start outside hiring process.
12		72.0	1.0	Evaluate job offer and notify personnel of candidate's decision.
13		16.0	1.1	If yes, notify manager that the job has been filled. If no, go to Activity 14.
14		8.0	0.1	Were there other acceptable candidates? If yes, go to Activity 12. If no, start outside hiring process.
15		48.0	0.3	Have new manager contact candidate's present manager and arrange for the candidate to report to work.
16				Start outside hiring process.

Total Cycle Time = 923 Hrs   Total Process Time = 16.5 Hrs

O = Start or stop the process O = Inspect ⇨ = Movement □ = Operation ◇ = Decision Point
D = Delay ▽ = Storage

Figure 4.9   Flowchart of internal job research process

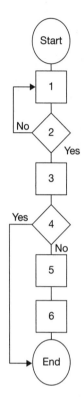

Activity	Processing Time (Hours)	Cycle Time (Hours)	Cost (Dollars)
1	3.0	3	192.00
2	0.3	72	19.20
3	2.2	200	140.80
4	1.0	72	64.00
5	2.0	48	128.00
6	1.0	120	64.00
Total	9.5	515	608.00

Figure 4.10 Part of the internal job research process flowchart

Functional Timeline Flowchart

A functional timeline flowchart adds processing and cycle time to the standard functional flowchart. This flowchart offers some valuable insights when you are doing a poor-quality cost analysis to determine how much money the organization is losing because the process is not efficient and effective. Adding a time value to the already defined functions interacting within the process makes it easier to identify areas of waste and delay.

Time is monitored in two ways. First, as you can see in Figure 4.10, the time required to perform the activity is recorded in the column entitled "Processing Time (Hours)." The column beside it is labeled "Cycle Time (Hours)" (i.e., the time between when the last activity was completed and when this activity was completed). Usually there is a major difference between the sum of the individual processing hours and the cycle time for the total process. This difference is due to waiting and transportation time.

In Figure 4.11, while the total processing time is only 16.5 hours, the total cycle time is 923.0 hours. Performing all the activities required only 1.8 percent of the total time that it took to fill one job. The cycle time analysis shows why it takes so much time to get even the simplest job done.

One common error is to focus on reducing processing time and to ignore cycle time. The result is focusing our activities on reducing costs

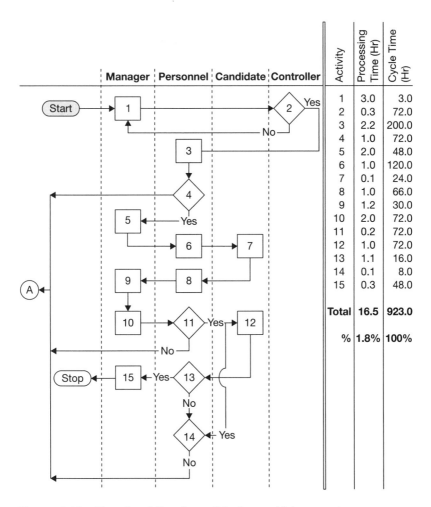

Figure 4.11   Functional flowchart of the internal job research process

without considering the business from our customer's viewpoint. Customers do not see processing time—they see only cycle time (response time). To meet our needs, we must work on reducing processing time. To have happy customers, we must reduce cycle time.

In one sales process, IBM was able to reduce processing time by 30 percent, thereby reducing costs by 25 percent. At the same time, the company reduced cycle time by 75 percent. An unplanned-for side effect was a more than 300 percent increase in sales (65 percent sales closure). There is no doubt that there is a direct correlation between cycle time, customer satisfaction, and increased profits.

The timeline flow concept can be applied to all types of flowcharts. Often, elapsed time is recorded using the time that has elapsed from the time the first activity in the process started. If this method had been used in Figure 4.11, the elapsed time recorded adjacent to the first three activities would be the sum of the cycle time recorded for Activities 1, 2, and 3, or 275 hours.

Figure 4.11 is a functional flowchart; it is sometimes also called a *swim-lane flowchart.* You'll notice that instead of recording the activity information within the activity block, it is recorded on the side, thereby allowing the flowchart to be collapsed into a smaller area. Table 4.2 presents the details related to each item on the functional flowchart.

Graphic Flowcharts

A graphic or physical layout flowchart analyzes the physical flow of activities. It helps to minimize the time wasted while work outputs are moved between activities.

Graphics flowcharting is a useful tool for evaluating department layout related to things like paperwork flow and for analyzing product flow by identifying excessive travel and storage delays. In SPI, geographic flowcharting helps in analyzing traffic patterns around busy areas like file cabinets, computers, and copiers. Figure 4.12 is a graphic flowchart of a new employee's first day at XYZ Company.

Value Stream Mapping

One of the ways to diagram a process is called value stream mapping, which became popular in the 1990s. Its main advantage over standard flowcharting is the additional information that is recorded on the diagram

Table 4.2 Functional Flowchart

Activity	Performed by
1. Recognize need. Complete payback analysis. Prepare personnel requisition. Prepare budget request.	Manager
2. Evaluate budget. If yes, sign personnel requisition slip. If no, return total package with reject letter to manager.	Controller
3. Conduct in-house search.	Personnel
4. If in-house candidates exist, provide list to management. If not, start outside hiring procedure.	Personnel
5. Review candidates' paperwork and prepare a list of candidates to be interviewed.	Manager
6. Have candidates' managers review job with the employees and determine those who are interested in the position.	Personnel
7. Notify personnel of candidates interested in being interviewed.	Candidates
8. Set up meeting between manager and candidates.	Personnel
9. Interview candidates and review details of job.	Manager
10. Notify personnel of interview results.	Manager
11. If acceptable candidate is available, make job offer. If not, start outside hiring process.	Personnel
12. Evaluate job offer and notify personnel of candidate's decision.	Candidate
13. If yes, notify manager that the job has been filled. If no, go to Activity 14.	Personnel
14. Were there other acceptable candidates? If yes, go to Activity 12. If no, start outside hiring process.	Personnel
15. Have new manager contact candidate's present manager and arrange for the candidate to report to work.	Manager
16. Start outside hiring process	Personnel

and its focus more on movement and inventory reduction. It also includes a sawtooth that depicts process and lead times.

Fat arrows are used to show flow of product, and triangles between process boxes are used to define inventory levels before each process activity. Recorded under the activity box is information related to that activity. (See Figure 4.13.)

Value stream mapping leaves a lot of latitude to the PIT. Many different symbols can be used, and the team is allowed to add additional

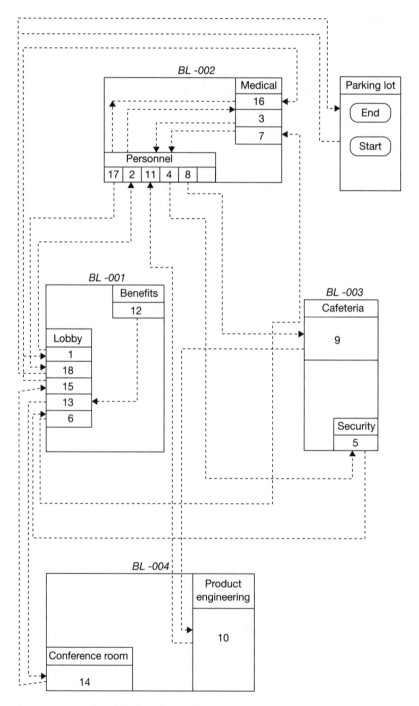

Figure 4.12 Graphic flowchart of a new employee at XYZ Company

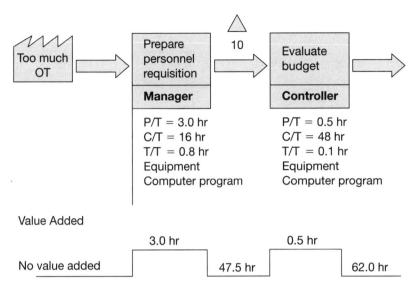

Figure 4.13   First two activities in internal job research process

symbols to meet its particular needs. (See Figure 4.14.) Some of the more common symbols are:

- *A truck.* To show that the movement is by truck
- *A train.* To show that the movement is by train
- *An airplane.* To show that the movement is by airplane
- *A stick figure.* To show that the movement is by people carrying the product from one spot to another
- *A triangle with a q inside.* To show that the product is in queue or waiting
- *A triangle with a capital I inside.* To show that the product is in inventory
- *A starburst.* To show that an activity has some improvement activities assigned to it
- *An elongated rectangle with FIFO inside.* To show that first in, first out is being practiced
- *A pair of eyeglasses.* To indicate that the team should look at this particular area
- *A thin line with an arrow.* To show it is a hard copy that is being transmitted
- *An irregular thin line with an arrow.* To show that the information is being sent electronically

Current-State Icons

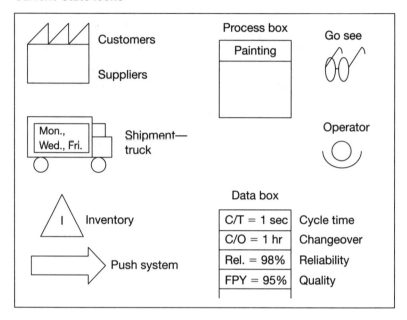

More Current-State Icons

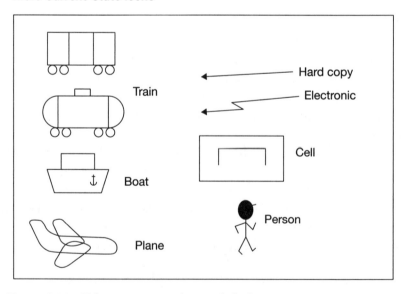

Figure 4.14   Value stream mapping symbols (icons)

Source: Strategy Associates

Figure 4.15 is a current-state value stream map of a process to get your driver's license.

The steps to create a value stream map are:

1. Form a PIT and prepare a charter.
2. Train the PIT on how to make and use value stream maps.
3. Collect data by doing a process walk-through.
4. Construct the value stream map for the current process.
5. Check the value stream map for the current process (80 percent accuracy is good enough).
6. Set targets for improvement for activity and area.
7. Draw a future-state map that defines what the process should look like based upon the defined improvements.
8. Get management's approval to make the changes.

Figure 4.16 is a current-state value stream map of a product's process, which consists of four major activities.

Figure 4.17 is the future-state value stream map of the same process prepared by the PIT as shown in Figure 4.16. You will note that the cycle time is reduced from 40 days to 7 days and processing time from 105 seconds to 91 seconds.

Value stream mapping is a good technique if it is made simple. Often the PIT members get so involved in making the value stream map that they lose sight of what the real objective is and it becomes cluttered and useless. We like to use it for simple processes that have few activities (less than 10). We find it works best when it is used as part of a Fast-Action Solution Technique (FAST) project.

Definition: Fast Action Solution Technique (FAST) is an approach that focuses a group's attention on a single process for a one or two day meeting to define how the group can improve the process over the next 90 days. At the end of the meeting, management approves or rejects the proposed improvements. For more detail, I recommend *Fast Action Solution Technique* (Harrington, 2010).

Driver's License Issuance: Current-State Map

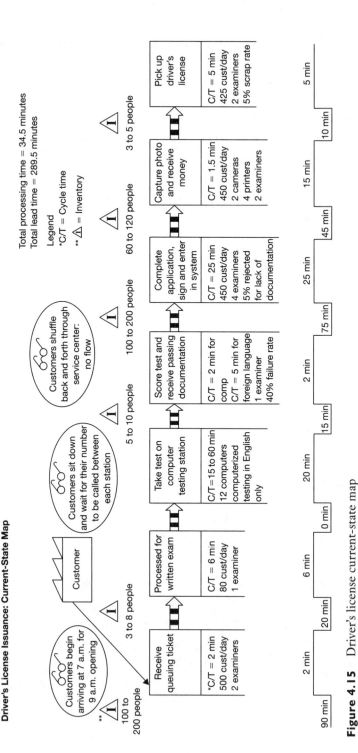

Figure 4.15 Driver's license current-state map

Source: *Quality Digest Magazine*, March 2006, p. 41

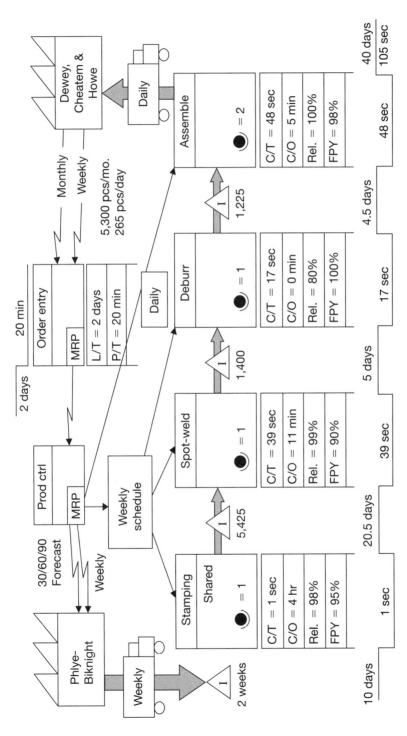

Figure 4.16 Current-state value stream map of a product process

Source: Strategy Associates

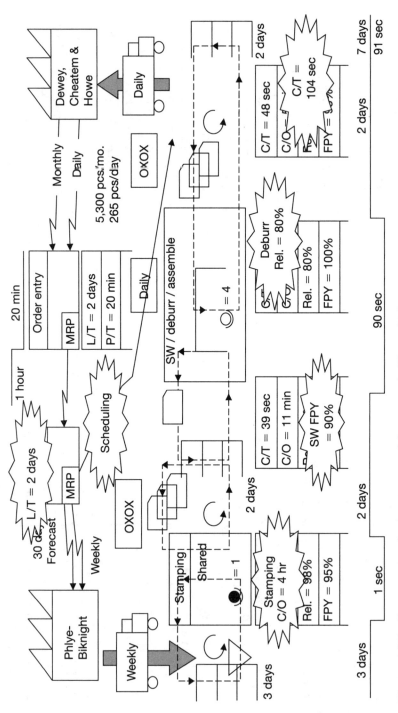

Figure 4.17 Future-state value stream map of the process in Figure 4.16

Source: Strategy Associates

Y = f(X) Process Charts

Processes are often analyzed as having *X* inputs that create *Y* outputs. To put it another way, *Y* (process outputs) is a function of *X* (inputs). This concept applies at the process activity or tasks levels. The *X* inputs include:

- Machines
- Manpower
- Materials
- Measurements
- Methods
- Mother Nature

Each of the process inputs can be classified into one of four subcategories based upon their variables designation. They are:

- *C (controllable).* The process owner has control over these variables regardless of what other controls are exercised.
- *N (noise).* Noise variables cannot be controlled or might be too expensive to control.
- *SOPs (standard operating procedures).* Standard operating procedures define the way the process is performed.
- *X (critical).* Critical input variables are other subsets of controlled variables; they are variables that have been determined to have significant impact upon one or more of the output variables.

Figure 4.18 shows three activities where the output from each activity is above the line and the inputs are below the line. You'll note that the inputs and outputs are numbers, and the variables designation for each input immediately follows the input. For example, 1.N stands for "input 1 is a noise input."

Information Process Flowcharting

In addition to the basic flowcharting we have discussed, there is also information diagramming, often with its own set of symbols. In general, these are more interesting to computer programmers and automated systems analysts than to managers and employees charting business

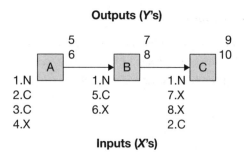

Figure 4.18   Typical value stream map

activities, but they are very important in designing an organizational structure. You make a set of these types of flowcharts that follow information through the process. As you prepare flowcharts, think of your organization's activities in terms of information processing, beginning with your organization's files. They are valuable because they contain information that is created or used by your business processes.

Figure 4.19 is a block diagram with its information-communication support system added to it with broken lines.

Next consider your employees. You and your coworkers have skills of various levels and types. Obviously even a single worker's knowledge is substantially more sophisticated than the information in the file, but the principle still holds. The employee's value to an organization depends upon his or her contribution of information. Whether it is how to load a pallet, introduce a new product, or resolve conflict, information is a resource. This is particularly true in the service industry, which in the twenty-first century employs over 80 percent of the U.S. labor force; all these people can be considered information processors and providers.

If you take an information processing view when preparing your flowcharts, it will create a common focus on getting and using quality inputs in order to produce quality outputs. At the same time, this type of view helps people determine who their interfaces are.

Process Knowledge Mapping

> *There will be an increased emphasis over the next few years on taxonomies, ontologies and knowledge.*
>
> —French Caldwell, Vice President, Information and
> Knowledge Management, Gartner Group

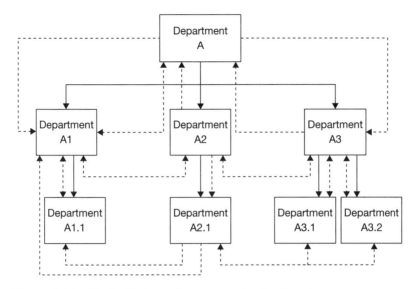

Figure 4.19 Typical information-communication flowchart

A process-based knowledge map is a map or diagram that visually displays knowledge within the context of the business process. It shows both the way knowledge should be used within the process and the source of this knowledge. Any type of knowledge that drives the process or results from execution of this process can be and should be met. This includes tacit (soft) knowledge or explicit (hard) knowledge. Tacit knowledge is defined as undocumented, intangible factors embedded in the individual's experience. Explicit knowledge, on the other hand, is documented and quantified knowledge that is recorded and can be easily distributed.

As you look at your process-based knowledge map, ask the following questions:

• What knowledge is missing?
• What knowledge is most valuable?
• What knowledge can be used in other processes?
• What knowledge is generated but not shared?

Knowledge management is often abstract, overly strategized, and weak in implementation. Process-based knowledge maps are concrete and tactical; they allow the business to really focus in on its key knowledge assets. Figure 4.20 is a typical knowledge map.

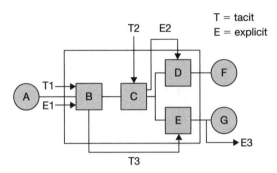

Figure 4.20 Typical knowledge map

Other Process Mapping Tools

We have only highlighted the major process mapping tools that we like to use. Some of the other major process mapping tools include:

- Organizational structure diagrams
- Hierarchical overview diagrams
- Global overview of processes and divisions diagrams
- Global process diagrams
- Detailed process diagrams
- Form management diagrams
- Form circulation diagrams
- Accounting system diagrams

For information on these diagrams and others, see *Business Process Improvement Workbook* (Harrington, Esseling, and Van Nimwegen, 1997).

Activity 2: Conduct a Benchmark Study

There is a big difference between a benchmark and doing benchmarking.
—H. James Harrington

Definition: A *benchmark* is a specific number or point that is used to compare another measurement or point against.

Definition: *Benchmarking* is a systematic way to identify, understand, and creatively evolve superior products, services, designs, equipment, processes, and practices to improve the organization's real performance. It is used to adapt or adopt the best part of the processes performed by other organizations into the process being studied.

At this point some of the PITs may question if the goals they set are realistic. Are they aggressive enough, or are they too aggressive? One way to answer this question is to benchmark similar processes in other organizations. This activity is usually done in parallel with Activities 1 to 4 in Phase II. It is important to note that benchmark studies are usually done if there is a question related to the goals set by the PIT.

By the end of Activity 4 in Phase II, the PIT members have an excellent understanding of the process they are studying and have it completely characterized. This puts the PIT in an excellent position to compare the process with other similar processes.

To start the benchmark process, the PIT needs to determine if the process is being conducted at any other place within its organization. We know of one organization (Organization X) that contacted an outside organization (Organization Y) asking for information about Organization Y's design review process. Organization Y responded that it had done a benchmarking study the previous year on the same process where it looked at 12 different organizations. Organization Y reported that it learned that Organization X had the best practice. Unfortunately these best practices were going on at another one of Organization X's locations, and there had been a lack of information exchange between X's locations.

It is usually easier to obtain data from other parts of your organization than from an outside source. The following are the benchmark tasks that should be performed:

- Develop a benchmark plan.
- Collect benchmark data from internal sources.
- Collect and analyze public-domain information.
- Collect data from:
  - External and internal experts
  - Professional associations
  - Consultants
  - Independent test firms
  - Universities
  - Company watches (brokerage firms)
  - Research organizations
  - Benchmarking clearinghouses

Many benchmarking clearinghouses are located around the world, such as the Quality and Productivity Center in Houston, Texas. The one I personally prefer is Business Performance Improvement Research (www.new.bpir.com) located in New Zealand. These organizations spend their time defining best practices based upon benchmarking studies and published literature throughout the world. They can save the PIT a lot of time and effort if they have relevant information. I personally don't like to rely on published data or on input from the experts, as usually it is more than two years out of date, making it obsolete or at least near obsolete. The major input that I get from these sources is the name and contact information for people working to improve the process that is being studied, but for many projects the information from the external and internal experts may be enough to determine if the goals set by the PIT are in line with world-class standards or at least in line with the level at which the organization needs the process to perform. Remember, all our processes do not need to be world class, just the ones that are customer-related or part of the organization's core capabilities and competencies. These are the processes that need to be better than 6 sigma. For the other processes, 3 sigma is often good enough unless there are financial benefits from improving them. We have seen processes that had improved from 3 sigma to 6 sigma in the support areas, but the cost to make the improvement was 300 percent more than what was saved by the improvement.

How do you go about obtaining detailed data from other organizations? The first step is to define organizations that will be benchmarked:

- Exchange benchmarking information with external benchmark organizations. Often the benchmark study performed in Phase II not only will identify an organization with which the PIT will want to exchange process information, but also will identify a contact person at that organization. If this is the case, one way you can get the contact information is to contact the organization's quality or sales department and explain what you want to do and ask for a contact person that you can work with. Another good way to get in contact with the organization is by looking it up on the Internet.
- Make a phone call to specific individuals at the potential benchmark sites to explain the project and get their agreement to participate.
- Send copies of the performance data from the process under study along with a survey to the external benchmark contact.

- Analyze the data that are returned from the external benchmark site and prepare a list of additional questions that it would like to raise. The PIT should also perform a gap analysis at this time.
- Conduct a conference call with the external benchmark coordinator to clarify any misunderstood data and to discuss negative gaps in the process being studied. The purpose of this phone call is to clarify any questionable data, define root causes for all negative gaps, and identify potential corrective action. This will usually give the members of the PIT the benchmark data they need and in some cases will be good enough to do benchmarking without visiting the benchmark partner location.

The second step in obtaining detailed data from other organizations is to prepare a benchmark comparison report and send copies to all the organizations that input data. Be very careful not to identify how the individual organization is performing unless you have the organization's approval.

For a comprehensive understanding of the benchmarking process, see *The Complete Benchmarking Implementation Guide* (Harrington, 1996).

Activity 3: Conduct a Process Walk-Through

The more you know about a process, the more you can improve it.
—H. James Harrington

The more we understand business processes, the more we can improve them. To do that, we must clearly understand several characteristics of business processes:

- *Flow.* The methods for transforming input into output
- *Effectiveness.* How well customer expectations are met
- *Efficiency.* How well resources are used to produce an output
- *Cycle time.* The time taken for the transformation from input to final output
- *Cost.* The expense of the entire process
- *Culture.* The beliefs and practices that drive the way the employees react to the process

Understanding these process characteristics is essential for three reasons. First, understanding them helps us identify key problem areas within the process. This information will provide the basis for streamlining the process. Second, the process characteristics provide the database needed for us to make informed decisions about improvements. We need to see the impact of changes not only on individual activities, but also on the process as a whole and on the departments involved. And third, understanding the process characteristics is the basis for setting improvement targets and for evaluating results.

In Activity 1 of Phase II, we reviewed how to flowchart a process based on documentation and the PIT's understanding of the process. A flowchart is the first step in changing a process. However, process documentation may not always reflect real life because of errors or misunderstandings. Therefore, you should verify the accuracy of the process documentation. You also should understand and gather information about other process characteristics (i.e., quality, cycle time, and cost). This provides valuable information about the location of existing problems.

The Employee and the Process

We have talked about the process as a "cold" thing—procedures, equipment, flowcharts, and techniques. The process is brought to life by people. Our people make the process work; without them, we have nothing. We need to understand how the people who bring life to the process feel about the process. What gets in their way? What are the parts of the process that they like? What bores them? The end process has to be a homogeneous marriage of people and methodologies, in which the equipment is the slave to the people, not the other way around.

In the long run, the success of the SPI activities will depend on the degree to which our people embrace the changes made to the process. Without considering the human side of the process, the PIT cannot be successful. There is only one way to gain the required understanding of the human side of the process—and the talents and the limitations our employees have—and that is to get out into the work environment. Talk to them. Ask for their opinions and ideas. Then implement their suggestions. If the people are involved, the end results will be much better and far easier to implement.

Process Walk-Through

The only way that you can really understand what is happening in the business processes is to personally follow the work flow, discussing and observing what is going on. This is called a *process walk-through*. In a process walk-through, the PIT physically observes each step in the process and discusses these steps with the people who are performing the activities.

Employees deviate from the process for a number of reasons; for example:

- They misunderstand the procedures.
- They don't know about the procedures.
- They find a better way of doing things.
- The documented method is too hard to do.
- They are not trained.
- They were trained to do the activity in a different way.
- They do not have the necessary tools.
- They do not have adequate time.
- Someone told them to do it differently.
- They don't understand why they should follow the procedures.

To conduct a walk-through, the PIT should physically follow the process as documented in the flowchart from the end to the beginning. Yes, I said "from the end to the beginning." If we start at the end and go backward, we have talked to the customer of the person we are interviewing. This provides the PIT with a very different view of the task being studied than if we didn't understand the customer's needs first.

To prepare for the process walk-through, the PIT should assign team members (usually groups of two or three people) to different parts of the process. Typically, one member of the walk-through team (WTT) will be from the department in which the activity is being performed. The people who are assigned to the WTT should have some understanding of the activity they will be evaluating. This facilitates review and verification of the process flow. Each WTT should:

- Become very familiar with all relevant, existing process documentation.
- Arrange with the department manager to interview his or her people.

- Interview a sample of the people performing the task to fully understand what is occurring in the process.
- Compare the way different people do the same job to determine what the best standard operation should be.

Preparation is the key to a successful walk-through. The WTT really must understand what should be happening in the process and be able to talk in terms that are relevant to the person performing the activity. This requires a lot of work prior to the interview process.

During the process walk-through, the WTT will have an opportunity to develop a list of the tasks required to support each activity. For example, let's look at the tasks required to support the activity of typing a letter:

- Read hand written memo.
- Check punctuation.
- Check spelling and proper names and obtain mailing address.
- Assign file reference number to document.
- Ensure that proper letterhead paper is inserted in printer.
- Turn on word processor; load program.
- Type letter.
- Use spell-check.
- Proofread letter.
- Print letter.
- Review printed letter to ensure that it is positioned correctly on the paper.
- Place in manager's incoming mail.

Doing the task analysis and documentation often reveals new suppliers to the process. It also provides keys to how to improve the process. The task analysis should be prepared in conjunction with the person performing the activity because that is the only way to know how the activity is being performed; the person performing the activity has the best understanding of what is involved.

The PIT should prepare a process walk-through questionnaire to collect needed information about the process. (See Appendix B.) Typical questions might be:

- What are the required inputs?
- How were you trained?

- What do you do?
- How long does it take on average to do your assignment? What is the maximum and minimum time?
- How do you know your output is good?
- What feedback do you receive?
- Who are your customers?
- How do you know what your customers' requirements are?
- What keeps you from doing error-free work?
- What can be done to make your job easier?
- How do you let your suppliers know how well they are performing?
- How is your output used?
- What would happen if you didn't do the job?
- Have you reviewed your job description?
- What would happen if each of your suppliers stopped providing you with input?
- What is the culture like in your department?
- What would you change if you were the manager?

The WTT should collect data related to the average, maximum, and minimum data for cycle times, processing times, and cost for each activity and for the total process.

Another element of success is the way the interview is conducted. Many employees feel threatened and intimidated being interviewed by the PIT. The small size of the WTT helps to make the employees feel more comfortable, but that is not enough. Dress to fit the environment. A black suit, white shirt, and tie are totally inappropriate for interviews conducted in a warehouse or service center. Take time to put the interviewee at ease. Before you ask questions, explain why you are talking to him or her. Show the interviewee the flowchart and explain how he or she fits into the big picture. Interviewing is an art. You should have interview training to get satisfactory results. A four-hour class on interviewing methods is very helpful.

Also during the process walk-through, the PIT will collect information that will be used to develop the current culture model. This model often differs from process to process and function to function. This analysis includes thing like:

- Organization structure and system analysis
- Diagnostic analysis

- Organization design effectiveness assessment
- Organization design impact assessment
- Organization fitness assessment

Immediately following each interview, the team should schedule a short meeting to review the interview and agree on:

- Task flow
- Required inputs
- Measurements
- Feedback systems
- Conformance to procedure and to other employees
- Major problems
- Cycle time estimates
- Value-added content
- Culture enablers and drivers
- Training requirement

It is often helpful to flowchart the tasks so that the team will gain a better understanding of the activity being evaluated and be in a better position to report its findings to the PIT.

The outcomes from the process walk-through should include:

- Differences between the documented process and present practice
- Differences between the way employees are performing the activity
- Identification of employees needing retraining
- Suggested improvements to the process (generated by the people performing the process)
- Process measurement points and measurements
- Activities that need to be documented
- Process problems
- Roadblocks to process improvement
- Suppliers that have input into the process
- Internal process requirements
- Elapsed cycle time and activity cycle time
- New training programs required to support the present process
- The way suppliers should receive feedback data
- A number of task flowcharts

We find that it is good practice to review the findings with the interviewees to be sure the team did not misinterpret their comments. A summary of the interviews of all members in a department should be reviewed with the department manager before they are reviewed with the PIT. The department manager and the WTT should agree on what action will be taken to eliminate differences among employees and between practice and procedure.

When the walk-through is complete, each WTT should present its findings to the PIT. This provides the total PIT with a better understanding of the process. Based on our experience, we find that the best way to present the data to the PIT is to follow the flowchart, starting at the beginning and working your way through to the end, marking up the flowchart as you go along.

The PIT will then redo the flow diagram (Figure 4.21) and prepare an Activity Analysis Form. (See Table 4.3.) This can vary based upon

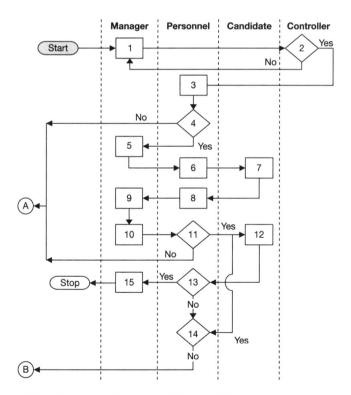

Figure 4.21 Functional flowchart of internal job research process updated after a process walk-through has been conducted

Table 4.3 Completed Activity Analysis Form

Activity Number: 1
Description: <u>Recognize need. Complete payback analysis. Prepare personnel</u>
<u>requisition. Prepare budget request.</u>
Activity performed by: <u>Manager</u>
Quantity Processes: <u>400/year</u>

Cycle time in hours	Maximum 40	Average 16	Minimum 4
Processing time in hours	Maximum 15	Average 13	Minimum 0.6
Applied time in hours	Maximum 0.9	Average 0.8	Minimum 0.6
Cost to perform the activity one time	Maximum $750	Average $150	Minimum $100
Value classification	RVA _____	BVA _X_	NVA _____
Quality of output	Poor _X_	Good _____	Very Good __

Equivalent employee hours: <u>1200 hours/year</u>
Target for improvement: YES _X_ NO _____
Comments: <u>The forms should be put on the computer as a standard form.</u>
Quick fix description: <u>Remove unused data from the forms.</u>
6A Activity Inputs: <u>Approved head count, approved budget, workload analysis, job description</u>
6B. Activity Output: <u>Filled out employee request.</u>
Data recorded by <u>C. Rogers</u> Date: <u>10/16/12</u>

the process. Table 4.3 includes the typical columns that would be used in an Activity Analysis Form.

The columns on the Activity Analysis Form are defined as follows:

- *Activity no.* The same number that is assigned to the activity in the flowchart.
- *Description.* A description of the activity.
- *Activity performed by.* The title or name of the individual doing the activity.
- *Cycle time in hours.* The time it takes from when the last activity was completed until this activity is completed. It includes the processing time plus transportation and wait time. You should record maximum, average, and minimum.
- *Quantity processed.* The number of times this activity is repeated per a specific time period.

- *Processing time in hours.* The actual time the individual spends to do the activity.
- *Applied time in hours.* The time it takes to perform the required tasks. It is usually less than the processing time by a considerable amount. For example, if you need some information and have to call someone to get it, the *processing time* would include the time it takes to look up the phone number, the time it takes to place the call, and all the conversation time. The *applied time* would be only the time during the conversation when the question was asked and answered.
- *Cost to perform the activity one time.* The cost to do the activity. It includes all the costs related to the cycle time. As a result, the cost of moving the output from one activity to the next is included here.
- *Value classification*
  RVA = real value-added
  BVA = business value-added
  NVA = no value-added
- *Quality level of output.* The view of the output from the next person receiving the output from the activity. It is typically rated as poor, OK, good, or very good. In some cases it is rated by the number of errors per hundred items processed.
- *Equivalent employee hours.* The number of equivalent full-time hours that are required to perform the activity. This is sometimes calculated by multiplying the average process time by the quantity process per year to obtain hours per year expended on this activity.
- *Target for improvement.* A PIT improvement objective as a result of the project.
- *Comments.* Anything related to the activity that will help in directing or documenting the improvement process.
- *Quick-fix description.* A description of things that should be fixed right away because they are easy to implement and save a lot of money or because they are causing a problem for the external customer.
- *Activity inputs.* This is the input to the activity that is required to perform the activity.
- *Activity outputs.* This is the product/output that the activity produces and delivers to the next activity in the process (customer of the activity).
- *Data recorded by.* The people who perform the audit of the activity

Usually, even at the end of the process walk-through, the PIT has not collected all the information that is required to fill out all the columns in the flowchart backup data worksheet. For example, the PIT members may not be able to define whether the activity is a value-added, business-value-added, or no-value-added activity. And in most cases they will not have defined improvement activities, as they are defined during Phase IV. However, in some cases, the people that the WTT are interviewing during the process walk-through may have defined corrective action that is needed, and so this part of the worksheet can start to be filled in. The worksheet approach turns out to be a very valuable and effective way of analyzing and improving the process. But you need to be careful—it is tempting to add up all the activity averages for processing time to calculate the total processing time. This can be misleading if there are process loops within the flow diagram. It is also tempting to add up all the minimum and maximum processing times to determine the minimum and maximum processing time for the process. Again, this often gives you a false indication because the maximum processing time at one activity does not mean that it would be the maximum processing time at all the other activities.

Some other headings we have used on worksheets are *difficulty, priority, reliability, change over time, first-pass yield, throughput yield, distance, on-time delivery, expediting costs,* and *inventory quantities.*

Action plans should be established for all the hot problems. These action plans should include:

- What action will be taken
- When the action will be taken
- Who will take the action
- How the PIT will know that the action was taken and that it is effective at eliminating the problem

The PIT members should go back to each person interviewed who described a problem or an idea to explain what action will be taken. If no action will be taken, the employee needs to be told why. This quick feedback will do a great deal to establish the credibility of the PIT and gain future cooperation.

We find that the team will perform better if a problem-tracking list is computerized. This computerized list should include:

- The statement of the problem
- The person who identified it and the date it was identified
- The person who will correct the problem and the date assigned
- The corrective action to be taken and the implementation target date
- Key checkpoints
- The date the corrective action was implemented
- The effectiveness of the corrective action

Reminders should be sent out to each individual one week before the due date for the action. The computerized list will also be used as an agenda item at the PIT meeting. This same type of computerized list is a good way to manage the PIT project plan.

Now that the PIT is familiar with all elements of the process, it should look at the whole process to determine the following:

- Are the boundaries appropriate? If not, has the process owner reported the recommended changes to the EIT?
- Does the process lend itself to being divided into subprocesses to increase the efficiency of the PIT? If so, the process owner should assign "sub-PITs" to concentrate on these smaller processes. The PIT still should meet to review the total activity to ensure that suboptimization does not occur.

Start your process walk-through from the end of the process so that you have first talked to the customer of the person you are interviewing.
—H. James Harrington

Activity 4: Perform a Process Cost, Cycle Time, and Output Analysis

It is very important that the PIT works with and makes decisions on real, factual data, not data that is the best estimate of the PIT members. This means that the PIT will need to develop a measurement plan for the effectiveness and efficiency measurements for the process they are assigned to improve. Much of the basic data should have been collected during the walk-through activity.

Historical Research

Although some processes are repeated only infrequently (i.e., new product introduction), cycle time is very important. In such cases, some historical research may be necessary to obtain dates documenting the beginning and end of these major processes. A good place to look is the old annual strategic operating plans. You may be shocked at some of these cycle times. Incidentally, this is one area in which Asian countries are far ahead of the United States. (The new product development process for Japanese cars is a good example. It is about 60 percent of the U.S. cycle time and about 50 percent of the cost.)

Scientific Analysis

Scientific analysis involves breaking down the process into smaller components and then estimating each component's cycle time. To help with this analysis, use the flow diagram to determine whether there are any subprocesses (or a series of activities) for which information can be gathered using either end-point measurements or controlled experiments. For other operations, use the knowledge of the people performing the work to estimate cycle time. These data should be collected during the walk-through. Combining all the resulting data will allow you to estimate total cycle time. Correctly done, this type of approach has an amazingly small error rate—frequently less than 5 percent.

Designed Experiment

Sometimes the only way to get the kind of data needed is to run a sample experiment in which a sample of the output is tracked through the process. It is important that the sample size be large enough to be able to have a high confidence that the result you get is correct. We like not only to run a sample that is big enough, but to run it over a long enough time cycle so that histograms can be constructed and sigma values can be calculated. This will give you a good understanding of the process variation. Be aware that samples tend to be handled with extra care which can result in better results than the process would deliver normally; you need to take this into consideration when you evaluate the data.

Processing Time versus Cycle Time

Consider the cycle time of a letter-writing process. (See Table 4.4.)

Table 4.4 Cycle Time of a Letter-Writing Process

Activity	Process Time (Hours)	Cycle Time (Hours)
1. Manager 1 estimates that it takes 12 minutes to write a one-page memo and place it in the outgoing basket.	0.2	0.2
2. Manager 1's secretary (secretary 1) picks up outgoing mail twice a day, at 9 a.m. and 1 p.m. Average delay time is 12 hours.	0.1	12.0
3. Secretary 1 assists three managers, answers phones, schedules meetings, processes incoming mail, retypes letters, and performs special assignments. All these activities have priority over typing. Average time before starting to type a letter is 26 hours.		26.0
4. Secretary 1 types the memo and puts it into manager 1's incoming mail.	0.3	0.3
5. Incoming mail and signature requests are delivered.		12.0
6. Manager 1 reads incoming mail at 5 p.m.	0.1	17.0
7. Secretary 1 picks up mail at 9 a.m.		16.0
8. Retyping is a priority activity and is returned in the 1 p.m. mail delivery. (*Note:* 60% of all letters are changed by managers.)	0.2	4.0
9. Manager 1 reads and signs letters at 5 p.m.	0.1	4.0
10. The memo is picked up by secretary 1 at 9 a.m.	0.1	16.0
11. The memo is put in the copy file and held for the next trip to the copy center at 2 p.m.	0.1	5.0
12. Secretary 1 walks to the copy center, makes copies, and addresses envelopes.	0.1	0.1
13. Secretary 1 takes memo to mailbox at 5 p.m.	0.2	2.5
14. Mail is picked up at 8 a.m.		15.0
15. The memo is held in the mailroom for afternoon mail delivery at 3 p.m.	0.1	17.0
16. Secretary 2 picks up mail and sorts at 4 p.m. Secretary 2 puts memo in manager 2's incoming mail.	0.1	1.0
17. Secretary 2 delivers incoming mail to manager 2 at 9 a.m.	0.1	14.0
18. Manager 2 reads mail at 5 p.m.	0.1	8.0
19. Manager 2 drafts answer and puts it into the outgoing mailbox, telling manager 1 to supply more information. It is classified "rush" because it is now overdue.	0.3	0.3
Total	2.2	170.4

While the process cycle time is 170.4 hours (over 7 working days, or 9 calendar days), only 2.2 hours were spent in actual work effort. The rest was wasted time. It is easy to see why we need to measure cycle time.

Cost

Cost is another important aspect of the process. Most organizations divide their financial information by department—because that is tradition. However, as we noted earlier, work flows across departments. Consequently, it is often impossible to determine the cost of the whole process.

The cost of the process, like cycle time, provides tremendous insights into process problems and inefficiencies. It is acceptable to use approximate costs, estimated by using current financial information. Obtaining accurate costs may require an enormous amount of work, without much additional benefit.

Typically, you will also need to understand the costs at a detailed level. What do the major subprocesses cost? What do the key activities cost? What is the cost of each output? Make additional estimates, and complete the form shown in Table 4.5.

- Identify the major subprocesses or activities, using the flowchart. For example, Table 4.5 shows nine activities ("Recognize needs," "Write requisition," "Review requisition," "Identify suppliers," and so on).

Table 4.5 Cost–Cycle Time Worksheet

	Cycle Time, Days			Cost, $ per Purchase		
Activity	Processing	Wait	Total	Personnel	Other	Total
1. Recognize needs.	0.1	1	1.1	30		30
2. Write requisition.	0.2	2	2.2	56		56
3. Review requisition.	0.1	5	5.1	28		28
4. Identify suppliers.	0.6	6.5	7.1	175		175
5. Negotiate terms.	0.2	0.5	0.7	58		58
6. Place order.	0.1	10.5	10.6	26	30	56
7. Receive materials.	0.1	7.5	7.6	26		26
8. Check with order.	0.2	1	1.2	54	38	92
9. Deliver to user.	0.2	1	1.2	50		50
Total	1.8	35	36.8	503	68	571

- Calculate the cycle time for each subprocess or activity, using the techniques discussed earlier. In this case, we estimated that the total processing time is 1.8 days per purchase and total cycle time is 36.8 days per purchase.
- Estimate the cost for each activity. This has two components: cost of personnel (including variable overhead) for the 1.8 days per purchase and other costs (e.g., computer systems), if they are significant. These are estimated at $571 for a single purchase, which may be for a $25 item.

We now have a good idea of what the cycle time and costs of the process are. You can depict this information on cost–cycle time charts to determine problem areas on which to work. The cost–cycle time chart in Figure 4.22 displays how a typical purchase of office supplies builds up costs over the 36.8 days that it takes from one end of the process to the other—from "Recognize needs" to "Deliver to user."

In the chart, the horizontal axis represents total cycle time, and the vertical axis represents cost for a single purchase. Upward lines indicate processing time for the activities, while horizontal lines indicate wait time when no direct cost is incurred. If you follow the chart, you can see that:

- The highest cost is incurred to "identify suppliers." Therefore, you should focus on the methods and processes used to identify suppliers.
- There are long wait times, when no activity is being performed, at the "Identify suppliers" and "Receive materials" stages. Expand these flowcharts to the task level to better understand why they take so much time and to determine how to improve the process.

Lew Springer, former senior vice president of Campbell Soup, points out that the storage cost for a can of soup is 43 cents on the dollar.

The objective of reviewing cost–cycle time charts is to analyze both the cost and the time components and to find ways to reduce them. This ensures that the effectiveness and efficiency of the process are improved. The next chapter discusses how to streamline the process.

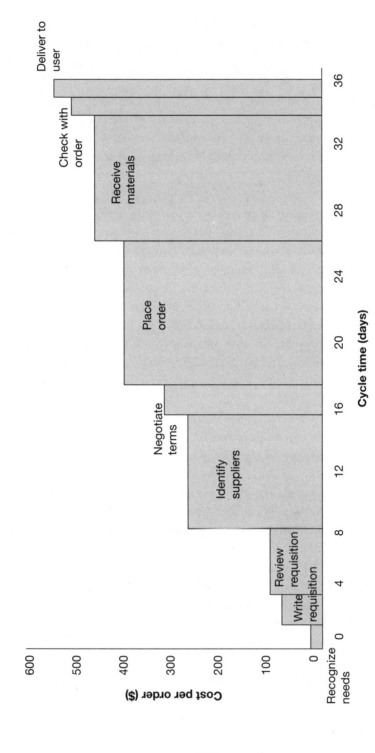

Figure 4.22 Cost–cycle time chart

Variation

Up to this point in the activity, we have been talking about average values. But you usually don't lose a customer based upon average values unless your competitor can produce the same product or service much faster and with better quality than you can. As you conduct the process walk-through, data about the worst- and best-case cycle times, processing times, cost, and error rates as well as averages should be collected. This will allow you to address the things in the process that give your customers major headaches. We are often surprised how good averages look and how bad 5 percent of the output is. It is this 5 percent of the output effectiveness and efficiency that is often the real cause of the organization's problems.

Table 4.6 uses the information presented in Table 4.5 and adds to it the cycle time minimum and maximum numbers. You can easily see how the process would be almost useless if an order were processed at the maximum cycle time for all the activities. In reality, some of the activities are always processed in less than the maximum time, and so the total is less than the sum of the maximum cycle time. For the type of analysis we are doing, we suggest you use the two sigma values, not the maximum value.

Cycle time is equal to processing time plus wait time, which includes transportation time. You will note that the cycle time varies from 6.43 (0.83 + 5.60) to 162.40 (16.40 + 146.00) hours, with an average of 38.80 (1.80 + 37.00). It is easy to see that if you told a customer that he or she would get something in 40 hours and it took 160 hours (4 times longer), the customer would be very unhappy and would be looking for another supplier.

Statistical Approach to Measuring Process Variation

The best way to understand process variation is by building a simulation model, and that is what we will discuss in the next part of this process. But often an organization does not have the required expertise in simulation modeling nor the software that is required to do it. It is also a very time-consuming activity. In spite of this, it is essential that you understand how the process is varying over time for the three key measurements—cost, cycle time, and quality. In this case the best approach is doing a statistical analysis to define process variability. For

Table 4.6   Minimum, Average, and Maximum Cycle Time Analysis

	Processing			Wait		
Activity	Min.	Avg.	Max.	Min.	Avg.	Max.
1. Recognize needs.	0.01	0.10	1.00	0.50	1.00	16.00
2. Write requisition.	0.01	0.20	2.00	0.10	2.00	16.00
3. Review requisition.	0.01	0.10	3.00	1.00	5.00	18.00
4. Identify suppliers.	0.20	0.60	4.00	1.00	8.50	40.00
5. Negotiate terms.	0.10	0.20	4.00	0.30	0.50	16.00
6. Place order.	0.10	0.10	0.10	1.00	10.50	24.00
7. Receive materials.	0.10	0.10	0.10	2.00	7.50	40.00
8. Check with order.	0.20	0.20	0.20	0.20	1.00	8.00
9. Deliver to user.	0.10	0.20	2.00	0.50	1.00	8.00
Total	0.83	1.80	16.40	5.60	37.00	146.00

purposes of this book, we will keep it simple, using no high-level mathematics, but you may need to learn some new terminology. Through the use of statistics, you can project how the process will vary over time using a small sample of the process data. This is accomplished by developing a histogram and calculating its standard deviation.

Let's start by providing some definitions:

- *Histogram.* A visual representation of the spread or distribution. It is represented by a series of rectangles or "bars" of equal-class size or width. The height of the bars indicates the relative number of data points in each class.
- *Mode.* The single number that occurs most frequently in the data you have collected.
- *Process capability index* (Cp). A measure of the ability of a process to produce consistent results. It is the ratio between the allowable process spread (the width of the specified limits) and the actual process spread at the plus or minus 3-sigma level. For example, if the specification was plus or minus 6 and the 1-sigma calculated level was 1, the formula would be 6 divided into 12 equals a Cp of 2.
- *Process capability study.* A statistical comparison of a measurement pattern or distribution to specification limits to determine if a process can consistently deliver products within those limits

- *Range.* The measurement of the spread of the numbers or data you have collected. You find it by subtracting the lowest number from the highest number in your data.
- *Sigma* (σ). The Greek letter that statisticians use to refer to the standard deviation of a population. *Sigma* and *standard deviation* are interchangeable. They are used as a scaling factor to convert upper and lower specified limits to *Z*.
- *Standard deviation.* An estimate of the spread (dispersion) of the total population based upon a sample of the population. As noted above, sigma (σ) is used to designate the estimated standard deviation.

Mean

Process mean is the most familiar and used statistical measure. The mean typifies the expected or most likely value of a parameter. Thus, it is also very important to understand that most of the measurements cluster around the mean. The mean is calculated by adding all the data points and dividing the sum by the number of data points.

The mean for data from a sample is denoted by $\bar{X}$, and the data from a population is denoted by the Greek letter μ. Each data point is represented by *Xi*.

Sample mean: $\bar{X} = \Sigma Xi/n$, for $i = 1$ to n

where $\Sigma X_i = x_1 + x_2 + x_3 + x_4 + \ldots + x_n$
n = sample size
Greek letter Σ = "sum of"

Population mean: $\mu = \Sigma Xi/N$, for $i = 1$ to N

where $\Sigma X_i = x_1 + x_2 + x_3 + x_4 + \ldots + x_N$
N = population size

Consider the data for an airline for the time to issue a ticket. The mean can be calculated using Excel or any statistical software. For an MS Excel worksheet, one uses the formula as '=AVERAGE (data cell range for variable x),' for example: '=AVERAGE (A2:A52)'.

In the case of our ticketing process example, the mean value would be 177.6 seconds.

Median

Median, similar to mean, is another measure of centrality. While the mean sums the data points and divides them by the number of observations, the median counts data points and determines the middle point in the data set. For an odd number of observations, the median is the middle value obtained by sorting observations in an ascending or descending order. For an even number of observations, the median is the average of the two middle values. Median is used when data are less variable in nature or contain extreme values; it provides an indication of the distribution of data points. The command in MS Excel is '=MEDIAN (data cell range for variable x)'.

In the case of our ticketing process example, the median value would be 177.5 seconds.

Mode

The mode is the value that occurs with greatest frequency. You may encounter situations with two or more different values with the greatest frequency. In these instances, more than one mode can exist. If the data have exactly two modes, we say that the data are *bimodal.* The Excel command using MS Excel is '=MODE (data cell range for variable x)'.

In the case of our ticketing process example, the mode value would be 178 seconds.

Range

The range is the simplest measure of variability. It is the difference of the largest and the smallest value in the data set. It has limitations because it is calculated using two values irrespective of the size of data. The range can be calculated by finding the maximum value (=MAX (data cell range for variable x)) and the minimum value (=MIN (data cell range for variable x)) and then subtracting the two.

In the case of our ticketing process example, the range would be 63 seconds.

Variance

Variance is a measure of inconsistency in a set of values (or in the process performance), using all data values instead of just the two values used in calculating range. It is a measure of variability that utilizes all the data.

The variation is the average of the squared deviations, where deviations are the difference between the value of each observation (x_i) and the mean.

Population (all data points) variance is denoted by σ^2:

$$\sigma^2 = \Sigma(x_i - \mu)^2 / N$$

Sample (subset of larger data set, or the population) variance is denoted by s^2:

$$s^2 = \Sigma(x_i - \bar{X})^2 / (n - 1)$$

Note: If the sample mean is divided by $n - 1$, and not n, the resulting sample variance provides an unbiased estimate of the population variance. Variance (using MS Excel): is determined with the command '=VAR (data cell range for variable x)'.

In the case of our ticketing process example, the variance would be 178.6.

Standard Deviation

Standard deviation is the square root of the variance.

For the sample standard deviation:

$$s = \sqrt{s^2}$$

For the population standard deviation:

$$\sigma = \sqrt{\sigma^2}$$

The command for calculating standard deviation using MS Excel is '=STDEV (data cell range for variable x)'.

In the case of our ticketing process example, the standard deviation would be 13.4 seconds.

Correlation Coefficient

A scatter plot represents the relationship between two variables such as between the experience of the employees and the passenger time spent at the ticket counter, as shown in Figure 4.23. The correlation

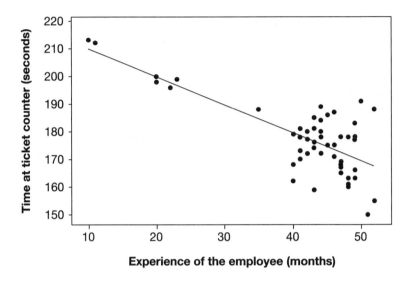

Figure 4.23 Scatter plot of the time at the airline ticket counters versus employee experience

Source: Minitab Inc. (2003). MINITAB Statistical Software, Release 14 for Windows, State College, Pennsylvania. MINITAB is a registered trademark of Minitab Inc.

coefficient is a statistical measure of the relationship between two variables. Depending upon the relationship of the data for two variables, the correlation and the correlation coefficient both can be negative or positive. The value of the correlation coefficient lies between 0 and ±1. A correlation coefficient of +1 indicates a direct positive relationship, and a value of −1 indicates a direct negative relationship. A zero value of the correlation coefficient implies no correlation, thus two independent variables.

The command for calculating correlation coefficient using MS Excel is '=CORREL (data cell range for variable x, data cell range for variable y)'.

In the case of our ticketing process example, the correlation coefficient would be −.75, which is expected because more experienced employees would be able to help the passengers faster.

Histogram

A histogram is a graphical representation of the frequency distribution of data. In a histogram, the horizontal axis (*X*) represents the measurement

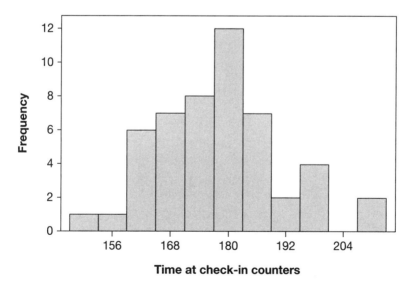

range, and the vertical axis (Y) represents the frequency of occurrence. The histogram is one of the most frequently used graphical tools for analyzing variable data. A histogram is like a bar chart except that it has a continuous X scale versus the separate and unrelated bars.

Histograms display central tendency and dispersion of the data set. If someone plots the limits around the process mean, one can tell what percentage of the data is beyond the limits. In business, this relates to being able to determine acceptable and reject rates of a process. One can also fit some known distributions visually or using software to estimate the probability of producing good product or bad product. By being able to determine the expected process performance, one can initiate a preventive action if necessary, rather than wait for it to happen and then correct it.

Figure 4.24 shows a histogram with central tendency and the dispersion for the time spent by the passengers at the airline ticket counters.

How to Use Histograms

Data gathered about any set of events, series of occurrences, or any problem will show variation. If the data are measurable, the numbers will be found to vary. The reason for this is that no two or more of the

Figure 4.24   Histogram of time spent by passengers at ticket counters

Source: Minitab Inc. (2003). MINITAB Statistical Software, Release 14 for Windows, State College, Pennsylvania. MINITAB is a registered trademark of Minitab Inc.

same item are identical. Absentee rates, sales figures, number of letters mailed, items or units produced, or any set of numbers will show variation. These fluctuations are caused by any number of differences, both large and small, in the item or process being observed.

If these data are tabulated and arranged according to size, the result is called a *frequency distribution.* The frequency distribution will indicate where most of the data are grouped and will show how much variation there is. The frequency distribution is a statistical tool for presenting numerous facts in a form that makes clear the dispersion of the data along a scale of measurement.

Description of a Histogram

A histogram is a column graph depicting the frequency distribution of data collected on a given variable. It visualizes for us how the actual measurements vary around an average value. The frequency of occurrence of each given measurement is portrayed by the height of the columns on a graph.

The shape or curve formed by the tops of the columns has a special meaning. This curve can be associated with statistical distributions that, in turn, can be analyzed with mathematical tools. The various shapes that can occur are given names such as *normal, bimodal* (or *multipeaked*), or *skewed.* A special significance can sometimes be attached to the causes of these shapes. A normal distribution causes the distribution to have a bell shape and is often referred to as a *bell-shaped curve.* It looks like Figure 4.25.

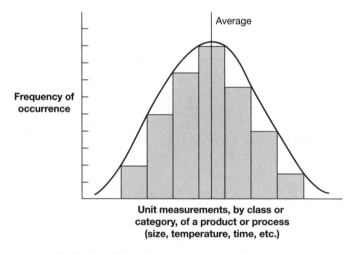

Figure 4.25   Bell-shaped histogram

Normal distribution means that the frequency distribution is symmetrical about its mean or average. To be technically correct, the bell-shaped curve would pass through the center point at the top of each of the bars. We have plotted it at the outside corner to make the histogram look less complicated.

Uses of Histograms

Histograms are effective tools because they show the presence or absence of normal distribution. Absence of normal distribution is an indication of some abnormality about the variable being measured. Something other than "chance" causes are affecting the variable, and thus the population being measured is not under *statistical control.* When any process is not under statistical control, its conformance to any desired standard is not predictable, and action needs to be taken. A histogram is also useful in comparing actual measurements of a population against the desired standard or specification. These standards can be indicated by dotted, vertical lines imposed over the histogram. (See Figure 4.26.)

Figure 4.26 indicates that even though all the parts that were sampled met the specification requirements, all the parts will need to be screened or a high percentage of defective products will be accepted. Consequently, histograms enable us to do three things:

- Spot abnormalities in a product or process.

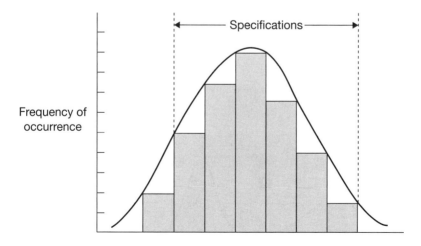

Figure 4.26   Histogram with specification limits added

- Compare actual measurements with required standards.
- Identify sources of variation.

Abnormalities are indicated when the data do not result in a bell-shaped curve, i.e., when there is not a normal distribution. (See Figure 4.27.)

Even when all the samples fall within the specifications, a skewed histogram (as in Figure 4.27) serves as a warning that the process is being affected by other than normal variations and is susceptible to drifting outside the standards. This has happened in Figure 4.27.

The second way to use histograms is to determine whether the process is producing units that fall within the established specifications or desired standards and, if not, to detect clues about what is needed to fix the situation.

In Figure 4.28, Histogram A shows an excessive spread, with both lower and upper limits being exceeded. This would indicate that, although the process is under control, action needs to be taken that will tighten up its range of variability. Histogram B shows a process also under control but the average value of which is too far to the right-hand side of the specifications. Action is needed to cause a leftward shift of

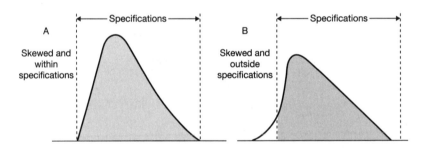

Figure 4.27   Abnormal distributions—skewed

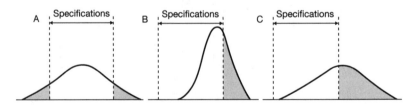

Figure 4.28   Outside established specifications

the population. Histogram C has two problems. The spread is too wide, as is the spread in Histogram A, and it is biased to the right, as is the spread in Histogram B. Both kinds of corrective actions are required to tighten up and shift the spread.

The third use of histograms is to reveal the presence of more than one source of variation in the population of the histogram. This is shown when the measurements of the data form a multipeaked curve. Figure 4.29 illustrates the bimodal curve that contains data measurements from two varying sources.

A histogram can be very distorted. (See Figure 4.30.) This type of distribution usually occurs when there is a natural barrier at one end of the measurement. A good example would be the following data from a phone call center:

- 34 percent of calls are answered on the first ring.
- 47 percent of calls are answered on the second ring.
- 8 percent of calls are answered on the third ring.
- 5 percent of calls are answered on the fourth ring or later.
- 6 percent of calls end in hang-ups.

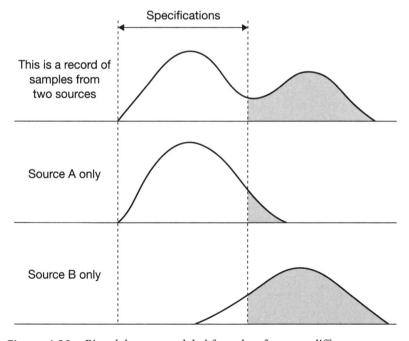

Figure 4.29   Bimodal curve modeled from data from two different sources

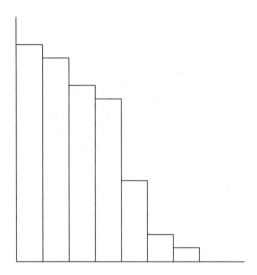

Figure 4.30   Distorted histogram

The natural barrier in this case is the expectation that the call center staff will answer the phone as soon as it rings. There could be a natural barrier at the other end as well, if the company installed a system that would transfer to voice mail all calls that remained unanswered after a certain number of rings.

Constructing a Histogram

The foregoing examples of histograms illustrate most of the different types. The following example is used to demonstrate the steps to be taken in constructing a histogram, using for our data the variations in the time required to complete a single method, Method A.

Step 1. Collect and Organize Data

To construct a histogram, you need data. The more data you have, the more accurate your histogram will be. A minimum acceptable number of data is from 30 to 50 measurements; there is no maximum number.

You need a certain type of data to properly construct a histogram. All the measures must be of the same item or process, and measurements should be taken in the same way. The measure could be how much time it takes to do a certain thing, measured each of the 50 times it is done on a certain day. Another measure could be how many units were processed in an hour, with a simple count being taken for each hour in a 40-hour week. The measurements are of items or processes that should be about the same.

Construct a data table to collect and record data. We can use Table 4.7 as an example. Find the range by subtracting the smallest measurement (15) from the largest measurement (37). In Table 4.7, the range is 22. Divide the range by 10. This tells you the width of the intervals (columns) to be plotted on the X (horizontal) axis of the histogram.

Step 2. Set Histogram Interval Limits
Put 11 marks along the X axis at equal intervals. Take the largest measurement on the data table (37) and record it on the right end of the horizontal axis. (See Figure 4.31.) Put the smallest measurement (15) on the left end of the horizontal axis. Then add to the smallest measurement the figure you got when you divided the range by 10 (2.2) to the smallest measurement and place this new figure (17.2) by the first interval on the horizontal scale. Continue moving to the right so that each interval point is increased by the same amount over the adjacent interval on the left.

Table 4.7 Data Table

Method A Length of Processing Time $n = 50$				
25	23	25.5	24	29
24	25	33	27	22.5
31	29	20.5	37	25.9
20	17	21	28.1	32.5
19	25.5	30.2	15	25
34	25	24	23.5	30
22	22.1	17.4	24.2	31
19.4	22	23	27	28
26.5	26	18	21.9	19.5
28.5	22	27.9	27.5	24

$37 - 15 = 22 =$ range
$22 \div 10 = 2.2 =$ width of each Column

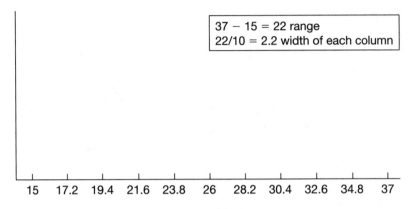

Figure 4.31 Setting histogram interval limits

The more data you have, the larger the number by which you should divide to determine the interval. Use the following as a guide:

Number of Measures	Divided By
50–100	6–10
100–250	7–12
Over 250	10–20

Step 3. Set the Scale for the Y Axis
Count the total number of measurements and divide this number by 3. You may round off the answer. The number 3 is used as a general practice, related to the probability that the highest frequency for any one interval is not likely to be more than 30 percent of the total measurements you have taken. This number—in our example, 50 ($50 \div 3 = 16.67$, rounded off to 17) —is plotted at the top of the Y (vertical) axis of the histogram. (See Figure 4.32.)

Step 4. Plot the Data
Count the number of measurements that fall between the first two numbers on the horizontal axis. Make a mark at the appropriate height. Do this for the remaining intervals along the horizontal line. In counting the number of measurements for each interval, a number that falls on the line between intervals is included in the column that begins with that number. For example, if you were plotting data on Figure 4.32 and the

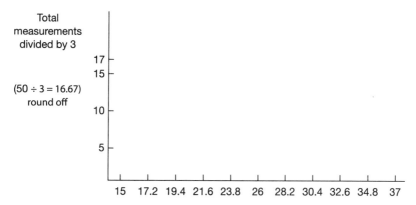

Figure 4.32 Setting the scale for the vertical (Y) axis

value of a specific measurement was 17.2, it would be plotted in the interval that is marked as 17.2 to 19.4. Then draw and fill in the columns.

Step 5. Label the Histogram
Add a legend telling what the data represent and where, when, and by whom they were collected. (See Figure 4.33.)

Histograms are extremely valuable in presenting a picture of how well a product is being made or how well a process is working. This is not something that can be readily detected by a mere tabulation of data. The simplicity of their construction and interpretation makes histograms effective tools for the analysis of data. Perhaps most importantly, histograms speak a language all can understand. They tell whether a process is under statistical control and whether the process is designed to meet its expected standard or specification.

The width of the histogram total population can be defined by calculating the standard deviation of the data. Standard deviation is an estimate of the spread of the total population based upon a sample of the population. As noted earlier, lowercase sigma (σ) is the Greek letter used to designate the estimated standard deviation. (*Note:* Standard deviation is presented later in this chapter.)

Process Capability Study

When the as-is process data is inadequate to determine how the process has been performing over time, it may be necessary to do a process capability study to define its variation in some of the key measurements.

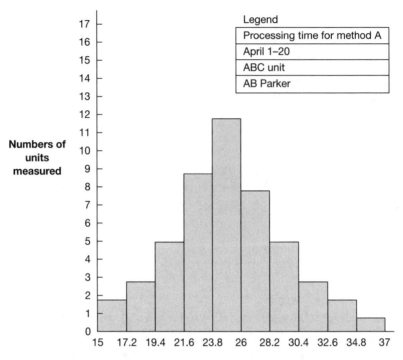

Figure 4.33   A completed histogram

This is an approach that is often used during Phase IV pilot run to predict the performance of the proposed process changes.

> *You have three options:*
> *Design the process so that it produces good output.*
> *Try to inspect quality into the output.*
> *Go out of business.*
> *I like option #1.*
>
> —H. James Harrington

How to Use a Process Capability Study

You will find that different statisticians, companies, and quality control texts vary in their notation of the formulas used to derive the process capability indices. This is not important as long as you understand what is being conveyed. All these formulas have as their basis the conventional statistical theory about probability distributions (frequency distributions);

that is, with a process under statistical control, exhibiting a normal distribution pattern, 99.73 percent of the output will fall within plus or minus 3 standard deviations of the mean of the distribution. The common base for computing the various indices is this 6 standard deviation (6-sigma) width. (See Figure 4.34.)

Cp—Inherent Capability of the Process

The baseline index (Cp) is the ratio of the tolerance width to the calculated plus or minus 3 standard deviation width. The formula is

$$Cp = \frac{\text{tolerance}}{\pm 3\sigma} \text{ or } Cp = \frac{\text{tolerance}}{6\sigma}$$

Therefore, if the tolerance width is exactly the same as the plus or minus 3 standard deviation width, the Cp index is equal to 1.0. (See Figure 4.35.)

Since the plus or minus 3 standard deviation limit only encompasses 99.73 percent of the output, even if the process is operated at the midpoint

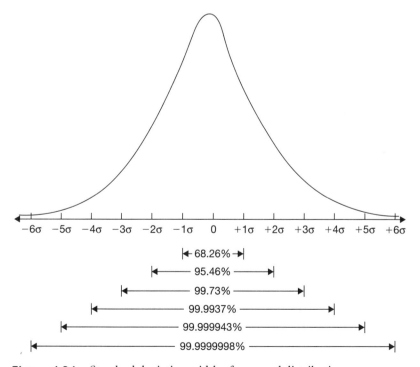

Figure 4.34   Standard deviation width of a normal distribution

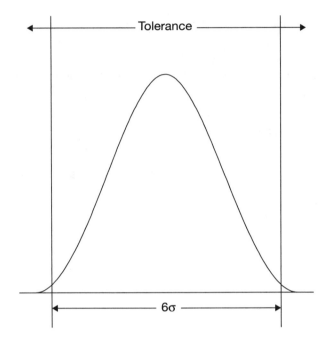

Figure 4.35 Example Cp = 1.0

Table 4.8 Cp Decision Table

Cp Value	Decision
Greater than 1.33	Process is capable.
Between 1.0 and 1.33	Process is capable, but should be monitored as Cp approaches 1.0.
Less than 1.00	Process is not capable.

of the tolerance, most companies establish a requirement that Cp = 1.33 (±4σ) before the process is considered capable. (See Table 4.8.) *Note:* Today many organizations are using a program called *Six Sigma* that has a Cp target of 2.0.

Relating Cp Location to Specification Limit

As stated above, the Cp index is useful only to compare the spread of the process with the spread of the specification limits (tolerance). It does not address the comparison of the locations of these two spreads.

Therefore, while a process may be inherently capable (Cp = 1.0 or higher), it might be operating off-center from the specification midpoint. (See Figure 4.36.)

Another index (Cpk) has been designed to accomplish a combined comparison of both the width and the location of the distribution to the specification limits. Two methods are used to derive a Cpk index. One makes a comparison between the process mean and the specification midpoint as a ratio of one-half the tolerance (called the K factor and used by the Japanese). (See Figure 4.37.) The other (used by Ford Motors) makes a measurement between the process mean and the nearest specification limit using a standard deviation as the unit of measurement (called Zmin). (See Figure 4.38.)

As can be seen, one uses the centers for comparison, and the other uses the distance to the nearest specification limit. We prefer the Zmin method because it depicts both the location and the spread of a process in a single index that can be used directly with a Z table to estimate the proportion of output that will be beyond the specification limit and therefore be defective. (See Table 4.9.) However, for those wishing to use the K-factor method, it, too, will be explained.

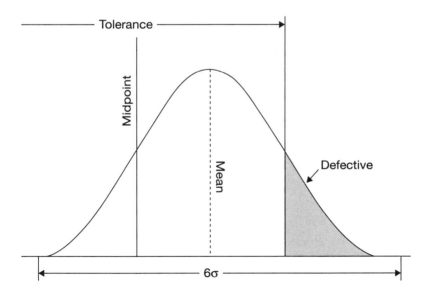

Figure 4.36   Inherently capable process operated off-center

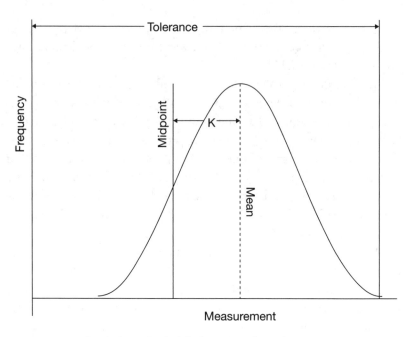

Figure 4.37 Deviation of a Cpk index using the *K*-factor method

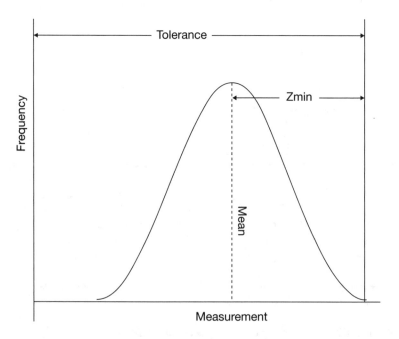

Figure 4.38 Deviation of a Cpk index based on Zmin

Table 4.9 Z Table
Entries in the body of the table represent areas under the curve between
$-\infty$ and z

z	0.00	0.01	0.02	0.03	0.04	0.05	0.06	0.07	0.08	0.09
0.0	0.5000	0.5040	0.5080	0.5120	0.5160	0.5199	0.5239	0.5279	0.5319	0.5359
0.1	0.5398	0.5438	0.5478	0.5517	0.5557	0.5596	0.5636	0.5675	0.5714	0.5753
0.2	0.5793	0.5832	0.5871	0.5910	0.5948	0.5987	0.6026	0.6064	0.6103	0.6141
0.3	0.6179	0.6217	0.6255	0.6293	0.6331	0.6368	0.6406	0.6443	0.6480	0.6517
0.4	0.6554	0.6591	0.6628	0.6664	0.6700	0.6736	0.6772	0.6808	0.6844	0.6879
0.5	0.6915	0.6950	0.6985	0.7019	0.7054	0.7088	0.7123	0.7157	0.7190	0.7224
0.6	0.7257	0.7291	0.7324	0.7357	0.7389	0.7422	0.7454	0.7486	0.7517	0.7549
0.7	0.7580	0.7611	0.7642	0.7673	0.7704	0.7734	0.7764	0.7794	0.7823	0.7852
0.8	0.7881	0.7910	0.7939	0.7967	0.7995	0.8023	0.8051	0.8078	0.8106	0.8133
0.9	0.8159	0.8186	0.8212	0.8238	0.8264	0.8289	0.8315	0.8340	0.8365	0.8389
1.0	0.8413	0.8438	0.8461	0.8485	0.8508	0.8531	0.8554	0.8577	0.8599	0.8621
1.1	0.8643	0.8665	0.8686	0.8708	0.8729	0.8749	0.8770	0.8790	0.8810	0.8830
1.2	0.8849	0.8869	0.8888	0.8907	0.8925	0.8944	0.8962	0.8980	0.8997	0.9015
1.3	0.9032	0.9049	0.9066	0.9082	0.9099	0.9115	0.9131	0.9147	0.9162	0.9177
1.4	0.9192	0.9207	0.9222	0.9236	0.9251	0.9265	0.9279	0.9292	0.9306	0.9319
1.5	0.9332	0.9345	0.9357	0.9370	0.9382	0.9394	0.9406	0.9418	0.9429	0.9441
1.6	0.9452	0.9463	0.9474	0.9484	**0.9495**	**0.9505**	0.9515	0.9525	0.9535	0.9545
1.7	0.9554	0.9564	0.9573	0.9582	0.9591	0.9599	0.9608	0.9616	0.9625	0.9633
1.8	0.9641	0.9649	0.9656	0.9664	0.9671	0.9678	0.9686	0.9693	0.9699	0.9706
1.9	0.9713	0.9719	0.9726	0.9732	0.9738	0.9744	**0.9750**	0.9756	0.9761	0.9767
2.0	0.9772	0.9778	0.9783	0.9788	0.9793	0.9798	0.9803	0.9808	0.9812	0.9817
2.1	0.9821	0.9826	0.9830	0.9834	0.9838	0.9842	0.9846	0.9850	0.9854	0.9857
2.2	0.9861	0.9864	0.9868	0.9871	0.9875	0.9878	0.9881	0.9884	0.9887	0.9890
2.3	0.9893	0.9896	0.9898	0.9901	0.9904	0.9906	0.9909	0.9911	0.9913	0.9916
2.4	0.9918	0.9920	0.9922	0.9925	0.9927	0.9929	0.9931	0.9932	0.9934	0.9936
2.5	0.9933	0.9940	0.9941	0.9943	0.9945	0.9946	0.9948	0.9949	0.9951	0.9952
2.6	0.9953	0.9955	0.9956	0.9957	0.9959	0.9960	0.9961	0.9962	0.9963	0.9964
2.7	0.9965	0.9966	0.9967	0.9968	0.9969	0.9970	0.9971	0.9972	0.9973	0.9974
2.8	0.9974	0.9975	0.9976	0.9977	0.9977	0.9978	0.9979	0.9979	0.9980	0.9981
2.9	0.9981	0.9982	0.9982	0.9983	0.9984	0.9984	0.9985	0.9985	0.9986	0.9986
3.0	0.9987	0.9987	0.9987	0.9988	0.9988	0.9989	0.9989	0.9989	0.9990	0.9990

Zmin

Zmin is the standard deviation from process mean to nearest spec limit.
In other words, Zmin is the distance between the process mean and the
nearest spec limit (upper or lower) measured in standard deviation
(sigma) units. The effect is to provide an index value in Z units that

readily conveys the capability of the process if one keeps in mind that plus or minus 3 standard deviations encompasses 99.73 percent of the output of a process in a state of statistical control. Its calculation can be stated as

$Z = \sigma$ (standard deviation)
$Z\text{min} = $ minimum of Z_U or Z_L

where U and L equal the upper and lower specification limits, respectively. It is graphically portrayed in Figures 4.39 and 4.40, where USL and LSL stand for upper and lower specification limits, respectively.

Cpk—Operational (Long-Term) Process Capability

As stated earlier, the Cpk index combines a measure of the inherent capability of the process with where it is operating in relation to its specifications(s). It converts the Zmin into units of 3 standard deviations. Zmin is in Z units, equaling standard deviation units, and so to convert Zmin to Cpk, the formula is

$$\text{Cpk} = Z\text{min}/3 = \text{minimum of } (\text{USL} - \bar{X})/3\sigma$$

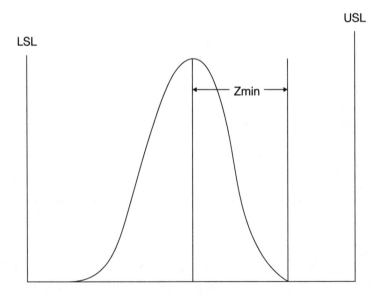

Figure 4.39 Example where $Z\text{min} = Z_U$

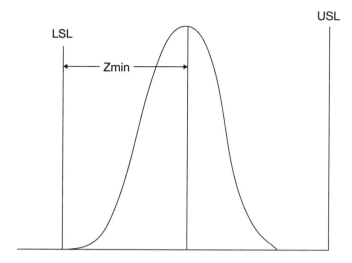

Figure 4.40 Example where Zmin = Z_L

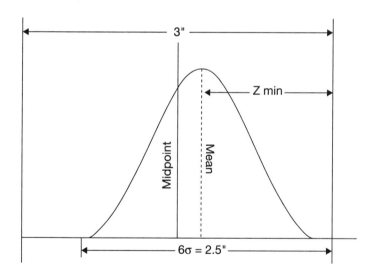

Figure 4.41 Example demonstrating comparison between Cp and Cpk with a process that is off-center

If Zmin = 3, by the formula Cpk = Zmin/3 we obtain a Cpk index of 1.0 when the minimum capability is 3 standard deviations. Since the Cp index of 1.0 also connotes a plus or minus 3 standard deviation capability when a process is centered, then Cpk = Cp. However, Figure 4.41

shows a condition where Cpk = 1.0 even when Cp = 1.2. This is caused by the process being off-center. Thus a Cpk that is lower than Cp indicates a process that is off-center.

CPU and CPL—Upper and Lower Process Capability Indices

In a normal histogram it is not unusual to have the measurements drift between the upper and lower three sigma levels. Control charts use the upper and lower three sigma values as control points to indicate that an unusual reading has been recorded.

$$Zmin = 3.0$$
$$Cpk = Zmin/3 = 1.0$$
$$Cp = \frac{\text{tolerance}}{6\sigma} = \frac{3.0''}{2.5''} = 1.2$$

As was shown above, a process that is off-center will have different Z values (standard deviation units) for the upper and lower specification limits and thus a different capability index value. In addition, there are times when only one tolerance applies. The CPU and CPL indices are designed to provide for these situations. The formulas are the same as for Cpk but for one specification limit only:

$$CPU = (USL - \bar{X})/3\sigma$$
$$CPL = (\bar{X} - LSL)/3\sigma$$

The computation of CPU and CPL is illustrated in the example below where

$$\bar{X} = 4.68$$
$$\sigma = 0.33$$
$$USL = 5.68$$
$$LSL = 3.0$$

Thus $CPL = \dfrac{4.68 - 3.0}{3 \times .33} = 1.68$ and $CPU = \dfrac{5.68 - 4.68}{3 \times .33} = 1.0.$

This process is marginally capable with 0.135 percent of the output expected to be outside the upper specification limit. (See Figure 4.42.)

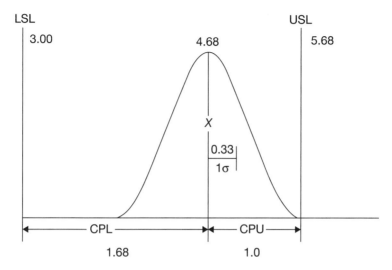

Figure 4.42 Example of off-center process showing CPL and CPU indices. For centered processes, CPU and CPL are equal to Cp.

It should be noted that Ford and its suppliers use a notation of Z_U and Z_L for this purpose. Since a Z unit is 1 standard deviation (not in 3 standard deviation units as are CPL and CPU), Z_U and Z_L will be 3 times the number of the CPL and CPU index.

One of the most valuable uses for a capability index is the determination of the proportion of the output that will be beyond either spec limit. In using the standard normal distribution (Z table) in Table 4.9, both sides of the distribution need to be considered in estimating the proportion of defectives from the process.

Cpk—Using the K-Factor Method

To determine Cp using the *K* factor method, first find *K*, which is the proportion of one-half the tolerance that the process mean varies from the spec mean.

The formula is

$$K = \frac{\text{process mean } - \text{ spec midpoint}}{\text{tolerance}/2}$$

The best value is zero, because that means that the process is being operated exactly at the midpoint of the tolerance. If *K* is positive

(Figure 4.43), the process mean is off-center toward the upper spec limit. Conversely, if K is negative (Figure 4.44), it is off-center toward the lower spec limit.

While the K factor is very helpful in portraying the centering of the process relative to the spec, it tells nothing about the relationship between the process spread and the tolerance spread. To overcome this deficiency, the K factor is combined with the Cp index and converted to 3 standard deviation values by the following formula:

$$Cpk = Cp(1 - K)$$

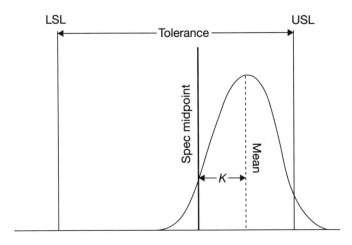

Figure 4.43 Example of a positive K factor

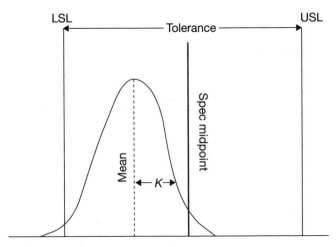

Figure 4.44 Example of a negative K factor

To illustrate, Figure 4.38, shown earlier to portray Cpk based on, Zmin, is repeated below and used to calculate Cpk using the *K*-factor method:

$$Cp = \frac{\text{tolerance}}{6\sigma} = \frac{3.0''}{2.5''} = 1.2$$

$$K = \frac{\text{process mean } - \text{ spec midpoint}}{\text{tolerance}/2}$$

$$= \frac{4.75'' - 4.5''}{3''/2} = \frac{.25}{1.5} = .167$$

$$Cpk = Cp(1 - K) = 1.2(1 - 0.167) = 1.0$$

It is noted that both methods produce the same Cpk result.

Using Process Capability Indices

The purpose of knowing about the capability of a process to meet its requirements is pretty obvious. It provides answers to two questions. Can a process as currently designed, equipped, and operated meet its requirements? If not, what proportion of the output is expected to be defective? The indices are just one of the tools for management to use to facilitate the investigation, analysis, and corrective actions necessary to bring the process capability up to the point of filling all its requirements.

There is a variety of conditions or stages of a process as it moves from design to full production, and there are a variety of depths of analysis that may be applied depending on many factors. A number of different terms are used to identify a given analysis in a given stage of the process. They might be called *process capability studies, process performance evaluations, process improvement programs, process optimization*, etc. What they are called is not too important; what is important is to realize that nothing is constant. Even if a process is capable today, it may not be tomorrow. Thus a never-ending effort is needed to maintain whatever level of proficiency has been achieved and to continuously strive to reduce the natural variation of all processes so that the levels of performance to requirements are improved and the goal of zero defects is sought.

It is necessary to understand that "process capability" as expressed by some index is not an absolute but rather an attempt to quantify and compare the degree to which the various processes can be expected to meet their requirements. For instance, the numerical value of a process capability index can differ for a number of reasons. If the index was derived from control chart samples of past history, it might not be the same as one derived from samples taken today. If the sample sizes and frequency of samples were to be changed, one might get a different value of the standard deviation of the process, thus changing the process capability index. To be more specific, if samples within a subgroup are taken very close together, the *the variation between the high and low reading (R)* will tend to be smaller than if the samples in the subgroup are taken over a longer period. The latter will increase the value of R, thus increasing the size of the estimated standard deviation. In turn, that broadens the control limits and decreases the process capability index. The point of this discourse is to help you realize the fallibility of process capability indices. They are very valuable tools, but they must be used with judgment and an understanding of the conditions under which they were derived.

Process Capability Analysis

As stated earlier, a number of different conditions will require process capability analysis. Typically a process will undergo several stages of development before it is ready for "full implementation." There exists a need to determine the capability of the various processes during these development stages. Unfortunately, the earlier the stage, the less hard data available.

During the design stage, any attempt to assure process capability will need to be done using estimates only. Because of the use of estimates, there is a need to provide for a greater margin of error; thus the use of a $Cp = 1.67$ $(\pm 5\sigma)$ as a target is desirable. As development proceeds and the process moves into pilot process, it will be necessary to consider the effect on process capability of such elements as the tools, cost, cycle time, and quality. While capability analysis during this stage can be computed from hard data, it is still difficult to predict what the full-blown process capability will be when the process is fully implemented.

Things like variation in cycle time and quality have a direct impact on the customer, while variation in cost has a direct impact on the organization's profits. It is therefore important that you can determine what percentage of the output will exceed the customer's requirements for quality and for cycle time.

Processes may be meeting all their requirements. However, through process optimization, better-quality products and reduced costs can be achieved.

Process Capability Study—Steps

Set forth below are typical steps that can be used when undertaking a process capability study.

Step 1. Preparation
Become familiar with the process to be studied. What physical conditions exist? At what point will the customer be dissatisfied with the output? What variables are to be studied? What historical data exist? What data need to be collected?

Step 2. Data Collection
The success of the study will be no better than the data that is collected. All too often we make bad decisions because we base them on bad data. It is absolutely essential that the PIT makes sure that the collected data is meaningful and accurate. This requires that the people who are collecting the data understand what they are required to do and that they have the right equipment.

- *Select the size and sequence of the subgroups to be measured.* Typically a rational subgroup of four or five process cycles is sufficient. These need to be taken from a single stream of output over a short interval of time (normally sequentially produced). They should represent, as nearly as possible, output under one set of conditions.
- *Decide the frequency of subgroups to be chosen.* Subgroups taken very frequently will reflect variations that occur with little external influence, while those taken less frequently will reflect the effect that changes in process and inputs to the process have on output from the process. The objective is to detect all the changes that the process will normally undergo.

Summing Up Activity 4

A key benefit of understanding an existing process is to facilitate the communication between the PIT and the stakeholders of the process. Having excellent communication with customers, management, process owners, process managers, and the employees involved in the process is crucial to getting buy-in to the future-state solution. You must understand the variation that is in the current process that causes you to have dissatisfied customers. If on an average you are able to fill a customer's order in 10 days and you tell your customer that is what he or she will get 50 percent of the time, you will not meet your customer's requirements. If only 1 percent of the orders are filled in 20 days, that 1 percent of customers will be very unhappy, and many of them will start looking for a new supplier.

(*Note:* This statistical approach to measuring process variation may look difficult to do if you are not mathematically inclined, but there are a number of software packages that will do all the statistical work for you. Three good software packages are QI Macros, Minitab, and JMP.)

You lose customers not on averages but when the process performs worse than the customer thought it would.

—H. James Harrington

Activity 5: Prepare the Simulation Model

Simulation modeling is the best answer to reducing variation in a process and to predict the impact changes will have on the process.

—H. James Harrington

It has been said, and I agree, that a picture is worth a thousand words. Well, if this is true, a picture that logically simulates tasks and collects data has to be worth a million words. Simulation models provide a picture that gives the appearance that it can think for itself. This modeling technique has the capability of considering complex interrelated tasks and structurally projected outcomes by exercising the many alternative combinations in a matter of seconds that would normally take months to do in the real process, and it can provide its user with validated results that can be very reliable. Simulation models can take on many different forms. Figure 4.45 is typical of one form.

It is not my intent to make process simulation modeling experts out of the PIT members as a result of reading this book. Simulation modeling is a complex process that requires training before it is undertaken.

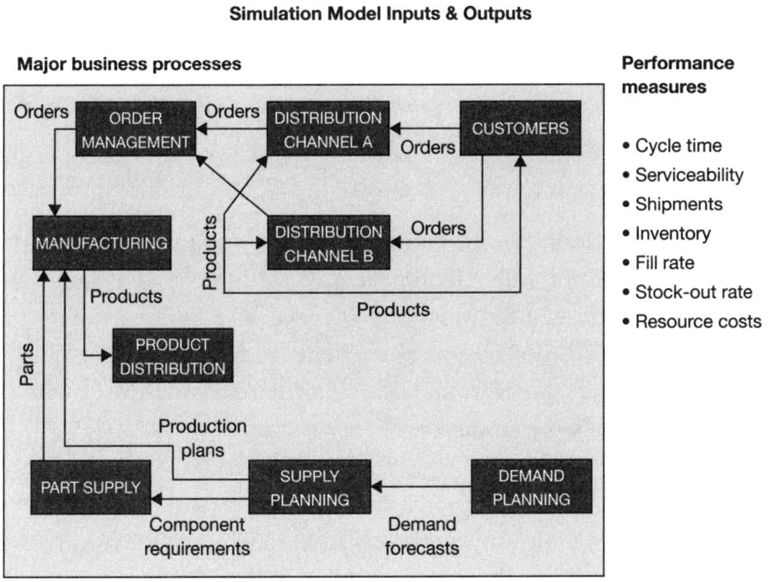

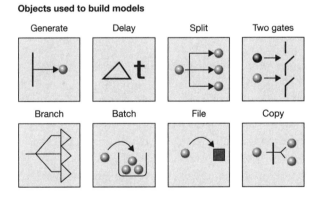

Simulation Model Inputs & Outputs

Figure 4.45 Typical simulation model form

Figure 4.46 Typical simulation objects

I recommend that you read the book *Simulation Modeling Methods to Reduce Risks and Increase Performance* (Harrington and Tumay, 1999) to get a detailed understanding of simulation modeling. However, there are a number of new objects that a person creating and using the models will need to become familiar with. Figure 4.46 shows some of them.

What Is Simulation?

Simulation is a means of experimenting with a detailed model of a real system to determine how the system will respond to changes in its structure, environment, or underlying assumptions.

—H. James Harrington

Simulation, by definition, allows for experimenting with a "model" of the system to better understand processes, with the goal of improving performance. Simulation modeling incorporates various inputs to a system and provides a means to evaluate, redesign, and measure or quantify customer satisfaction, resource utilization, process streamlining, and minimizing of time spent.

Process Simulation in SPI

SPI is a means by which organizations attempt to almost reinvent themselves. This effort involves redesigning processes—finding new and innovative and therefore more effective, efficient, and productive ways of doing business.

One of the many tools used to assist SPI is process simulation. Simulation is a powerful means by which "now processes or existing processes" may be understood, streamlined, evaluated, and visualized without running the risks associated with conducting tests on a real system. Dynamic process simulation allows organizations to study their processes from a systems perspective, providing a better understanding of cause and effect in addition to allowing better prediction of outcomes. This strength of simulation allows for evaluating the overall process performance under different conditions very rapidly to:

- Define the problem and variation in the current process.
- Address customer satisfaction and quantify it for the new process or system.
- Utilize resources in the new streamlined process or system.
- Minimize time to produce an output

All these capabilities make simulation an ideal tool in a SPI effort. (See Figure 4.47.)

Ernst & Young uses process simulation to help clients redesign their businesses. Simulation plays a powerful role in the analysis of the current state as well as the future-state vision for the redesigned processes.

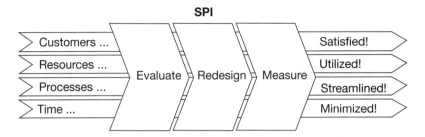

Figure 4.47   Inputs and outputs from a simulation model

Simulation could assist in the following areas in a SPI effort:

- *Feasibility analysis.* Examining the viability of the new processes in the light of various constraints
- *Cost-benefit analysis.* Conducting a cost-benefit analysis or process evaluation
- *Visioning.* Exploring the possibilities for the system in the future state
- *Performance characteristics.* Examining the performance metrics of a system in either the current state or future state, thus providing an understanding of performance
- *Prototyping.* Once a vision for the future state for the reengineered processes is generated, implementing planning and risk assessment and also helping to begin detailed process design
- *Communication.* Disseminating the workings of the newly redesigned process to the organization

Why Simulate?

This is a fair question to which there are a number of good answers:

- *Simulation can assist in creative problem solving.* Fear of failure prevents people from coming up with ideas. Simulation will allow creative experimentation and testing and then selling the idea to management, thus encouraging an optimistic "let's try it" attitude. Simulation provides a means for creative problem solving.
- *Simulation can predict outcomes.* Management in all organizations needs to be able to predict. Simulation educates people on how a system might respond to changes. For example, simulation could help in predicting response to market demands placed on the business system. This allows for analyzing whether the existing infrastructure

can handle the new demand placed on it. Simulation can thus help in determining how resources may be efficiently utilized and in predicting outcomes for various changes to process inputs.

- *Simulation can account for system variances.* Conventional analytical methods, such as static mathematical models, do not effectively address variance, as calculations are derived from constant values. Simulation allows the PIT to look at variance in a system incorporating interdependence, interaction among components, and time. This approach allows for examining variation in a broader perspective. It is very important to understand the variation in the current process because you don't lose customers over average performance. It is the "extremes" that are not normal which upset your customer, i.e., when you tell him or her the order will be delivered in three days and it actually takes three weeks.

- *Simulation promotes total solutions.* Simulation allows modeling entire systems and therefore promoting total solutions. Simulation models provide insight into the impact that process changes will have on input to and output of the system as well as system capabilities. Simulation models can be designed to provide an understanding of the systemwide impact of various process changes. Thus simulation provides a means of examining total systemwide solutions.

- *Simulation can be cost effective.* As organizations try to respond quickly to changes in their markets, a validated simulation model can be an excellent tool for evaluating rapid responses. For example, a sudden change in market demand for a product can be modeled using a validated system model to determine whether the existing system can cater to this need. Additionally, simulation modeling allows for experimenting with system parameters without having to tamper with the real system. Simulation provides more alternatives, lowers risks, increases the probability of success, and provides information for decision support without the cost of experimenting with the real system. Simulation thus provides a cost-effective way to rapidly test and evaluate various solutions to respond to market demands.

- *Simulation can help quantify performance metrics.* Simulation can help quantify performance measures for a system. For example, the aim of a system may be to satisfy the customer. Using a simulation model, this requirement could be translated to time to respond to a customer's request, which can then be designated as the performance measure for customer satisfaction. Simulation can help measure trade-offs associated with process designs and allow for further analysis on parameters such as time to market, service levels, market requirements, carrying costs, and SKU levels. Simulation thus provides a quantitative approach to measuring performance.

- *Simulation is an effective communication tool.* A simulation model can be used to communicate the new redesigned process in a dynamic and animated fashion. This provides a powerful means of communicating the function of various components to those who will use the new system, helping them understand how it works.

Why Do You Need Process Simulation?

Let's take a look at a very simple order fulfillment process and see the reasons why process simulation is needed. The process map in Figure 4.48 shows three activities: orders are received, they are processed, and they are shipped.

Let's define some parameters about how the process works:

- On the average, 10 orders are received every day.
- There are two types of orders, standard and high priority. Forty percent of the orders are standard, and 60 percent of the orders are high priority.
- On the average, standard orders take two hours per order to process, while high-priority orders take four hours per order.
- Four workers process orders working eight-hour shifts each day.

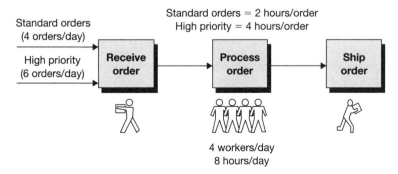

Figure 4.48 Order processing example

Based on simple calculations shown in Table 4.10, one can quickly conclude that the customers will always receive their orders on time and that the order fulfillment process is optimized with its resources at 100 percent utilization!

Let's look at a typical day's activities where the order arrival rate is rather random; i.e., customers place their orders at random times throughout the day. A manual simulation of the process for 10 orders is shown in Table 4.11. The table includes the event times (receipt and shipment) of each order, the order number and type, and the event type.

Table 4.10   Simple Order Fulfillment Process Calculations

Standard orders = 4 orders/day × 2 hours/order = 8 hours/day
High-priority orders = 6 orders/day × 4 hours/order = 24 hours/day
Total capacity required = 32 hours/day
Total capacity available = 4 workers/day × 8 hours/day = 32 worker hours/day
Percent utilization = capacity required/capacity available = 32/32 = 100%

Table 4.11   Manual Simulation of the Order Processing Example

Event Time	Order Number	Order Type	Event Type	Number in Queue	Number in Process	Time in Queue	Time in Process
9:00 a.m.	1	Standard	Receive	0	1	-	-
9:00 a.m.	2	Standard	Receive	0	2	-	-
10:00 a.m.	3	Standard	Receive	0	3	-	-
11:00 a.m.	1	Standard	Ship	0	2	-	2 hr
11:00 a.m.	2	Standard	Ship	0	1	-	2 hr
11:00 a.m.	4	High priority	Receive	0	2	-	-
12:00 p.m.	3	Standard	Ship	0	1	-	2 hr
12:00 p.m.	5	Standard	Receive	0	2	-	-
12:00 p.m.	6	High priority	Receive	0	3	-	-
12:30 p.m.	7	High priority	Receive	0	4	-	-
1:00 p.m.	8	High priority	Receive	1	5	-	-
1:00 p.m.	9	High priority	Receive	2	6	-	-
1:00 p.m.	10	High priority	Receive	3	7	-	-
2:00 p.m.	5	Standard	Ship	2	6	-	2 hr
3:00 p.m.	4	High priority	Ship	1	5	-	4 hr
4:00 p.m.	6	High priority	Ship	0	4	-	4 hr
4:30 p.m.	7	High priority	Ship	0	3	-	4 hr
6:00 p.m.	8	High priority	Ship	0	2	1.5 hr	5.5 hr
7:00 p.m.	9	High priority	Ship	0	1	2 hr	6 hr
8:00 p.m.	10	High priority	Ship	0	0	3 hr	7 hr

The first two orders arrive at 9:00 a.m. The third order arrives an hour later at 10:00 a.m. The first three orders are standard orders. At 11:00 a.m., the first two orders are shipped. Also at 11:00 a.m., a high-priority order is received. At noon, the third standard order is shipped, while two new orders arrive. Of the two orders that are received at noon, one is standard and the other is high priority. At 12:30, another high-priority order arrives. At 1:00 p.m., three more high-priority orders are received. By 4:30 p.m., the workers have shipped seven orders. Three workers stay on and complete the remaining three orders by 8:00 p.m.

The last four columns of Table 4.11 contain the vital statistics that are recorded each time an event takes place in the simulation. For example, the number of orders in queue reaches its peak of three at 1:00 p.m. At the same time, the total number of orders in process peaks at seven. The last three orders spend 1.5 hours, 2 hours, and 3 hours in queue, respectively. Table 4.12 summarizes the performance measures of the manual simulation.

Although the process appeared to be designed perfectly, randomness associated with the arrival rate of customer orders caused queuing and subsequent delays in processing time.

Now let's take a look at three other possible scenarios:

- *Scenario #1.* What if the daily demand varies in a way such that the business receives anywhere from 8 to 12 orders a day (most likely daily demand remains at 10)?
- *Scenario #2.* What if the order processing time for high-priority orders takes anywhere from three to five hours (most likely processing time remains at four)?
- *Scenario 3.* What if the order mix is random?

Table 4.12 Performance Measures of the Manual Simulation

Average cycle time for standard orders = 8 hours /4 orders = 2 hours/order
Average cycle time for high-priority orders = 30.5 hours /6 orders = 5.08 hours/order
Average queue time = 6.5 hours/10 orders = 0.65 hour/order
Maximum queue time = 3 hours
Average service level = 7 orders on time/10 orders = 70%
3 workers had to work a total of 6.5 hours of overtime to complete orders
Total queue time = 6.5 hours

How long will it take to fulfill an order (cycle time) given the new demand, process times, and product mix? The answer is even more difficult to compute by hand. Why? More variability in the process means more variability in performance. Possible results for the cycle time statistics for three scenarios may look like the outcomes in Table 4.13. The table shows the average values as well as the values for the mathematical variance (σ) in terms of the 2-sigma variance.

Mathematical variance is a very important consideration when analyzing the performance of a process. Figure 4.49 shows a normal distribution curve with 1-sigma, 2-sigma, and 3-sigma variances. (See Harrington's *Statistical Analysis Simplified*, 1998, for calculating sigma.) Assuming that the observations are from a normally distributed population, the 2-sigma band

Table 4.13 Outcomes of Cycle Time Measures

Scenario #	Avg. Cycle Time	Max. Cycle Time (2σ)	
1	5.26	7.13	Variable demand
2	5.35	9.23	Additional variability in process time
3	5.77	10.84	Additional variability in demand

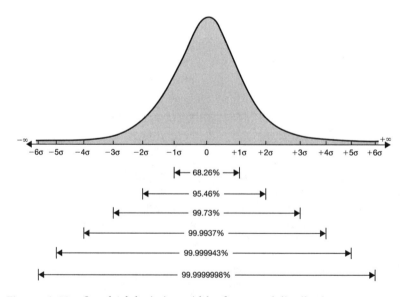

Figure 4.49 Standard deviation width of a normal distribution

contains 95.46 percent of the observations and the 3-sigma band contains 99.73 percent of the observations.

Organizations lose customers most often because of exceptionally bad performance, not because of average performance. In the potential scenarios described above, the maximum cycle time values are outside the 2-sigma band representing exceptionally bad performances. That is, the likelihood of a high-priority order taking 7.13 hours (in Scenario #1) is less than 5 percent. Even though this seems like a small percentage, that is all it may take for a major customer to consider doing business with a competitor.

Of course, when such a rare event as an exceptionally bad performance occurs, management begins asking questions like, How many customers were lost? What additional costs, such as overtime, were incurred to recover from the situation? How much will be spent in marketing to lure back customers that were lost? Based upon our research, the following are typical cost ratios:

- Cost to keep a present customer: $1\times$
- Cost to get a new customer: $10\times$
- Cost to win back a lost customer: $100\times$

Your priority should always be placed upon keeping your present customers because you cannot afford to try to win them back.

Although the exercise is an overly simplistic view of an order fulfillment process, it clearly demonstrates the effect of process dynamics on cycle time, service level, and process costs. It also demonstrates clearly why complex processes cannot be adequately analyzed without the use of process simulation modeling. In other words, as random behavior and interdependencies of resources increase in a process, it becomes impossible to predict performance without process simulation. (See Figure 4.50.)

Process Simulation at Ernst & Young

Ernst & Young uses process simulation as part of its methodological approach to business process innovation and performance improvement. Simulation is used to understand and analyze the current state of a system as well as visioning the future state of the redesigned system. Simulation offers a powerful means by which management consultants are able to

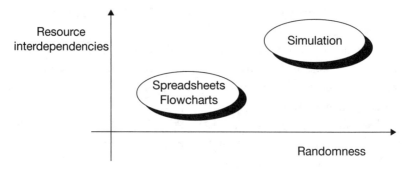

Figure 4.50 When do you need process simulation?

provide clients with better suggestions for improving or innovating their systems.

Ernst & Young has used simulation to assist clients in improving just parts of their systems or their entire systems. Examples of processes in which simulation was used include:

- Order processing and management with the purpose of improving service levels and shortening time to respond to customer requests
- Inventory management to help evaluate various options so as to select a cost-effective system and layout
- Customer support and service to help redesign processes so as to shorten response times and improve service levels
- Service delivery with the goal of improving quality of service delivered with efficient utilization of resources using streamlined processes
- Claims processing with a view to minimizing cycle time through streamlined processes so as to improve customer satisfaction
- Critical-path evolution to help improve system response to external market requirements

In each situation, process simulation provided a means to analyze the system and allowed for an innovative approach to arriving at better solutions.

Simulation Tool Suppliers

Process simulation is not something that the PIT can do by hand. It requires a good software support package and skill in using it. Many software packages are available today. Appendix C lists some of them.

Introduction to ProModel

ProModel is a typical simulation software that I used when I worked at Ernst & Young. ProModel is a Windows-based simulation system. The package facilitates rapid modeling in a specific environment. It provides built-in restrictions for specific applications, thereby allowing the user to select specific constraints that are relevant to the process being studied without having to use programming statements. Additionally, the package comes in three versions—ProModel for the manufacturing environment, ServiceModel for the service industry, and MedModel for the health-care industry. Each package uses icons representative of the industry, thereby providing for environment-specific modeling.

ProModel provides detailed statistical reports of model outputs. In addition to these reports, ProModel offers graphical means to display model results and outputs.

Here are some commonly used graphical outputs produced by ProModel:

- *Content history graphs.* Illustrate variation of customers in a queue over time, providing an understanding of service levels in critical areas.
- *Resource utilization pie charts.* Break down utilization. For example, the chart could show how much time a manager spends in moving from his or her office to the sales desk to answer a subordinate's queries compared with the time spent doing managerial work such as sales calls.
- *Resource-state graphs.* Reveal bottlenecks caused by staff or equipment. This kind of graph shows the utilization of all resources in a comparative fashion, allowing staff to analyze areas for redeploying resources to utilize them more efficiently.
- *Plot of variables.* Graphical depiction of variables such as time spent in the system, allowing staff to examine system performance metrics. This type of comparison of system parameters in the current and future states can be accomplished with relative ease using a simulation model. This feature of the software allows for a quantitative comparison of benefits in the future and current states of the system.
- *Graphical layout.* High-resolution printout of the graphical layout of a model developed in ProModel. The layout shows various locations and on-screen performance metrics and is animated. This feature is ideal to communicate a process.

Process Variation Analysis

During Phase II a simulation model is primarily used to do process variation analysis. As people began to understand the true complexity of processes, it became apparent that customers were lost, not over average values of the process measurements, but as a result of the extreme negative part of the population. For example, the repair cycle for the average TV is 1.5 hours, but 5 percent of the time it takes 2 weeks or more. Well, few are going to be really unhappy about not having a television for 1.5 hours, but if you have to wait for 2 weeks to get your TV repaired, you will probably look for a new repair shop the next time.

Many things can cause variation in the process. Some of them are:

- Uneven work flow
- Differences in complexity of the individual work item
- Changes in the input drivers
- Workload buildup because people are out
- Equipment downtime
- Seasonal variation

Variation is occurring simultaneously in each activity, and the variation is occurring in random patterns. It is unrealistic to calculate the total process performance by using the 2-sigma limits of the process measurements because of the low probability of that combination occurring. Process variation analysis uses random number generation tables to calculate a realistic total process performance distribution for each of the key measurements. This is the only way an effective Monte Carlo analysis can be performed. Monte Carlo methods (or Monte Carlo experiments) are a class of computational algorithms that rely on repeated random sampling to compute their results. Monte Carlo methods are often used in simulating physical systems. Monte Carlo methods are especially useful for simulating systems with many coupled degrees of freedom. They are used to model phenomena with significant uncertainty in inputs, such as the calculation of risk in business. When Monte Carlo simulations have been applied, their predictions of failures, cost overruns and schedule overruns are routinely better than human intuition or alternative "soft" methods. The PIT can use it to predict projected extremes of variation in the output from the current and future state process.

> **Definition**: *Process variation analysis* is a way of combining the variation that occurs at each task or activity in a process so that a realistic prediction of the total variation for the entire process can be made.

Process Flow Animation

Up to the development of process flow animation, the process designer was limited to a static picture of the process. But with process flow animation, the flowchart on the computer screen comes to life. (See Figure 4.51.) It is able to show how transactions through the process and how bottlenecks affect the process performance. For example, animation can show waiting customers in a queue while the service agents are busy serving other customers. Or animation can show idle resources with unused capacity due to transportation delays. (See Figure 4.52.)

> **Definition**: *Process flow animation* is a process model that pictorially shows how transactions move within the process and how variability and dynamics affect process performance.

Figure 4.51 Simulation model

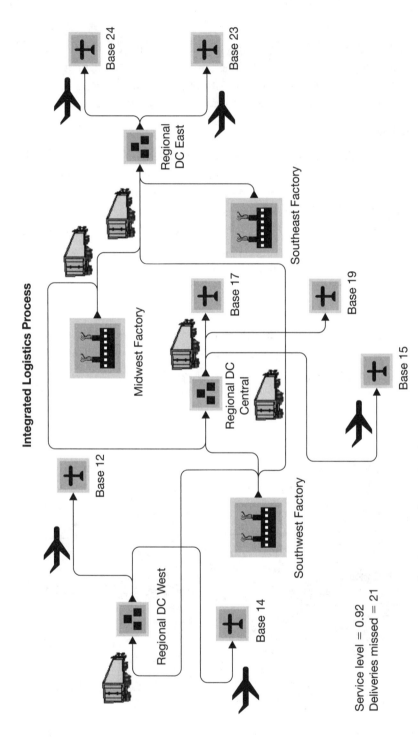

Integrated Logistics Process

Base 24

Base 23

Regional
DC East

Southeast Factory

Midwest Factory

Base 17

Base 19

Regional DC
Central

Base 15

Base 12

Southwest Factory

Regional DC West

Base 14

Service level = 0.92
Deliveries missed = 21

Figure 4.52   An example of process flow animation

Work Flow Monitoring

This is an online model that is used to track transactions through the process. Each time a transaction enters an activity, it is logged in; and when it leaves the activity, it is logged out. The information is computer-analyzed so that the exact status of each transaction is known at all times. Typically, the maximum time that a transaction should be in each specific activity is preset in the computer program so that exceptions are highlighted and priorities reestablished. (See Figure 4.53.)

> **Definition**: *Work flow monitoring* is an online computer program that is used to track individual transactions as they move through the process to minimize process variation.

How Is Simulation Used in SPI Projects?

Each time that a proposed change to the process is considered, the simulation model should be changed and exercised so that the impact of the change can be evaluated. The new future-state solution that is developed supposedly represents the new process after the suggested changes are installed. The problem is that with the methodology, the PIT that develops the future-state solution has to make a number of assumptions that may or may not be correct in designing the new process. These important assumptions are then used to estimate the benefits that the organization will receive as a result of implementing the new process.

It is important to realize that the processes to which these breakthrough methodologies were applied are the critical processes within most organizations and, as a result, make or break the organization's performance. Because of this, no organization can afford to implement the future-state solutions that are developed by the PIT without some way of verifying the correctness of the PIT's assumptions before the organization commits the resources required to implement the recommended changes. Often management is literally betting the organization's future on the results of these changes.

Due to the critical nature of these changes, simulation models of the future-state solution are critical to each part of the SPI methodology. They allow the PIT members to evaluate the correctness of the

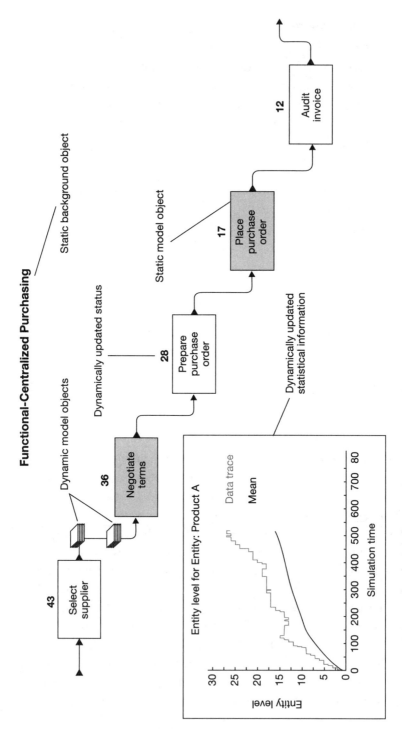

Functional-Centralized Purchasing

Static background object

Dynamic model objects

Dynamically updated status

Static model object

Dynamically updated statistical information

43 Select supplier

36 Negotiate terms

28 Prepare purchase order

17 Place purchase order

12 Audit invoice

Entity level for Entity: Product A

Data trace

Mean

Entity level

30
25
20
15
10
5
0

0   100 200 300 400 500 600 700 80

Simulation time

Figure 4.53 Example of work flow monitoring

assumptions they made. These simulation models put the complex paper model into a virtual operating mode that verifies work flow and identifies bottlenecks. The simulations also allow the PIT to adjust the proposed process to correct for weaknesses in the design and to quickly collect data that measure the effectiveness of any change that is made to the process.

Simulation modeling by itself is not adequate to evaluate the correctness of the new process design because it is created using estimates generated by the PIT. It turns out to be only the first step in the piloting process. A typical piloting process for a new complex process could be:

- Simulation modeling
- Conference room pilot
- In-process pilot

You can simulate many things. For example, a child watches a Western on TV and wants to ride a horse just like John Wayne. Her mother, as Figure 4.54 shows, resolves the situation by providing the child with a rocking horse to play on—a poor simulation, but it is better than the alternative.

Figure 4.54   You can simulate many things.

Preparing a Process Simulation Model

The following are the six steps required to prepare a process simulation model.

Step 1. Plan the simulation project.
Step 2. Collect and analyze data.
Step 3. Build the model.
Step 4. Verify and validate the model.
Step 5. Conduct experiments.
Step 6. Analyze, document, and present results.

Benefits of Process Simulation

Significant value-added process simulation and analysis occurs because it has the ability to do dynamic analysis of costs based on the event-driven simulation. Because the simulation model keeps track of resource interdependencies and captures the random nature of processes, the process performance statistics are far more accurate than results obtained from static analysis. The primary benefits of process simulation are:

- Focus on cycle time
- Strategic pricing
- Process variation
- Evaluation of capital investments
- Evaluation of organizational changes

These are detailed below.

Focus on Cycle Time

Successful companies understand that minimizing waste can make real process improvement. Non-value-added activities include such things as doing rework, putting things in stock, moving things from one place to another, and checking other people's outputs; these activities are all wasted time that can sometimes constitute 95 percent of the total cycle time. Process simulation facilitates the focus on cycle time by modeling non-value-added activities and showing their impact on total process time.

Strategic Pricing

Life cycles of products and services are becoming shorter and shorter. The up-front costs of developing, testing, and marketing are not recouped until revenue is generated. Understanding the cost trade-off between life-cycle stages is critical to strategically pricing the products. That is, understanding when the total investment in product development can be recouped is valuable information for strategic pricing. Process simulation allows simulation of the process changes during the life cycle of a product or service for strategic or time-based pricing.

Process Variation

Process simulation allows organizations to study the performance variation and reduce its magnitude by defining the activities that have the greatest impact upon the total process variation. Understanding the impact of variability in customer demand or activity times on cycle time can help managers minimize waste.

Evaluation of Capital Investments

SPI applied to business processes requires a trade-off between the benefits and costs of making process improvement changes. Without the trade-off, executives and managers are faced with making large investment decisions based on gut feel. Process simulation provides an analytical tool for accurate evaluation of capital investments.

Evaluation of Organizational Changes

Decisions about centralizing, decentralizing, or even eliminating an organizational function are difficult management decisions that impact customers, employees, and stakeholders of a business. Mergers and acquisitions require corporations to constantly evaluate these alternatives and make quick decisions. Powerful resource and hierarchical process modeling functions of process simulation allow visualization and evaluation of alternatives before making these risky organizational change decisions.

Limitations of Process Simulation

Like any other technique, process simulation has its limitations:

- Process simulation is a process management technique, not a project management technique.
- Process simulation is a planning and analysis technique, not a scheduling technique.

- Process simulation is primarily a technique for measuring process efficiency; it does not measure effectiveness or adaptability.

These limitations are usually overcome with the application of other techniques, such as project management, scheduling, or optimization.

Don't simulate life. Live every day to its fullest.
—H. James Harrington

Summing Up Activity 5

It may not be necessary to develop a simulation model for every process, but it is really helpful when one is prepared. Figure 4.55 presents a Siemens example.

Process simulation helps organizations predict, compare, or optimize the performance of a process without the cost and risk of disrupting existing operations or building a new process. The interactions of people with processes and technology over time result in a large number of scenarios and outcomes that are impossible to comprehend and evaluate without the help of a computer simulation model. The ability to visualize how a process would behave, measure its performance, and try "what-ifs" in a

The Bottom Line...

Results:

"The improved capabilities of the new facility, fine-tuned by simulation, have enabled SSI to realize significant production improvements. The new clean room is saving the cell-fabrication department roughly $7.5 million annually."

Mike Fahner, Project Manager
Siemens Solar Inc.

Figure 4.55 Siemens example

computer model makes process simulation an invaluable technique for decision making.

Successful implementation of process simulation involves a three-phase approach:

- Assessment and planning
- Implementation
- Measurement and continuous improvement

Simulation modeling is the best way to optimize performance.
—H. James Harrington

Activity 6: Implement Quick Fixes

SPI is a relatively long-term commitment. Future-state solutions require as much as three months to identify and another three months to implement. By analyzing the current process, a number of quick wins can be identified that will bring about positive change in the process—change that often more than pays for the entire cost of the streamlining methodology.

As the members of the PIT conduct Activities 1 through 3 in Phase II, they often identify things that can be changed within a short period of time that improve quality, reduce cycle time, or reduce cost. These are usually very simple things to correct. These changes are ones that cost little or nothing to implement but have a measurable impact upon the process. We call them "quick fixes," or as I like to put it, "Stop doing dumb things."

As a general ground rule, quick fixes should be implemented within 30 days, and the savings from the change should outweigh the cost of making the change. The reason that all the identified improvements are not implemented at this time is that the redesign process may not include the activity being addressed, and as such, making the change would be a waste of effort. All the identified improvement opportunities will be considered during the next phase, Phase III: Streamlining the Process.

Implementing the quick fixes is an important activity because very often the savings from this activity early in the SPI cycle will save more money than the cost of the total project. This makes quick believers out of top managers who may have been skeptical when the project started.

Example of a Quick Fix

We were conducting a process walk-through when one employee pointed out that she had to work every Saturday and often on Sunday to generate a very complex report for the manager of production control. She was told that the report had to be on his desk on Monday morning when he arrived. She pointed out that she had never seen him use the report and that if he could wait until Tuesday for the report, she wouldn't have to work so much overtime. We contacted the manager and asked him if it could be put off until Tuesday. His answer was, "Sure, as far as I am concerned. I don't even use it." When we pointed out that she prepared the report only for him, he stated: "I will stop the report. It is just a waste of paper." (*Note:* The next Saturday she went to a friend's wedding instead of preparing this report.)

> *Let's stop doing dumb things.*
>
> —H. James Harrington

We have seen processes that are well documented, but the process design was not being followed. In some of these cases, if the employee follows the documented process, the process problems would be eliminated.

In other cases, one or more employees have identified much better ways to operate and the process procedures were obsolete. Most of the problems and costs were caused by people who were trying to follow the documentation that management supplied to them even though they knew there was a better way to perform the related activities.

In both these cases it is important to align the process and procedures. This simple act has on occasion corrected the problems so that the PIT could skip Phases III and IV and go directly to Phase V: Continuous Improvement.

Activity 7: Develop a Current Culture Model

One of the primary causes for the breakthrough methodologies' high failure rate is the lack of good organizational change management structure to support the change activities. During Phase II the PIT should develop a cultural model of the current process and its related environment. The model should be based upon the following cultural enablers:

- Management style
- Organizational structure
- Performance management
- Compensation benefits and rewards
- Education and development
- Communication
- Behavioral models
- Environmental factors

Typical behavior changes that will need to be considered are:

- Trust in management
- Team orientation
- Communications
- Constraints
- Commitment
- Flexibility
- Respect
- Proactivity
- Responsibility
- Pride

In addition to these formal analyses, management interviews and personal observation will be conducted and documented in order to develop the current-state culture model. In Phase III the PIT will compare the new culture model for each solution with the present-state model to define the gap between plus and minus. The greater the gap between the proposed change and the present process, the greater the risk of failure.

Activity 8: Conduct Phase II Tollgate

The end of Phase II is an excellent time to do a complete review of the Phase II deliverables. The tollgate should be chaired by the project sponsor, and the total EIT should be invited to attend. During this toll-gate, the following questions should be addressed:

- Has the PIT developed all the necessary flow diagrams needed to streamline the process?
- Have the key measurement data been collected? Has the variation in the key measurement been defined?
- Are all the PIT members participating as they should?
- Is the project on schedule and within the cost defined in the budget?
- Has the project progressed to the point that the PIT should start Phase III?

When these questions are answered in the affirmative, the project is ready to move into the streamlining phase.

Summary

Phase II is an important phase in the SPI methodology, but the PIT needs to be careful not to make it a "career." We find that often PITs will spend far too much time analyzing and collecting data on the current process. The objective of SPI is to improve the current process, not to document it. The purpose of Phase II is to understand the current process in order to determine where the problems and improvement opportunities are within the current process. The data collected is also used to determine what impact the proposed changes will have on the processes' key measurements. Keeping this in mind, spend enough time and effort to understand the magnitude of the improvement opportunities so that the PIT can determine which, or even if, the opportunities are worthy of expending the effort to include them.

Make your improvements based upon facts, not guesswork, to get the best results.

—H. James Harrington

CHAPTER

Phase III: Streamlining the Process

You are creative when you come up with a new idea, and you become real-value-added when you implement it.

—H. James Harrington

Introduction

Wikipedia encyclopedia defines the word *streamliner* as follows: "a vehicle incorporating streamlining in a shape providing less resistance to air." In SPI we refer to streamlining as a way to optimize the process that is being studied. Process optimization is the discipline of adjusting a process to optimize some specific set of parameters without violating other constraints. The most common goals are minimizing costs and maximizing throughput and effectiveness. This is one of the major qualitative tools in organizational decision making. When optimizing a process, the goal is to maximize one or more of the process specifications while keeping all others within their targeted values.

Frequently there are three parameters that can be adjusted to affect optimal performance:

- *Equipment optimization (including software).* The first step is to determine whether the existing equipment is being used to its fullest advantage by examining operating data and identifying bottlenecks.
- *Operating procedures.* These may vary widely from person to person and from shift to shift. Operating procedures can help significantly,

but they will be of no help if the operators take control and run the organization manually.

- *Control optimization.* In a typical organization there are hundreds or even thousands of control loops. Each control loop is responsible for controlling one part of the process. If the control loop is not properly designed and tuned, the process runs below its optimum. The process will be more expensive to operate, and equipment will wear out prematurely. It is important to note that for each control loop to run optimally, you must identify the sensors and values that turn problems into solutions. It has been very well documented that over 35 percent of the control loops typically have problems.

Often during this phase some very special approaches—such as forced-idea relationships and lateral thinking—are used. A forced-idea relationship is a lot like lateral thinking, as it relates to words and idea associations to generate new ideas. Lateral thinking is sidewise thinking, i.e., thinking across categories. Lateral thinking combines word associations with creative cross-categorical thinking. These approaches will be discussed in more detail later on in this chapter.

The streamlining phase is the most critical and the most interesting. It is during this phase that the creative juices of the PIT members are really put into action. The streamlining phase consists of six activities. (See Figure 5.1.) They are:

- Activity 1: Apply Streamlining Approaches
- Activity 2: Conduct a Benchmarking Study
- Activity 3: Prepare an Improvement, Cost, and Risk Analysis
- Activity 4: Select a Preferred Process
- Activity 5: Prepare a Preliminary Implementation Plan
- Activity 6: Conduct Phase III Tollgate

In his book *Great Ideas on Innovation and Creativity*, David Tanner states: "Creative thinkers

- Are discontent with the status quo
- Seek alternative solutions to problems or opportunities
- Are alert to things around them that may trigger ideas
- Turn a negative into a positive by viewing it from different angles
- Work hard at it"

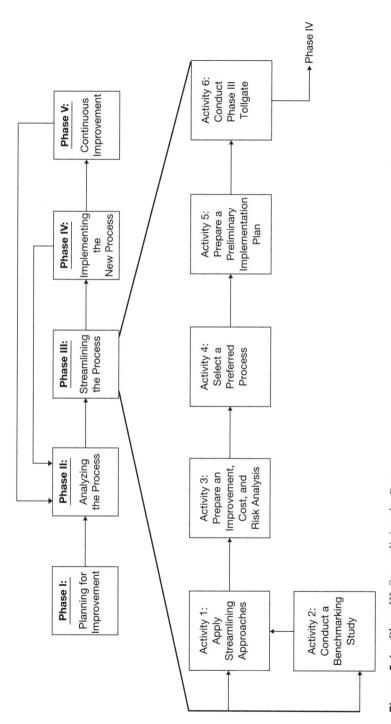

Figure 5.1 Phase III: Streamlining the Process

Streamlining Phase

Now the fun begins. This is the part in the methodology where the PIT members can use their creativity to create a new and better process. It is a process of discovery and growth. Good ideas are set aside for even better ones. The PIT will be using a very systematic approach to evolve solutions that are so good that it will even surprise the PIT members. As the PIT works through the activities in this phase old beliefs and concepts will give way to new and exciting ones. Hold on to your hats— the rollercoaster is at the top of the grade and the ride is about to begin.

Activity 1: Apply Streamlining Approaches

Ask the question, "Why do we do what we do and why do we do it the way we do it?"

—H. James Harrington

The streamlining approach takes the present process and removes waste while reducing cycle time and improving process effectiveness. It focuses on the elimination of the seven types of waste. (See Figure 5.2.)

Waste is the enemy of SPI. We need to wage a war on waste with the objective of eliminating as much as possible. The following is a list of typical waste creators as defined by Lean Six Sigma and their impact:

- *Production waste.* This can fall into two categories: making too much and making too little.
  - Making too much causes:
    - Excessive inventory
    - Increased rework and updating
    - Obsolescence

```
• Production
• Wait time
• Transportation
• Processing
• Inventory
• Motion
• Errors
```

Figure 5.2 Seven types of waste

  - ◆ Additional handling
  - ◆ Bottlenecks
  - ◆ Increased cost
  - ■ Making too little causes:
    - ◆ Unused capacity
    - ◆ Your customers to be upset
    - ◆ Missed shipped dates
    - ◆ Poor utilization of resources
- *Wait-time waste.* This is caused by:
  - ■ Absentee people that are not backfilled
  - ■ Other priorities
  - ■ Delivery delays
  - ■ Low inventory levels
  - ■ Scrap and rework
  - ■ Slow decision making
  - ■ Equipment downtime
  - ■ Lost or misplaced items
  - ■ Activities whose cycle time is greater than takt time

Definition: *Takt time* is the rate that a completed product needs to be finished in order to meet customer demand. If you have a takt time of 15 minutes, that means every 15 minutes a complete product should be delivered from the process in order to meet the customers' needs. If the output is less than 15 minutes, the process is building up inventory.

- *Transportation waste.* Transportation waste is usually the consequence of poor scheduling and can be broken down into internal and external problems:
  - ■ Internal transportation waste results in:
    - ◆ Movement between departments in different parts of the organization
    - ◆ Movement between desks or workstations within a department
    - ◆ Movement into stock when parts are sent from suppliers
    - ◆ Increased product quantities to make up for transportation time

- ◆ Increased workload to handle transportation scheduling, packaging, unpackaging, and storage
    - ◆ Increased paperwork related to transportation scheduling
  - ▪ External transportation waste into the organization results in:
    - ◆ Suppliers located at distant points
    - ◆ Delays related to recognizing a problem and correcting a problem
    - ◆ Handling damage
    - ◆ Increased packaging and shipping costs
- *Processing waste.* Operations, activities, and tasks that don't add true value include:
  - ▪ Inspection operations
  - ▪ Duplicate activities
  - ▪ Just-in-case activities
  - ▪ Redundant records and files
  - ▪ Unused outputs
  - ▪ Data that aren't analyzed or used
  - ▪ Unnecessary storing of information
  - ▪ Rework operations
  - ▪ Approval activities
- *Inventory waste.* It can fall into two categories: excessive inventory and insufficient inventory.
  - ▪ Excessive inventory or stock results in:
    - ◆ The use of additional space
    - ◆ The organization's money being tied up
    - ◆ Additional tracking
    - ◆ Stock becoming obsolete
    - ◆ Stock frequently getting damaged
    - ◆ A slowdown in cycle time
  - ▪ Insufficient inventory or stock results in:
    - ◆ Shipment delays
    - ◆ Unhappy customers
    - ◆ Emergency work orders
    - ◆ Production defects as workaround procedures are used
- *Motion waste.* Every movement that an individual makes should be directed at real-value-added activities. Many of the motions that go on are no-value-added. For example:
  - ▪ Looking in a file for a paper
  - ▪ Looking up phone numbers

- Getting an eraser from the desk drawer
- Waiting for the computer to come up
- Putting away something to use later
- Laying out the tools necessary to do a job
- *Error waste.* This refers to both production and administrative activities. Everyone makes errors that waste time and money. Typical errors are:
  - Producing parts that don't meet specification
  - Dialing the wrong phone number
  - Filing away documents in the wrong file
  - Misspelling a word in a report
  - Providing inadequate data
  - Draft-typing correspondence
  - Sending documents to people who don't need them
  - Managers not listening to their employees
  - Not being prepared for a meeting

After the process is simplified and automated and current-state IT approaches are applied, the process will go through an amazing transformation that greatly improves its efficiency, effectiveness, and adaptability measurements. It would typically result in a 30 to 60 percent decrease in process cycle time and cost and a 100 percent improvement in process effectiveness.

SPI is the most frequently used BPI methodology because the risks are lower and costs are less than in other methods. It is the right answer for approximately 80 percent of the business processes that an organization is interested in improving.

Streamlining guidelines include the following:

- Combine several activities into one.
- Eliminate rework activities.
- Have the workers make the decisions.
- Standardize the process and the way it is performed.
- Centralize data and decentralize operations.
- Capture data as close to the source as possible using IT techniques.
- Integrate parallel activities.
- Reduce business-value-added and eliminate no-value-added activities.
- Perform the steps in the process in a natural order.
- Ensure that processes have multiple versions.

- Perform work where it makes the most sense.
- Reduce checks and controls.
- Minimize reconciliation.
- Use a case manager as a single point of contact.
- Make use of hybrid centralized and/or decentralized operations.

There are two factors that play important roles in driving the process improvement activities—the implementation framework and the best established practices. Table 5.1 presents survey results that identify the key implementation framework drivers (Mansar and Reijers, 2007). Table 5.2 identifies the most popular best practices.

Variation is the enemy of all processes. It doesn't matter if it is variation in cost, cycle time, or a specific measurement. The more variation within a process, the less precise and predictable it is. The whole concept behind Six Sigma was to minimize variation to less than 50 percent of the acceptable tolerance.

The Six Sigma methodology is based upon the concept that the more variation is reduced around the midpoint of a specification, the less chance there is to create defects or errors. (See Figure 5.3.)

This is a concept that was well accepted in the 1940s during World War II. As early as the 1920s, Shewhart set the standard of performance in his control charts at plus or minus 3 sigma. The folks at Motorola felt that Phil Crosby's Zero Defects performance criteria were unattainable, and so they set a specification to variation target of performance at 6 sigma. This will result in a process capability of 2.0 (Cp). Motorola felt that over time the process would drift plus or minus 1.5 sigma, so the actual long-term process capability target was set for 1.5 (Cpk) or spec to the actual variation target of 4.5 sigma. (See Figure 5.4.)

The change in target variation from 3 sigma to 6 sigma is where Six Sigma got its name. At the 6-sigma level, the long-term process capability results in 3.4 errors per million opportunities, not 3.4 errors per million items or transactions. This is near to perfection without requiring perfection. It is a goal to be sought after, not a performance standard that has to be met.

Another important point is that it is related to opportunities, not to the total output. For example, a car could have a million opportunities for failure due to its complexity. In this case, at the 6-sigma level there would be an average of 3.4 defects per car produced. This is the reason

Table 5.1 Best Practices Classified According to an Implementation Framework

Framework Components	Best Practice Name	Definition
Customers	Control relocation	Move controls toward the customer.
	Contact reduction	Reduce the number of contacts with customers and third parties.
	Integration	Consider integration with a business process of the customer or a supplier.
Products	None	
Operation view	Order types	Determine whether tasks are related to the same type of order and, if necessary, distinguish new business processes.
	Task elimination	Eliminate unnecessary tasks from a business.
	Order-based work	Consider removing batch-processing and periodic activities from a business process.
	Triage	Consider the division of a general task into two or more alternative tasks. Or consider the integration of two or more alternative tasks into one general task.
	Task composition	Combine small tasks into composite tasks and divide large tasks into workable smaller tasks.
Behavioral view	Resequencing	Move tasks to more appropriate places.
	Knockout	Order knockout decisions in a decreasing order of effort and in an increasing order of termination probability.
	Parallelism	Consider whether tasks may be executed in parallel.
	Exception	Design business processes for typical orders and isolate exceptional orders from normal flow.
External environment	Trusted party	Instead of determining information oneself, use results of a trusted party.
	Outsourcing	Consider outsourcing a business process in whole or in part.
	Interfacing	Consider a standardized interface with customers and partners.

(Continued)

Table 5.1 Best Practices Classified According to an Implementation Framework (*Continued*)

Framework Components	Best Practice Name	Definition
Organization: structure	Order assignment	Let workers perform as many steps as possible for single orders.
	Flexible assignment	Assign resources in such a way that maximal flexibility is preserved for the near future.
	Centralization	Treat geographically dispersed resources as if they are centralized.
	Split responsibilities	Avoid assignment of task responsibilities to people from different functional units.
	Customer teams	Consider assigning teams out of different departmental workers that will take care of the complete handling of specific sorts of orders.
	Numerical involvement	Minimize the number of departments, groups, and persons involved in a business process.
	Case manager	Appoint one person as responsible for the handling of each type of order, the case manager.
Organization: population	Extra resources	If capacity is not sufficient, consider increasing the number of resources.
	Specialist-generalist	Consider making resources more specialized or more generalized.
	Empower	Give workers most of the decision-making authority and reduce middle management.
Information	Control addition	Check the completeness and correctness of incoming materials and check the output before it is sent to customers.
	Buffering	Instead of requesting information from an external source, buffer it by subscribing to updates.
Technology	Task automation	Consider automating tasks.
	Integral technology	Try to elevate physical constraints in a business process by applying new technology.

Table 5.2 Most Popular Best Practices

	Best Practice	Definition
1.	Task elimination	Eliminate unnecessary tasks from a business process.
2.	Task composition	Combine small tasks into composite tasks and divide large tasks into workable smaller tasks.
3.	Integral technology	Try to elevate physical constraints in a business process by applying new technology.
4.	Empower	Give workers most of the decision-making authority and reduce middle management.
5.	Order assignment	Let workers perform as many steps as possible for single orders.
6.	Resequencing	Move tasks to more appropriate places.
7.	Specialist-generalist	Consider making resources more specialized or more generalized
8.	Integration	Consider integration with a business process of the customer or a supplier.
9.	Parallelism	Consider whether tasks may be executed in parallel.
10.	Numerical involvement	Minimize the number of departments, groups, and persons involved in a business process.

that every car that rolls off the Toyota assembly line still has its breaks checked to be sure they work.

In Phase I we defined the variation in key measurements such as cost, cycle time, and quality. Throughout the 12 streamlining steps, the PIT will evaluate the impact the proposed change has on decreasing variation in these key measurements. Remember it is not the averages that make your customer unhappy; it is the extremes. It is when you tell a customer it will cost $100 and charge him or her $200, or you tell your customer the product will be ready in three days and it takes a week. It is therefore very important that we not only reduce the average cost, cycle time, and error rate, but reduce their variation over time.

The flowchart and simulation model prepared in Phase II serve as the road map to many improvement opportunities. Look for decision diamonds, loops, and branches to focus on eliminating them. (See Figure 5.5.)

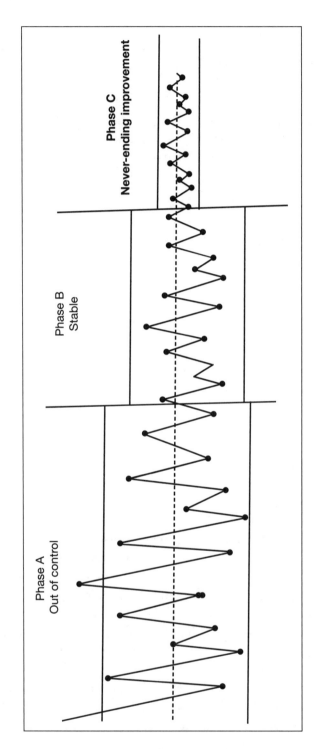

Figure 5.3 Reduced variation around the midpoint

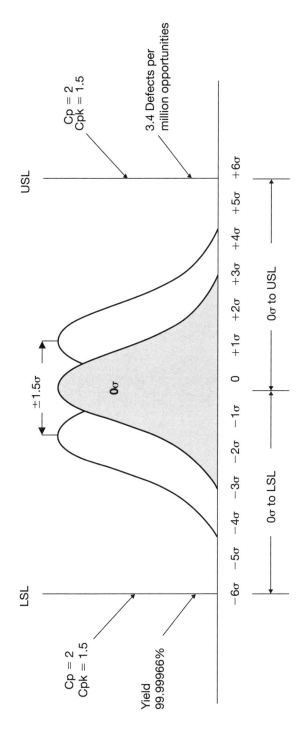

Figure 5.4 Process drift versus time

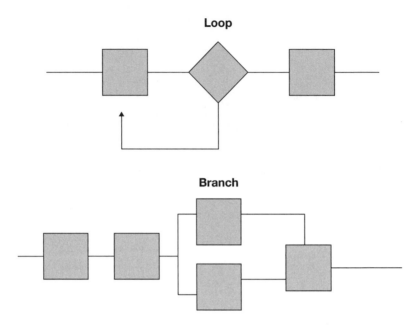

Figure 5.5 Typical loops and branches

Each symbol on the flowchart provides an opportunity for improvement. Specific questions that the PIT could ask relate to the specific symbols that follow:

- *Operation symbols.* Are all the operations necessary? Can they be reduced? What would happen if this operation wasn't done? Could the flow of manual operations be streamlined? Can operations be combined together? Are some of the operations duplications? Are some operations in conflict with others? Can any of the manual operations be eliminated or simplified through the use of technology?
- *Decision symbols.* Are there a lot of decisions indicating complex work flow? Does the decision block result in a rework procedure? If so, how can the defect be eliminated? Have all the possible decisions from the decision block been flowcharted? Can any of the decisions be automated through the use of technology?
- *Inspection symbols.* Is this inspection necessary? Can the inspection be done by the person performing the task? Is the inspection done close to where the activity that is being inspected is performed so that quick feedback can be implemented? If the inspection is

necessary, are data being collected to understand what the problem is so that it can be eliminated and thus the inspection activity will not be needed?

- *Delay symbols.* Are all the delays necessary? Can the work flow be changed to eliminate the delays? Can operations be combined to eliminate delays?
- *Documentation symbols.* Is the documentation necessary? What would happen if it were eliminated? Is the information coming to an activity being used, or does it need to be stored for a later use? Are copies only being distributed to people who need to use them? Is the document a duplication of some other document? Is the information on the document available someplace else? Is the documentation format designed for the person recording the information or for the person using the document? Could the documentation be created automatically using technology?
- *File symbols.* What would happen if the document was not filed? Are the document files in many different places? Is the method of storage effective? Have the documents periodically been purged from the filing system? If so, how often and by whom? How frequently are the documents retrieved from the files for value-added purposes?
- *Transportation symbols.* Why is the transportation necessary? Could the activity or operation that is receiving the transportation be combined with the one that was inputted into the transportation? Is the method of transportation the most effective? Can technology help? What can be done to minimize the distance traveled? What can be done to minimize the handling during transportation?

Twelve different tasks are used during Activity 1. (See Figure 5.6.) They are:

1. Bureaucracy elimination
2. Value-added analysis
3. Duplication elimination
4. Simplification
5. Cycle time reduction
6. Error proofing
7. Supplier partnership
8. Technology

Phase III: Streamlining the Process
Activity 1: Apply Streamlining Approaches

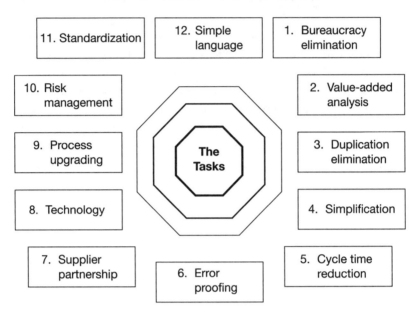

Figure 5.6   Twelve tasks of Activity 1

9. Process upgrading
10. Risk management
11. Standardization
12. Simple language

How Simulation Modeling Is Used in Phase III

The simulation model was very useful in defining the variation in the current process. Now that we are about to define ways to improve the process, it will become even more valuable. When the PIT defines a potential improvement, there needs to be a way of projecting the improvement's impact upon the process. Without a simulation model the impact upon the process is just the best estimate of the PIT members. But if you have a simulation model, you can include the improvement in the simulation model software, and in a matter of minutes you will have data that are equivalent to a full year of process activities.

With the simulation model you can predict the impact each improvement will have on the process considering the impact that the other proposed changes will have upon the process. This is a very important ability because often changes to the process are made that are not needed since the problem had already been solved by another change. By *not* installing good ideas that are not needed, you can reduce cost and process complexity. Simulation modeling also helps you understand when a problem is resolved and improvement effort should be shifted to another part of the project or to another project.

Each time an activity within the process is under consideration to be removed or changed, the simulation model should be updated to determine the impact upon the total process. Frequently an activity that is changed may have a positive impact upon a specific part of the process but a negative impact on the total process. The simulation model allows you to quickly determine the total impact. In many cases, an activity can be changed in a number of different ways. Each of the options needs to be evaluated from the total process standpoint before one is selected. Continue to look for the best option, not the first way of eliminating a root cause.

This systematic approach is designed to minimize waste throughout the process as well as reduce activities that don't benefit the external customer. As we outlined earlier in this chapter, Lean Six Sigma has categorized seven main waste creators—here we have added two more.

1. *Errors, rework, and scrap*
   - **Definition:** Any time an output does not meet the internal or external customer needs the first time.
   - **Results:** Increased costs, added labor, poorer reputation, increased checks and balances, and added frustration.
2. *Waiting*
   - **Definition:** Any time an individual is waiting to go to a meeting or has idle time because the information or input has not reached him or her, or any time an output is waiting for the next activity to be applied to it.
   - **Results:** Increased cycle times, larger inventories, and poorer utilization of space and personnel.

3. *Over/under production*
   - **Definition:** Buying or producing more than is needed for immediate use or sales.
   - **Results:** Large stocking areas, higher costs, increased floor space, and obsolete parts.
4. *Inventory*
   - **Definition:** Excessive stock in the form of raw materials, in-process inventory, and finished-goods inventory.
   - **Results:** Valuable cash flow being tied up, increased storage space and the labor to maintain it.
5. *Transportation*
   - **Definition:** Movement of things from one activity to another.
   - **Results:** Longer cycle times, increased lead times, poorer communications, and higher labor costs.
6. *Movement/motion*
   - **Definition:** Excessive movement of anything, which includes people, machinery, and materials.
   - **Results:** Higher labor costs, longer cycle times, reduced productivity, and increased employee physical effort.
7. *No-value-added activities*
   - **Definition:** Activities that are unnecessary or redundant and that are not required for supporting the business or for meeting the external customers' requirements.
   - **Results:** Increased costs, increased cycle times, increased bureaucracy, and decreased morale.
8. *Underutilized people*
   - **Definition:** People who don't have a full day's work to do. They have the capabilities of doing more if it was assigned and the timing was right.
   - **Results:** Longer cycle times, added costs, unnecessary delays, low morale, and high turnover.
9. *Staffing*
   - **Definition:** Products stop moving because someone is out ill or on vacation and no one has been assigned to fill in. People that are assigned to do the job are not trained.
   - **Results:** Increased costs, increased cycle times, and increased errors.

Task 1. Bureaucracy Elimination (Figure 5.7)

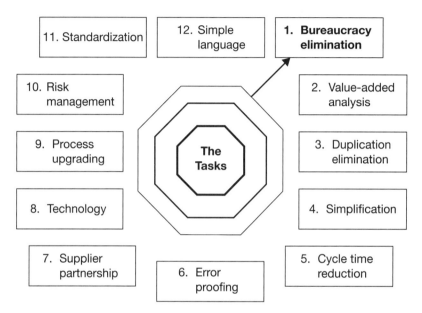

**Phase III: Streamlining the Process
Activity 1: Apply Streamlining Approaches**

Figure 5.7   Task 1. Bureaucracy Elimination

*42% of the white-collar workers have considered quitting over bureau-
cratic hassles.*
                                        —The Conference Board, *Chief Executive Magazine*

We like to start with bureaucracy elimination because everyone hates
"the Big B" (bureaucracy). Management doesn't like it, customers resent
it, employees hate it, and unions fight it. This is the one thing that everyone will help identify and eliminate. To start this task, the members of
the PIT will review the flowchart (see Figure 5.8 and note that the flowchart is in black and white, not in color as it would be if it were created by
a PIT) or simulation model and color in each of the bureaucracy activities in blue. They will then review each of these activities to determine if
the results justify the costs. All too often, bureaucracy activities are put in
place because 0.1 percent of the people in the organization are dishonest,

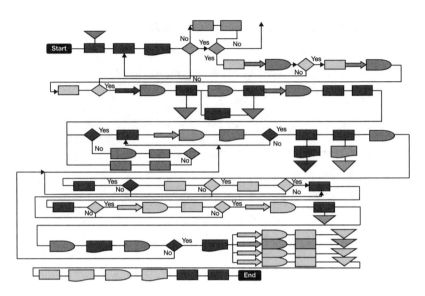

Figure 5.8 Gray scale of a flowchart with bureaucracy activities

and as a result, the other 99.9 percent—the honest people—are punished by adding more bureaucracy to their lives. (Here's an example: when an employee gets caught taking home a pad of paper, the organization might require the security guards to start looking in each employee's purse or briefcase to be sure that no one is stealing office supplies.)

In many organizations that we have worked with, the chief financial officer (CFO) frequently has to approve the capital equipment requests even if they are in the budget. In one such organization we asked the CFO to justify this approval procedure; he replied that it only takes a minute for him to sign the purchase request so there was no need for him to justify what he was doing because its cost was zero. When we then asked him why he signed it, he explained that he needs to check to see that it is in the budget for the department, that the department is not over budget already, and that there are three legitimate quotations. When we questioned if he could do all that in one minute, he hemmed and hawed for a while and then stated that it actually took him five minutes. Then we checked the purchase orders on his desk and found that the previous signature on average was five to seven days old. Getting the CFO's signature delayed processing the purchase order. If the equipment saved $10,000 per month, the loss of savings would run between $2,500 and $5,000. When we asked him how many are rejected by him, he estimated about 10 percent, mainly because they didn't have three quotations. He admitted that the rejected ones came back about five days later and most of them were purchased from the original recommended supplier. This is a good example of a rework cycle that added no value and increased cost and cycle time. It is usually hard to justify why a CFO needs to sign off on purchase orders. Processes should be designed for the majority of the employees, and management should have the courage to fire the dishonest ones.

Task 2. Value-Added Analysis (Figure 5.9)

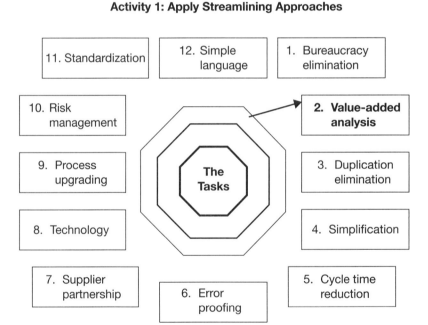

Phase III: Streamlining the Process
Activity 1: Apply Streamlining Approaches

| 11. Standardization | 12. Simple language | 1. Bureaucracy elimination |

| 10. Risk management | | 2. **Value-added analysis** |

The Tasks

| 9. Process upgrading | | 3. Duplication elimination |

| 8. Technology | | 4. Simplification |

| 7. Supplier partnership | 6. Error proofing | 5. Cycle time reduction |

Figure 5.9   Task 2. Value-Added Analysis

David Fran, past member of the Economic Development Council of New York City, stated: "Value is the relative cost of providing a necessary function or service at the desired time and place with the essential quality. Value analysis is concerned with identifying the unnecessary costs that do not add essential reliability or quality to the product" (Fran, 1974).

Value-added analysis (VAA) is an analysis of every activity in the business process to determine its contribution to meeting end-customer expectations. The objective of VAA is to optimize real-value-added activities and minimize or eliminate no-value-added activities. The organization should ensure that every activity within the business process contributes real value to the entire process.

Value is defined from the point of view of the external customer. (See Figure 5.10.) There are three classifications of value activities:

- *Real-value-added (RVA) activities.* These are the activities that, when viewed by the external customer, are required to provide the output that the customer is expecting.
- *Business-value-added (BVA) activities.* These are activities that need to be performed in order to run the organization but that add no value from the external customer's standpoint, for example, preparing budgets, filling out employee records, or updating operating procedures.
- *No-value-added (NVA) activities.* These are activities that do not contribute to meeting external customer requirements and could be eliminated without degrading the product or service function or the business, for example, inspecting parts, checking the accuracy of reports, reworking a unit, or rewriting a report. This category includes activities already classified as bureaucracy activities. There are two kinds of NVA activities:
    1. Activities that exist because the process is inadequately designed or the process is not functioning as designed. Examples include movement, waiting, setting up for an activity, storing, and doing work over. These activities would be unnecessary to produce the output of the process, but they occur because of poor process design. Such activities are often referred to as part of poor-quality cost.
    2. Activities not required by the external customer or the process and activities that could be eliminated without affecting the output to the external customer, such as logging in a document.

What every organization has is a huge hidden office made up of BVA and NVA activities. Together they often account for 80 percent of the total effort, while RVA activities only account for 20 percent of the organization's total effort. (See Figure 5.11.)

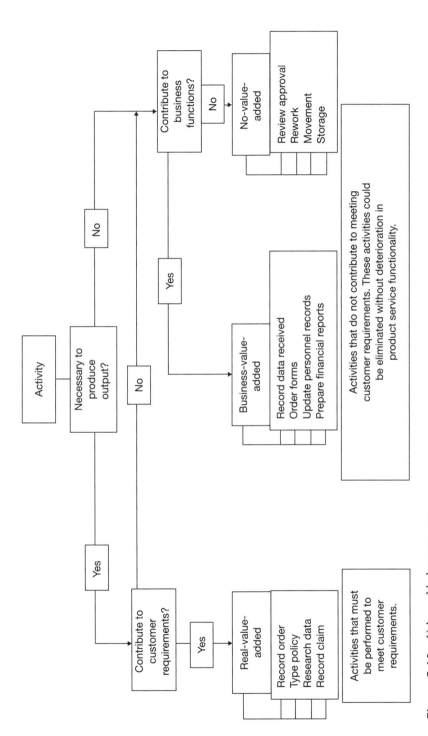

Figure 5.10 Value-added assessment

213

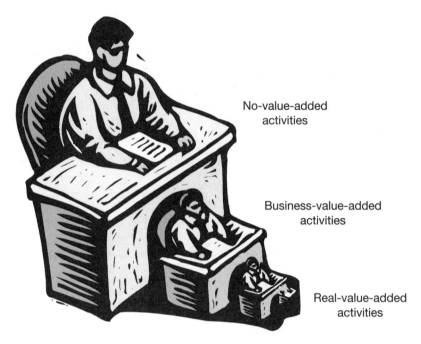

No-value-added
activities

Business-value-added
activities

Real-value-added
activities

Figure 5.11   The hidden office

Figure 5.10 shows how the evaluation is done. RVA activities contribute directly to producing the output required by the external customer. The PIT should analyze each activity and task on the flowchart and classify it as an RVA, a BVA, or an NVA activity. (*Note:* The bureaucracy activities will also be classified as BVA or NVA activities.)

Use a yellow highlighter to designate each BVA activity on the flowchart. Color in the NVA activities with a red highlighter. You have now turned your flowchart into a rainbow flowchart (Figure 5.12 is a gray tone copy of a rainbow flowchart). Typically, as PIT members go through this phase of the analysis, they are astonished at the small percentage of costs that are RVA activities. Even more alarming is the mismatch of processing time for RVA activities compared with total processing time. For most business processes, less than 15 percent of time is spent in RVA activities.

Obviously, this indicates something very wrong, and managers are often disturbed when they learn of these numbers. But there are several explanations:

• As the organization grows, processes break down and are patched for use, thereby making them complex.

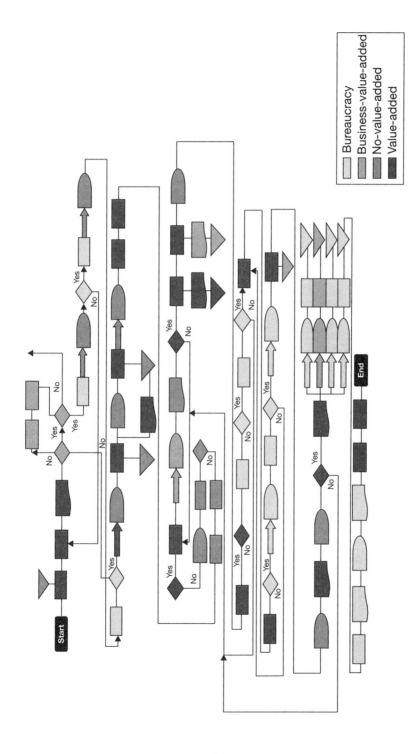

Figure 5.12 Gray tone copy of a rainbow flowchart

215

- When errors take place, additional controls are put in place to review outputs rather than change the process. Even when the process is corrected, the controls often remain.
- Individuals in the process seldom talk to their customers and hence do not clearly understand the customers' requirements.
- Too much time is spent on doing internal maintenance activities (such as coordinating, expediting, and record keeping) instead of RVA work.

The PIT should now answer the following questions:

- How can the RVA activities be optimized?
- Can the RVA activities be done at a lower cost with a shorter cycle time?
- How can the NVA activities be eliminated? If they cannot, can they be minimized?
- Why do we need the BVA activities? Can we minimize their cost and cycle time?

The PIT has to be very creative in coming up with solutions and should not be constrained by the current culture, personalities, or environment.

- Rework can be eliminated only by removing the causes of the errors.
- Moving documents and information can be minimized by combining operations, moving people closer together, or automating processes.
- Waiting time can be minimized by combining operations, balancing workloads, or automating processes.
- Expediting and troubleshooting can be reduced only by identifying and eliminating the root causes.
- NVA outputs can be eliminated if management agrees.
- Reviews and approval can be eliminated by changes in policies and procedures.

When you need to generate some new ideas, Harold R. McAlindon, author of the book *Great Ideas on Innovation and Creativity*, suggests that you SCAMPER:

- Substitute
- Combine
- Adopt
- Magnify/minimize
- Put to other uses
- Eliminate
- Reverse/rearrange

Challenge everything. There is no sacred cow in SPI. Every activity can always be done in a better way. The end result of this analysis is an increase in the proportion of RVA activities, a decrease in the proportion of BVA activities, a minimizing of NVA activities, and a greatly reduced cycle time. (See Figure 5.13.) This concept is so important that all employees should learn to use it in their daily work. The results will be powerful.

As you analyze each BVA and NVA activity, drive the analysis down to determining the root cause for the activity's existence. Pay particular attention to rework and scrap cycles. We find that the Five Whys approach is a simple way of defining the root cause of the activity's

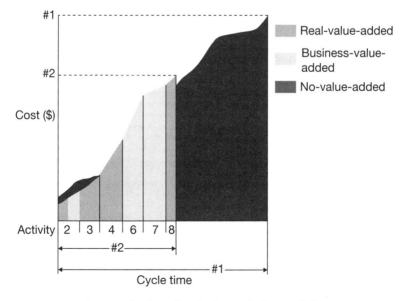

Figure 5.13   Cost–cycle time chart before and after applying VAA

existence. Once the root cause is defined, a decision can be made to eliminate, modify, or leave the activity alone. Recently there have been some breakthroughs in using computer software to help define root causes. We are using a program called Anticipatory Failure Determination produced by I-TRIZ. It is a systematic procedure for identifying the root cause of a failure or other undesirable phenomenon in a process and for making corrections in a timely manner.

Let's take a look at an example of a process we worked on. The object was to eliminate the need for any of the decision blocks. We were working on a decision activity that asked the question, "Does the customer live in a location where the service can be provided?" *Answer:* "Yes, but the location was not in your qualified records."

The following are the results of using the Five Whys approach:

- *Question 1.* Why isn't the location qualified?
  Answer: It is a new area and not in our records.
- *Question 2.* Why isn't it in our records?
  Answer: Because no one told us they were building in that area.
- *Question 3.* Why weren't we told?
  Answer: Because we didn't look at the records.
- *Question 4.* Why didn't we look at the records?
  Answer: Because no one was assigned to do it.
- *Question 5.* Why was no one assigned?
  Answer: Management didn't realize that it would be a problem.
- *Action:* Department 375 will assign John to review the building permits each week and update the records.

This is a very simple example of how this approach drilled down to correcting the problem very effectively. It is amazing how many of these activities can be eliminated through extremely simple methods, eliminating much of the complexity that we are facing today.

> *If you figure out what is causing the exceptions, you can streamline the process.*
>
> —Mark Robertson, EDS Headquarters

A Typical Value Analysis Cycle

All of us are flowcharting our processes, but once they are flowcharted, the real challenge begins. The question is, How can you streamline the process? The following is one simple approach that has worked for me:

Step 1. Review each block in the flowchart to define which of the following classifications each of the blocks fits into.

- *Real-value-added activities.* These activities are directly related to the product or service that will be delivered to the external customer. These are the activities that the customer would be willing to pay for (*examples:* machining a part, cooking a meal in a restaurant, writing out a sales order).
- *Business-value-added activities.* These activities are needed to run the organization but are not the things that the external customers want you to do for them (*examples:* preparing budgets, filling out employee records, updating operating procedures).
- *No-value-added activities.* These activities are unnecessary (*examples:* inspecting parts, checking the accuracy of a report, reworking a unit, rewriting a report). They include activities already classified as bureaucracy activities.

Now ask yourself if the things you classified as real-value-added are truly what the customer wants to pay for. The answer in most cases is yes *and* no. Most real-value-added activities have no-value-added or business-value-added parts. For example, let's look at the activity of contacting a customer to give him or her the date when an order will be delivered. It is obvious that this is an activity that the customer wants you to do, but is it all real-value-added—probably not. The input to the activity is the order delivery date sent to you over the internal network from production control. Let's focus on the tasks that make up this activity. (See Table 5.3.)

As you can see from Table 5.3, the only part of the activity that is real-value-added is the part of the conversation when you provided the customer with the date of the delivery. This was about five seconds of the conversation when you said, "Your order #175 for 50 wheel lugs will be delivered on July 17 in the morning." The rest of the task was business-value-added or no-value-added.

You can see that even in the activities classified as real-value-added activities there are significant opportunities to improve. Most of the activities classified as real-value-added activities have less than 20 percent of the cost devoted to real-value-added work.

Be careful—you can have a big problem if you don't consider the *non-value-added* cost. (Business-value-added plus no-value-added equals non-value-added.) Table 5.4 shows a product-cost estimate from the

Table 5.3 Tasks to Contact Customer for Delivery Status

Turn on your computer.	No-value-added
Search through the inputs until you find the customer order status.	No-value-added
Read the status to be sure it covers all that the customer ordered.	Business-value-added
Find your scheduling notebook.	No-value-added
Record the data in your notebook.	Business-value-added
Look up the customer's phone number.	No-value-added
Place the call to the customer.	No-value-added
Customer calls back.	No-value-added
Find your scheduling notebook and find the status of the order.	No-value-added
Provide the customer with the date the order will be delivered.	Real-value-added
Record in your scheduling notebook that you have completed the task.	Business-value-added
Put your scheduling notebook away.	No-value-added

Table 5.4 Total Cost versus Functional Cost

	Product Cost			
	Normal Cost	**VA Cost**	**NVA Cost**	**Total Cost**
Material	$35.00	$27.50	$7.50	$35.00
Direct labor	$4.50	$3.50	$1.00	$4.50
Storage cost			$6.00	$6.00
Internal moving cost			$2.25	$2.25
Utility cost		$1.80	$0.30	$2.10
Scheduling cost		$0.80		$0.80
Machine cost		$2.00	$1.40	$3.40
Interest		$0.60	$0.60	$1.20
Other mfg. cost		$2.08	$1.04	$3.12
Overhead	$10.00	$7.28	$11.59	$18.87
Engineering		$1.20	$0.80	$2.00
Accounting		$1.00	$0.50	$1.50
Mfg. admin		$2.00	$1.60	$3.60
Personnel		$0.75	$1.25	$2.00
Marketing		$4.00	$1.80	$5.80
Sales		$1.20	$2.20	$3.40
Total selling, general, and admin cost	$8.00	$10.15	$8.15	$18.30
Total cost	$57.50	$48.43	$28.24	$76.67
Sales price	$69.99			$69.99
Profit	$12.49			−$6.68

normal cost standpoint and then what the real costs are when non-value-added costs are considered.

Figure 5.14 is a simple four-block flowchart. The first operation is machining a part, which is real-value-added; the second operation is recording the time that it takes to machine the part, which is business-value-added; and the third operation is inspecting the part to see if it is good or bad, which is no-value-added.

Step 2. To highlight these differences, we recommend coloring in the real-value-added activities in green, business-value-added activities in yellow, and no-value-added activities in red. As noted earlier, this is called a rainbow flowchart. Often bureaucracy-type, no-value-added activities are colored in blue to set them apart.

Step 3. For the activities that are classified as no-value-added, define the ones that are inspection or audit activities.

Step 4. For the inspection and audit activities, define what the activity cost is and how much the activity delays the process. Next compare the activity cost with the real-value-added savings that the inspection or audit adds because it keeps defective items from moving on to later, higher-cost activities. If the real-value-added content is less than the cost of doing the audit or inspection, consider eliminating the activity. If the real-value-added savings is greater than the cost of doing the activity, then continue doing the activity but start a corrective action project to correct the problem to the point that the no-value-added activity can be eliminated. *One word of caution:* Often, people do a better

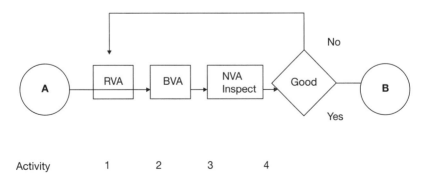

Figure 5.14 Process flow diagram

job because they know that their output will be reviewed or inspected by another person, and so if the inspection or audit is dropped, the quality of the work may become unacceptable.

Step 5. For those inspection and audit operations that will remain, collect the defect, error, or deviation data and plot them using a Pareto diagram. (See Table 5.5 and Figure 5.15.)

For the top 50 to 60 percent of the defects, use the Five Whys technique to define the root causes. In some cases a more sophisticated root-cause analysis may be required.

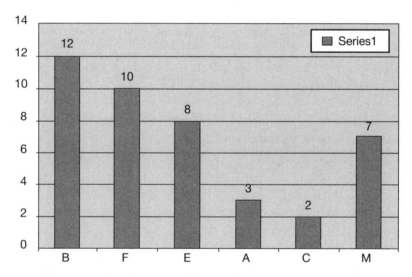

Figure 5.15 Pareto diagram of defects

Table 5.5 Number of Defects by Defect Name

Defect Name	Quality
A	3
B	12
C	2
D	0
E	8
F	10
Misc.	7

Step 6. Perform a root-cause analysis on the three highest defects: B, E, and F. Table 5.6 shows the results.

For defect B, two root causes were defined (BR1 and BR2), and only one root cause was defined for defects E and F (ER and FR).

Step 7. Now for each of the root causes a corrective action plan needs to be developed. (See Table 5.7.)

Step 8. We will now analyze each corrective action to define what impact it would have on the process and organization. Each corrective action is evaluated as a stand-alone item. (See Table 5.8.)

It is important to understand that a single corrective action can have an impact in a number of ways. For example, by reducing variation in a process, process cycle time and cost can be decreased and quality and customer satisfaction can be improved. With this in mind, in Table 5.8 we analyzed each corrective action in the following ways:

- Dollars saved
- Reduced variation

Table 5.6   Root Cause per Defect

Defect	Root Cause
B	BR1
	BR2
E	ER
F	FR

Table 5.7   Root Causes and Their Related Corrective Action

Root Cause	Corrective Action
BR1	BR1C1
BR2	BR2C1
	BR2C2
	BR2C3
ER	ERC1
	ERC2
	ERC3
FR	FRC1
	FRC2

Table 5.8 Impact of Corrective Action

Corrective Action	$ Saved	Reduced Variation	Quality Improvement	Cycle Time Reduction	Inventory Reduction	Increased Customer Satisfaction	Processing Time
BR1C1							
BR2C1							
BR2C2							
BR2C3							
ERC1							
ERC2							
ERC3							
FRC1							
FRC2							

- Quality improvement
- Cycle time reduction
- Inventory reduction
- Increased customer satisfaction
- Processing time

Step 9. The next activity is to study the impact that each of the corrective actions has on the different defects. (See Table 5.9.)

Step 10. For each corrective action, next evaluate its cost, cycle time, difficulty to implement, and workload. (See Table 5.10.)

Table 5.9 Corrective Action Impact on Defects

Corrective Action	Defect Types						
	A	B	C	D	E	F	Misc.
BR1C1	+	+ +	−	0	+	+	0
BR2C1	+	+ +	+	+	0	0	0
BR2C2	−	+ +	0	0	+	0	+
BR2C3	0	+	0	0	0	0	0
ERC1	0	X	−	0	+ +	0	0
ERC2	0	+	0	0	+ +	+	0
ERC3	0	0	0	0	+ +	0	0
FRC1	0	+	0	0	+	+ +	+
FRC2	+	0	0	−	−	+	0

+ Positive   + + Very positive   0 No impact   − Negative   − − Very negative

Table 5.10 Corrective Action Implementation Analysis

Corrective Action	Cost ($)	Cycle Time (Days)	Difficulty to Implement	Work-load (Days)
BR1C1	10,000	30	Medium	5
BR2C1	2,000	10	Low	1
BR2C2	25,000	45	Medium	30
BR2C3	3,000	5	Medium	6
ERC1	1,000	4	Medium	1
ERC2	18,000	18	Medium	10
ERC3	28,000	30	High	60
FRC1	5,000	3	Low	1
FRC2	15,000	10	Medium	8

Step 11. By analyzing Table 5.10, you can define the sequence in which the improvements will be implemented. As you define the implementation order, add the improvement to the impact table. (See Table 5.11.)

In Table 5.11 we recorded the percentage of the defect problems corrected by the corrective action. Some people prefer to analyze the number of defects that would be eliminated by each corrective action instead of the percentage of the problem that will be eliminated. For example, Corrective Action BR2C1 would reduce the three defects in Problem A in Table 5.11 by one defect instead of 33 percent. Both approaches are acceptable.

Each corrective action must assume that the problem has been reduced as defined by the previous corrective action. For example, if the previous corrective action eliminated the burrs on a part by using a new tool, a later corrective action could not claim that it had eliminated the burrs by changing the materials.

In analyzing the projected impact of improvement for the first three corrective actions, you will note the following results: defects for Problem B are completely eliminated, defects for Problem A are reduced by 66 percent, Problem F is solved, and defects for Problem E are decreased by 85 percent.

In the Problem E example, after the first three corrective actions were selected and the impacts analyzed, additional improvement was still needed. So the fourth corrective action that was planned for ERC2. The combination of these four corrective actions was enough to correct the process, and five of the potential corrective actions did not need to be implemented.

This approach is a simple and straightforward way of completing a thorough problem-analysis cycle. The first step defines the root causes, and the next steps analyze the potential corrective actions to optimize the positive effects of implementing these corrective actions on the total process.

Other Approaches

Although the Five Whys is an effective way to drive to the root cause of a problem, there are many other ways to come up with effective corrective action. The following are three of them:

1. Creative questioning
2. Forced-idea relationships
3. Lateral thinking

Table 5.11 Implementation Impact

Corrective Action	% Defects Reduction							$ Savings	Cycle Time (Hours)	Customer Satisfaction	Inventory Reduction
	A	B	C	D	E	F	M				
BR2C1	33	40	10	0	0	0	10	25,000	−10	+	+
FRC1	0	30	0	0	15	75	10	30,000	0	+	0
BR1C1	33	30	−10	0	20	25	0	1,000	−5	+	+
ERC2	0	0	0	0	50	0	20	1,000	0	0	0
Total	66	100	0	0	85	100	40	57,000	−15	3+	2+

Creative Questioning
Alex Osborn originally developed this technique. It has been used extensively in creative activities such as value analysis and visioning. The technique involves identifying an object such as an activity in a process or a physical product and asking a series of questions about how that object might be changed. Creative questioning may be used either individually or as an aid to brainstorming in a group.

Forced-Idea Relationships
This technique is a lot like lateral thinking and *morphological* analysis, as it relates to words and idea association to generate new ideas. It usually begins with a brainstorming activity. The group is next asked to force-associate at random words that are on the brainstorming list. This forced association then generates creative thinking.

Lateral Thinking
Lateral thinking is sidewise thinking, i.e., thinking across categories. Lateral thinking combines word associations with creative cross-categorical thinking. The three primary ways to associate words are:

1. *Similarity.* You combine words and ideas based upon some common type or category.
2. *Contrast.* You associate words and ideas based upon their differences.
3. *Proximity.* You associate words and ideas based upon a cause-and-effect relationship or order sequence.

To accomplish these techniques, the group is given key words and is asked to develop other associated words that are combined in a matrix. By examining the matrix, the team comes up with unique associations between key words and the associated words that can lead to innovation.

Directed Evolution
Although these tools do a good job at defining root causes, there are some tools that go much further and help to define the correction to the problem. Directed Evolution is one such tool. It is based upon the 40 TRIZ Principles for Conflict Resolution—these are 40 one- or two-word statements that describe approaches to resolving technical conflict

(problems and contradictions) that were defined by Genrich Altshuller based upon his study of over 200,000 patents. These 40 TRIZ Principles have a twofold purpose:

- Within each principle resides guidance on how to conceptually or actually change a specific situation or system in order to be rid of a problem.
- The 40 principles also train users in analogical thinking, which is to see the principles as a set of patterns of inventions or operators applicable to all fields of study. (See Figure 5.16.)

The principles also make use of the 39 Characteristics of a Technical System. These are the 39 engineering parameters for expressing technical contradictions defined by Genrich Altshuller in the late 1960s. (See Figure 5.17.)

To make this combination usable, Directed Evolution has combined them into Patterns of Evolution. They are a set of terms or statements that define trends that have strong, historically recurring tendencies in

1	Segmentation	21	Rushing through
2	Extraction	22	Convert a harm into a benefit
3	Local conditions	23	Feedback
4	Asymmetry	24	Mediator
5	Combining	25	Self-service
6	Universality	26	Copying
7	Nesting	27	Disposable object
8	Anti-weight	28	Replacement of a mechanical system
9	Prior counteraction	29	Use a pneumatic or hydraulic construction
10	Prior action	30	Flexible film or thin membranes
11	Cushion in advance	31	Use of porous material
12	Equipotentiality	32	Changing the color
13	Inversion	33	Homogeneity
14	Spheroidality	34	Rejecting and regenerating parts
15	Dynamicity	35	Transformation of physical and chemical states
16	Partial-excessive action	36	Phase transition
17	Shift to a new dimension	37	Thermal expansion
18	Mechanical vibration	38	Use strong oxidizers
19	Periodic action	39	Inert environment
20	Continuity of a useful action	40	Composite materials

Figure 5.16 Altshuller's 40 TRIZ Principles for Conflict Resolution

1 Weight of moving object	21 Power
2 Weight of non-moving object	22 Waste of energy
3 Length of moving object	23 Waste of substance
4 Length of non-moving object	24 Loss of information
5 Area of moving object	25 Waste of time
6 Area of non-moving object	26 Amount of substance
7 Volume of moving object	27 Reliability
8 Volume of non-moving object	28 Accuracy of measurement
9 Speed	29 Accuracy of manufacturing
10 Force	30 Harmful factors acting on object
11 Tension, pressure	31 Harmful side effects
12 Shape	32 Manufacturability
13 Stability of object	33 Convenience of use
14 Strength	34 Reparability
15 Durability of moving object	35 Adaptability
16 Durability of non-moving object	36 Complexity of device
17 Temperature	37 Complexity of control
18 Brightness	38 Level of automation
19 Energy spent by moving object	39 Productivity
20 Energy spent by non-moving object	

Figure 5.17   Altshuller's 39 Engineering Parameters for Expressing Technical Contradictions

the development and evolution of man-made systems. There are 8 major patterns (some people use 12 major categories in place of the 8). They are often presented in a spider diagram. See Figure 5.18 for the 8 Patterns of Evolution and Figure 5.19 for the 12 Patterns of Evolution.

Each of the Patterns of Evolution is subdivided into many Lines of Evolution. Lines of Evolution describe in greater detail typical sequences of stages (positions on a Line) that a system follows in a specific Pattern of Evolution in the process of its natural progress. Once these positions are known, the system's current position on a Line can be identified, and the possibility of transitioning to the next position can be assessed (for example, become flexible or use microlevel properties of materials utilized).

Aligned with each Line of Evolution is a group of possible corrective actions called *Operators* that can be used to correct the problem or improve the product or process. An Operator is a little nugget of wisdom (recommendation, suggestion) on changes to the system designed to trigger you into thinking how to solve the problem or to improve the process under evaluation. Operators could also be used in moving the

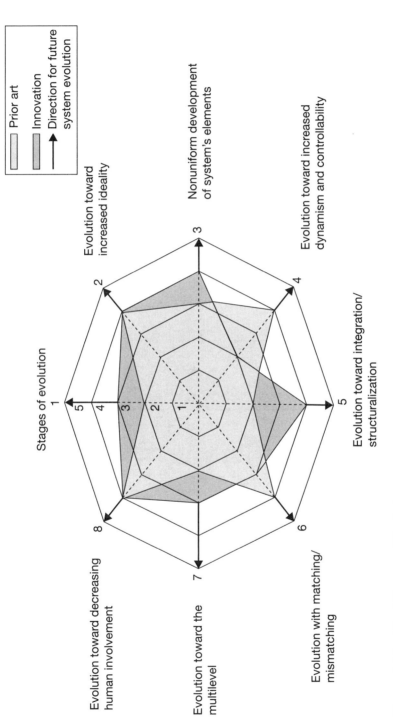

Figure 5.18 The 8 Patterns of Evolution

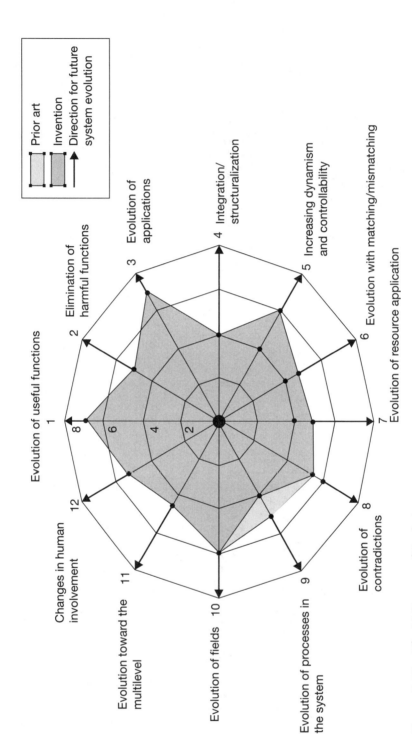

Figure 5.19 The 12 Patterns of Evolution

system to the next position on the Line if this step requires a creative solution. Operators are drawn from the successful results of previous actions that resolved difficult technological problems and process problems. Operators are used to solve problems in existing systems and to change the system position on the relevant Lines of Evolution, for example by suggesting to employ a hinge or use special physical effects. In some situations, a position on the Line could be described via an applied Operator, so a Line could include a number of Operators or positions that are or were applied or achieved in a certain sequence. The 40 TRIZ Principles were the first Operators discovered; there are about a thousand of these Operators available today.

It helps me to think of Lines of Evolution as taking a long trip with many cities along the way. Each one is a destination unto itself. The Operators are the GPS (Global Positioning System) that tells you the best way to get to the next destination.

HU Diagrams

The Directed Evolution approach also makes use of HU diagrams (*H* stands for harmful functions, and *U* stands for useful functions). These diagrams show the relationships between the functions. The model helps us identify the areas of the system that can be improved. Every time you define a corrective action (useful function), you also may create a counterreaction (harmful function). (See Figure 5.20.)

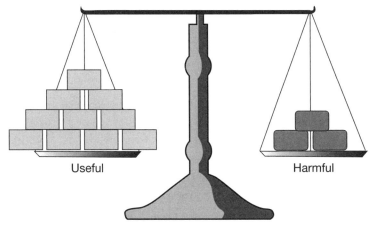

Useful   Harmful

Maximize the ratio of useful to harmful.

Figure 5.20   The ultimate goal

The object of the HU exercise is to maximize the ratio of useful to harmful functions. This is accomplished by creating an HU diagram. (See Figure 5.21.)

HU diagrams focus on defining a solution. This is a very different objective compared with that of most problem-solving tools used by the improvement professional in the past; previously the objective would have been to define the root cause. HU diagrams also help to reduce the risks related to the new process. To understand how to construct and use an HU diagram, see Appendix H.

Best-Value Analysis

Figure 5.22 shows the impact of having a bigger percentage of a process in real-value-added activities.

The materials or process may be real-value-added, but is it the best way to accomplish the desired function? Best-value analysis is another effective approach used to evaluate if the item being studied is designed to provide maximum value to the customer at the lowest possible price. Best-value analysis (sometimes just called value analysis) consists of five phases:

- Information phase
- Specification phase
- Analysis phase
- Execution phase
- Reporting phase

The following is a detailed explanation of each of these five phases:

- *Information phase.* The information phase asks three questions: What is it? What does it cost? What does it do? Function is what makes a product, process, or procedure work or sell. A function can be either primary or secondary. For example, the function of a drill might be to drill holes, but this would restrict it to making holes. A better definition would state that the function of a drill is to remove materials. Likewise, if we ask what the function of a power cable is, we might say it is to conduct electricity. A better definition would say that the function of a power cable is to transmit energy.
- *Specification phase.* Creativity equals knowledge times imagination times evaluation. The specification phase asks the question, What

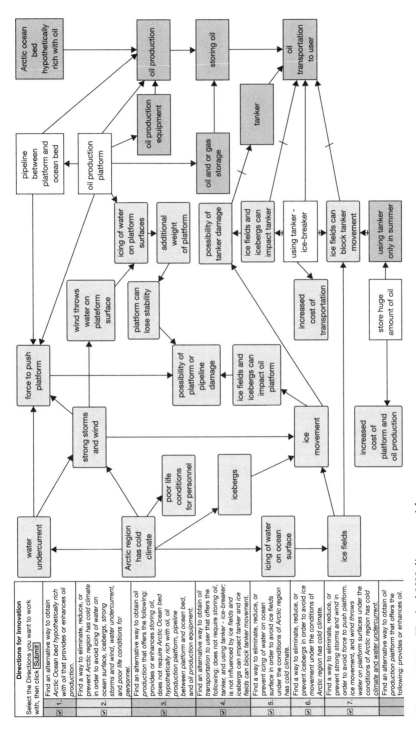

Figure 5.21 Typical HU diagram with comments

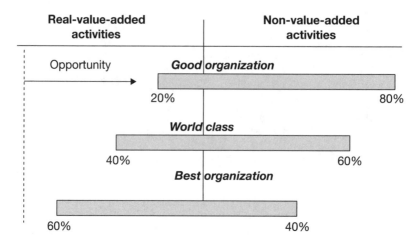

Figure 5.22 The difference between the good and the best organizations

else will do the job? After doing something the same way for 2 years, look it over carefully. After 5 years, be suspicious. After 10 years, throw it out and start all over again. The brain contains about 13 million nerve cells. About one-third are used in a normal lifetime. Only 5 percent are in constant use. So there are a lot of no-value-added nerve cells available for you to use to make you more creative. To keep the creative flow going, don't critique ideas during a brainstorming session. Just think how much faster you travel on a freeway than down a street in your town. Each time you come to a red light and put your brakes on, your vehicle stops. Creativity stops whenever it is interrupted. In addition, our studies reveal that the best ideas do not appear during the beginning of the brainstorming session. The second half is where 80 percent of the good ideas originate.

- *Analyze phase.* The analyze phase asks the questions: Will it work? What will it cost?
- *Execution phase.* In this phase the future-state solution becomes a reality.
- *Reporting phase.* In this phase the results of the changes are measured to verify that the projected improvements were realized (Fran, 1974).

The following are typical examples where creative thinking got rid of non-value-added waste to bring about some big improvements in performance. A good example of a wrong material selection occurred at a motor manufacturing factory—a stainless-steel bellow was used as a coupler between a small electric motor and a variable condenser. By replacing it with a plastic tube, the cost was reduced 95 percent (Fran, 1974).

Typical examples include Union Carbide—it used process breakthrough techniques to remove $40 million out of its fixed cost in just 3 years. And Blue Cross of Alaska's improvement efforts increased productivity 20 percent in 15 months. CEO Betty Woods stated: "It was more difficult than we ever imagined but it was worth it."

Task 3. Duplication Elimination (Figure 5.23)

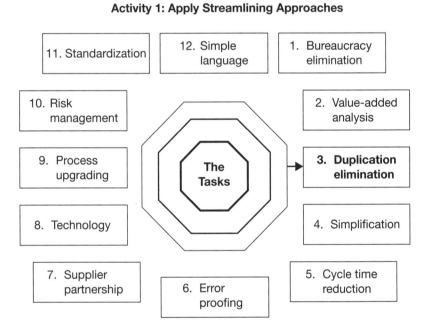

Phase III: Streamlining the Process
Activity 1: Apply Streamlining Approaches

11. Standardization

12. Simple language

1. Bureaucracy elimination

10. Risk management

2. Value-added analysis

9. Process upgrading

The Tasks

3. **Duplication elimination**

8. Technology

4. Simplification

7. Supplier partnership

6. Error proofing

5. Cycle time reduction

Figure 5.23   Task 3. Duplication Elimination

To eliminate duplication, the PIT will look at the process to define where the process is recording the same data in more than one place in the process and will also look to see if the same data are recorded in another process that could eliminate the need to record those data in the process under study. As well, the PIT will check for activities that are done in two places in the process or are done in other processes that could be eliminated or be combined so that the activities do not have to be done in both places. A typical example is where the manager and the personnel department are keeping separate employee attendance records. Frequently these duplications end up by confusing rather than helping, for often one set of records doesn't agree with another set of records. (See Figure 5.24.) This results in a lot of additional work to resolve the differences when what should have been done was to refine the process so that the data that are collected are correct.

> *Start with an article that suits and then study to find some way of eliminating the entirely useless parts. This applies to everything—a shoe, a dress, a house, a piece of machinery, a railroad, a steamship, an airplane. As we cut out useless parts and simplify necessary ones, we also cut down the cost of making.*
>
> —Henry Ford, Sr.

Figure 5.24   Problems with two sets of data

Task 4. Simplification (Figure 5.25)

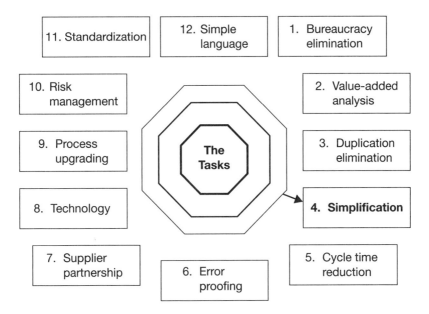

Phase III: Streamlining the Process
Activity 1: Apply Streamlining Approaches

11. Standardization

12. Simple language

1. Bureaucracy elimination

10. Risk management

The Tasks

2. Value-added analysis

9. Process upgrading

3. Duplication elimination

8. Technology

4. Simplification

7. Supplier partnership

6. Error proofing

5. Cycle time reduction

Figure 5.25 Task 4. Simplification

Henry Ford, Sr., wrote in his book *My Life and Work,* "The foremen and superintendents would only be wasting time were they to keep a check on the costs in their departments. There are certain costs—such as the rate of wages, the overhead, the price of materials, and the like, which they could not in any way control, so they do not bother about them" (Ford, 1922).

Simplification is an approach that the Japanese have defined and used to create an advantage over their competitors. While the rest of the world has been focused on installing very complex systems to manage their processes, the Japanese have looked for ways to simplify them and to eliminate the need for the very costly software approaches. Companies like Toyota look for ways that they could complete the same task without the cost or complication of the popular software programs. As a result, they are using very simple approaches that could eliminate the need for expensive and complex Supply Chain Management and customer relationship management systems used by their competitors in the United States. This is one of the major reasons that Toyota is now the number one car producer in the world, replacing General Motors and Ford.

Simplification is another important concept in streamlining. Let's begin by trying to understand the term. We live in a world of ever-present and increasing complexity. Complexity means that life has more of everything: more parts, more systems, more relationships, more dependencies, more problems, and more imperatives. Today, goals, requirements, and volume are changing, and so the processes are adapted accordingly. More steps, more tasks, more people, more inter-dependencies are added. When new tasks are added, support tasks usually follow (for example, preparation, filing, or putting away work), making the process more complex.

The increase in complexity results in increasing difficulties everywhere as activities, decisions, relationships, and essential information become more difficult to understand and to manage. In an era of rapidly increasing complexity, it is essential to actively and continuously be engaged in simplification as a counterforce to evolving complexity.

When you apply simplification to a business process, you evaluate every element in an effort to make it less complex, easier, and less demanding. When an organization fails to make continuous simplification efforts, it invites difficulty and poor performance.

The following list illustrates the application of the concept in relatively simple but time-consuming everyday activities:

- *Eliminate duplication and fragmentation of tasks.* The first step is to identify the duplications and fragmentations that occur during various parts of the process and then, second, to combine related tasks and eliminate redundancies.
- *Address complex flows and bottlenecks.* These can be managed by changing the order of tasks, combining or separating tasks, and even balancing the workload of different individuals.
- *Simplify memos and other correspondence.* These can be simplified by making them shorter, more direct, better formatted, and more readable.

- *Manage meetings.* An agenda (sent well in advance) is a basic simplification device. Presentation materials should be simple and easily understood. Meeting protocol should be established and followed, and meeting attendees should be trained in protocol.
- *Combine similar activities.* Can similar or consecutive activities be combined to make one job more rewarding to the person performing the assignment and reduce cost, errors, and cycle time?
- *Reduce amount of handling.* Can you reduce the amount of handling by combining responsibilities? Can the person doing the activity evaluate the output to ensure that it is correct? Can a phone call eliminate the need to mail a document to another building?
- *Eliminate unused data.* Do you use all the data that are recorded? If not, why record them? Each thing that is recorded (word by word) should be challenged to be sure it is needed.
- *Eliminate copies.* Are all the copies of letters and computer reports used? In most cases, they are not.
- *Refine standard reports.* Meet frequently with the people who receive standard reports to find out what parts of the report they use and how they use them. Put all the standard reports in similar formats.

Let's look at an example of the simplification concept: writing checks, recording the transactions in a journal, and tracking the receipts. With the traditional, old-fashioned manual method, these are three separate activities, tedious and time consuming. Simplification combines them into one activity. The method is called the *one-write system of check writing.* Simultaneously, you can write a check, make a duplicate, and record the transaction in a journal. This system accomplishes the same objective as the three-step process but with less effort, less time, and less chance for error.

In trying to find ways to apply the principles of simplification, we would again begin by asking questions such as:

- Is this process effectively systematized or performed haphazardly?
- Would a different process be more effective, more efficient?
- Would a different layout make work smoother and easier, with less handling and less wasted motion?
- Can the forms be filled out without adding another document?

- Can this activity or stage be combined with another?
- Could a single activity produce a combined output?
- Are instructions immediately available, easy to understand, self-explanatory?
- Would a backup process eliminate rework or wait time?
- Does this activity require someone to stand by idly while the task is being done?
- Would simpler language speed up reading and improve understanding?
- Does the way it is done create more unnecessary work downstream?
- Is time lost looking for information or documents?
- Do interruptions of the work flow add to complexity?
- Could a template be used to simplify the activity?
- Does the work flow smoothly around the area?
- Is there unnecessary movement?

And the list goes on and on ...

Sometimes it is helpful to start your simplification analysis for an activity by asking the question, What is your output? Then design a process for the simplest way of generating that output and compare this new process design with the original process. After the comparison has been made, combine the two processes, taking the best of each.

To summarize simplification, you need to:

- Make the process less complex.
- Make the process less demanding.
- Include fewer pages.
- Include fewer steps.
- Include fewer tasks.
- Ensure fewer interruptions.
- Make the process easier to learn.
- Make the process easier to do.
- Make the process easier to understand.
- Ask yourself, Does it really even need to be done?

When Boeing focused on simplification, the company was able to cut six manuals down to one that was smaller than any one of the six. When IBM Brazil focused on simplification, it eliminated 50 procedures and

450 forms and reduced the number of documents it produced each year by 2.5 million.

One part of an electronic music organ was made up of 163 parts. It provided the vibration tones similar to that of a violin when it is played. By analyzing its functions and streamlining it, it was reduced down to 51 parts that improved the quality of the tone (Fran, 1974).

Task 5. Cycle Time Reduction (Figure 5.26)

Phase III: Streamlining the Process
Activity 1: Apply Streamlining Approaches

| 11. Standardization | 12. Simple language | 1. Bureaucracy elimination |

| 10. Risk management | | 2. Value-added analysis |

| 9. Process upgrading | **The Tasks** | 3. Duplication elimination |

| 8. Technology | | 4. Simplification |

| 7. Supplier partnership | 6. Error proofing | **5. Cycle time reduction** |

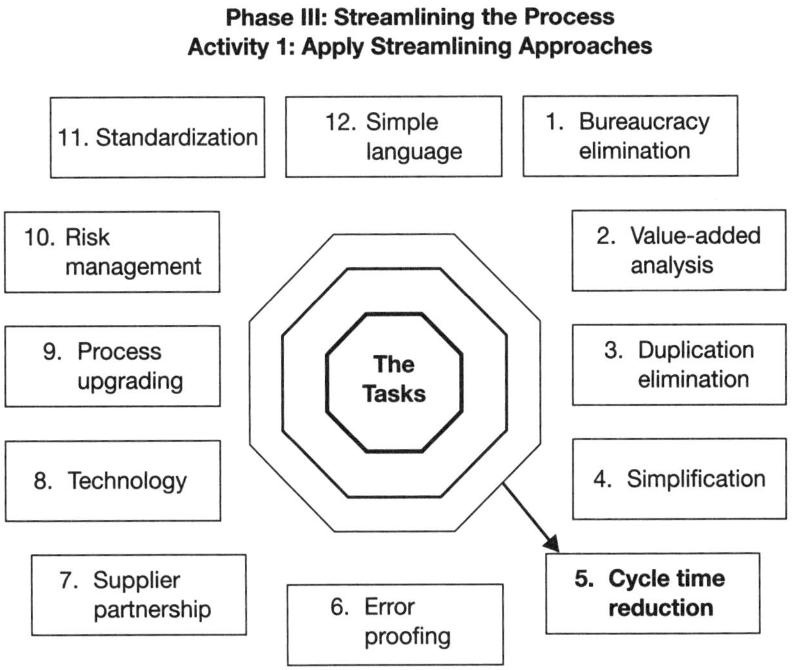

Figure 5.26   Task 5. Cycle Time Reduction

Time is the only thing that you can't get more of.
—H. James Harrington

Reducing cycle time is critical to success today. The organization that gets there first with the most is always the winner. Every product has a market window. Long development processes miss the critical beginning portion of the market window that sets the theme for the total buying activities. Long cycle times increase cost and cost the organization customers.

The objective of this task is to reduce cycle time. To do this, the PIT needs to focus on activities that take long cycle times in the current process.

When your product isn't moving, you have a problem.
—H. James Harrington

A number of things can be done to reduce cycle times. Some of them are:

- Do activities in parallel versus serially.
- Stop batch processing.
- Change activity sequence
- Eliminate wait time.
- Reduce interruptions.
- Improve timing (when an employee receives output).
- Reduce output movement.
- Set different priorities.
- Reduce inventory.

At G&G Machine Inc. a list of improvement ideas came out of each value stream map (VSM), resulting in about a 50 percent reduction in lead time and similar reduction in work-in-process (WIP) inventory. One of the improvement ideas from the VSM was to implement a Pull/*Kanban* system to keep material flowing through the shop and minimize WIP (Southwest Research Institute, 2010). Henry Ford, Sr., was the U.S. father of just-in-time production. He did not believe in warehouses. To him stock represented money wasted. In 1922, he stated:

> We have found in buying materials that it is not worthwhile to buy for other than immediate needs. We buy only enough to fit into the plan of production, taking into consideration the state of transportation at the time. If transportation were perfect and even flow of materials could be assured, it would not be necessary to carry any stock whatsoever. The carloads of raw materials would arrive on schedule and in the planned order and amounts, and go from the railway cars into production. That

would save a great deal of money, for it would give a very rapid turnover and thus decrease the amount of money tied up in materials. With bad transportation one has to carry larger stocks.

This is the step where critical path analysis and the theory of constraints become very important tools to help you reduce cycle time. The critical path method (CPM) constructs a model of the project or process that includes the following:

- A list of all activities required to operate the process
- The time (duration) that each activity will take to completion
- The dependencies between the activities

Using these values, CPM defines the longest path of activities from the beginning to the output of the process that is being analyzed. The critical path is the sequence of activities that add up to the longest overall duration to produce an output. This determines the shortest time possible to complete a process cycle. An additional parallel path through the process with the total durations shorter than the critical path is called a subcritical or noncritical path.

The theory of constraints is based on the premise that the rate of goal achievement is limited by at least one constraining process. Only by increasing flow through the constraint can overall throughput be increased.

When things sit on a person's desk or in the stock room, it is just adding to the cycle time and the cost. Just-in-Time, Zero Inventory, and Single Item Processing all add up to reducing cycle time, saving money, and improving customer satisfaction. After all, cycle time is what the external customer lives with, not processing time.

One of the most effective ways to reduce cycle time is through CPM. Every process has a critical path; it is the combination of activities and tasks that gate the takt time of the process. The PIT can determine the critical path by analyzing each path that the item can go through in the flow diagram and adding up the time it takes in each of the activities, including transportation and wait time. Although it is possible to define the critical path by hand, it is much more practical to do it using a computer program like Microsoft Project. In this case, with the touch of a button you can immediately define and highlight the critical path. Once the critical path is defined, prioritize elements that are on the critical path to work on and reduce their cycle time. Frequently there are one or two activities that are going to make the difference. Once the critical path is streamlined, another critical path will immediately come up. Keep working with these critical paths until your cycle times meet the requirements as defined in your project charter.

Hughes Aircraft analyzed the steps required to construct a space satellite. The company found out that many of them were not required. By cutting out or combining these steps, the team reduced the time required to build key components of the shuttle from 45 to 22 weeks, saving millions of dollars (Tomasko, 1993).

Combining several activities into one can result in:

- Eliminating rework activities
- Having the workers make the decisions
- Standardizing the process and the way it is performed
- Centralizing the data and decentralizing operations
- Capturing data as close to the source as possible using IT techniques
- Integrating parallel activities
- Reducing business-value-added activities and eliminating no-value-added activities
- Reducing cycle time

Let's take a look at what reducing cycle time did for IBM's special-bid process. The old special-bid process took 90 days, and the company closed 20 percent of the bids. After streamlining the process, IBM was able to process a bid in 15 days, reducing the cost to process a bid by 30 percent. But even more important, the bid closure jumped from 20 to 65 percent wins—more than a 300 percent improvement in sales.

Owens Corning was able to cut its budgeting cycle from 5 months to 60 days, starting in October and having the board of directors' approval in December. Budgets were due the middle of October. Two weeks later, all the regional presidents met together in a two-day planning meeting where they presented their numbers and justifications. At the end of the two-day meeting, goals for the next year were completed, and the chairman took these goals to present them to the board of directors in December.

We are not afraid to try new things now. Sometimes they work and are useful, other times not. If everything we did worked, we would know we weren't trying hard enough.
—Charlie Chambers, Owens Corning
Reporting and Forecasting (*CFO*, 1996)

We cut our process from 20 steps to 9 steps and added one so the change was significant.
—John Trabulsi, Dun & Bradstreet
Accounts Payable and Purchasing

The concerns always come back to controls—how would this new process minimize fraud with so few steps? ... The idea was to do each step only once and only if it was needed. Steps had been added over time to take the thinking out of the process. We wanted to put the thinking back in.
—(John Trabulsi, Dun & Bradstreet, Accounts
Payable and Purchasing, *CFO*, 1996).

Batch processing in production and in the support areas increases cycle time. For example, if forms are batched in quantities of 50 and it takes 2 minutes per form, the first form processed waits 98 minutes before it moves on to the next operation. If each form is processed as an individual unit, then it would only be a 2-minute delay before it moves to the next station.

The following is another example of serial versus parallel activities. A typical engineering folder would go from development engineering to product engineering, manufacturing engineering, manufacturing field service, purchasing, and QA and then back to development engineering. If it takes 2 days in each of the areas plus 1 day to transport, that is 15 days or 3 weeks. If you hold a meeting where you bring all six people together, you could reduce that time to minutes.

When it is not moving, that is an improvement opportunity.
—H. James Harrington

Task 6. Error Proofing (Figure 5.27)

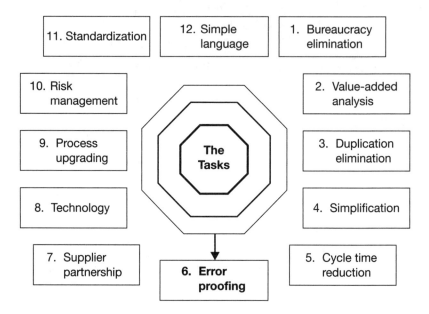

Figure 5.27   Task 6. Error Proofing

To err is human, but to be paid for it is divine.

—H. James Harrington

Error proofing is a task that requires a very deliberate focus since we have a tendency to accept errors as a way of life. We live with them, we put up with them, and we do little to prevent them. As much as we dislike errors, there are many reasons why we don't eliminate them. Some of them are:

- *Lack of time.* "I don't have the time now." The reason we don't have the time to fix it today is that we didn't take the time to do it right yesterday.
- *Lack of problem ownership.* "It's not my problem—Joe did it wrong; let him fix it." The lack of problem ownership causes many problems to stay with us when they could have been solved in a very simple way.

- *Lack of recognition.* "Sure, I could tell Joe that he is doing it wrong and show him how to do it right, but that doesn't give me any points with my boss. All it does is put me behind schedule and make Joe look better." Management needs to find ways to recognize people who go out of their way to help correct problems, who take the time to do the job right every time.
- *Errors as a way of life.* "Mistakes are bound to happen—we're only human." This type of attitude is the beginning of the end for a company.
- *Ignorance of the importance of the problem.* "It is just a little burr; it will fall off sometime." But what if it sometimes occurs in a precision servo system that is used to navigate a plane and it jams the gears? Every job is important; it if isn't, it should not be done. An error that is repeated is unforgivable.
- *Belief that no one can do anything about some problems.* "You can't do anything about it" is no answer to a real problem. It may cost too much to prevent it from recurring, but don't stop short of finding out what it would cost.
- *Poor balance by upper management among schedule, cost, and quality.* If management places priority on quality, schedules and cost will take care of themselves. Remember, the bitterness of shipping poor quality lingers long after the sweetness of meeting schedules.
- *People who try to protect themselves.* All too often, people are more interested in proving that the problem was not caused by them than in solving the problem. When such people realize that a problem is coming close to their front porch, they add a detour route so that the problem takes much longer to solve than it should have.
- *Head hunting by management.* If management is more interested in placing blame than eliminating the problem, the error-prevention program is doomed.

There are three major ways to protect your customers from receiving errors:

- Eliminate errors at their source before they occur.
- Detect an error in the process of doing it before it results in a defect.
- Detect an error after it has been created but before it reaches the next operation.

Negative Analysis—Reverse Thinking

To error-proof our processes, we use a technique called *negative analysis* which is sometimes called *reverse thinking*. When using this approach, we ask ourselves, What would we do if we want the process to fail? Then we will design a process to prevent the identified conditions from occurring.

Let's assume you were opening a restaurant and you wanted it to fail. Some of the things that would cause it to fail are:

- Poor food
- Poor parking
- Poor attitude of waiters and waitresses
- Poor location
- No or little signage identifying the restaurant
- Poor menu choices
- Dirty dining area
- Uncomfortable seating
- Dirty glasses

Looking at just one of the reasons—dirty glasses—you would be sure, in your quest to prevent errors, that the automatic dishwasher would remove lipstick from glasses and that the glasses would be stored on a closed shelf.

Typical error-proofing methods are:

- Put all letters in envelopes with plastic windows to reveal the name and address. Not only does this save much typing time, but also it eliminates letters being sent to the wrong person.
- Use different-colored paper for different jobs to help direct correspondence to the right location. Different-colored paper for each day quickly tells everyone what needs to be done today. Different-colored folders for different jobs give the same message. Proper use of colors will greatly reduce errors.
- Put confidential information on paper preprinted with the words "Do not copy" in large thin letters on each page. This is more effective than typing "confidential" on the page, but do both if it makes you feel more comfortable.
- Use preprinted lists for repetitive mailing. It is more accurate to delete names for one-of-a-kind mailing than to retype the names.
- Use longer paper if you want the document to be given special care. If you normally use $8\frac{1}{2} \times 11$, go for legal-size paper so that the document will stand out.

- Use computer programs that check spelling, and check the input to ensure that letters, not numbers, and vice versa, are recorded in the correct places on a form. This double-check saves a lot of errors.
- Make sure the on-off switch is out of the way on your computer so that you can't turn it off in error and lose your data.
- Select a phone without a disconnect button. Too often, employees hit the disconnect button instead of the hold button, and a customer is lost.
- Ensure effective communication by asking employees to repeat instructions to be sure they are understood.
- Write down any directions to employees for their future reference.
- Use cross-checking when totaling a number of columns.

You need to error-proof your communications also. (See Figure 5.28.)

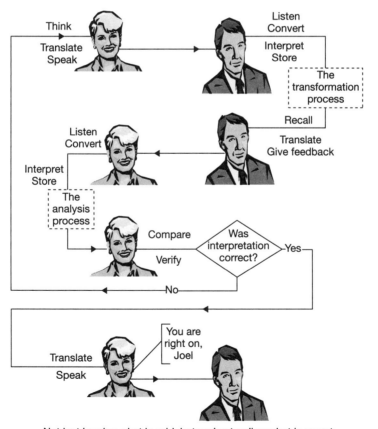

Not just hearing what is said, but understanding what is meant.

Figure 5.28 Error-proofing the communication process

Task 7. Supplier Partnership (Figure 5.29)

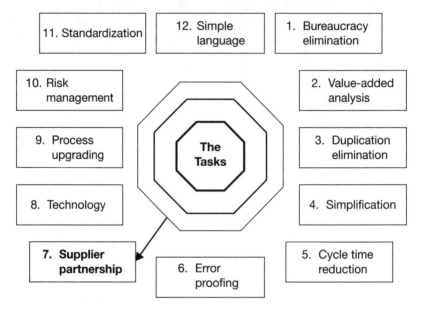

Figure 5.29 Task 7. Supplier Partnership

> *If your people are your most important asset, then your suppliers run a very close second.*
>
> —H. James Harrington

The relationship between you and your suppliers should be a lot like the relationship between a husband and a wife. It should be a partnership (see Figure 5.29) in which both parties need to go more than 50 percent of the way if it's going to be successful. The old attitude of "I give them 100 percent good money; they should give me 100 percent good inputs" is gone. When things go wrong today, it is usually the result of a complex situation where both parties suffer. (See Figure 5.30.) (*Note:* In the Figure 5.30 case the second delay was caused because the employee supplied accounting bad data in the first place.) Today suppliers and customers need to develop a partnership-type relationship that provides a win-win environment for both parties.

Figure 5.30 Suppliers are important

The PIT now looks at each input to each activity and asks questions like:

- Did the receiving party (customer) define to the supplier exactly what is needed, and have the parties agreed on how it is to be measured?
- Is the supplier providing more than the receiving party requires?
- Does the input come into the receiving party (customer) in the most usable format?
- Does the input arrive too early, causing storage problems?
- Does the input come late, slowing down the process?
- Is the quality good enough so that the receiving party (customer) does not need to check it?
- What would happen if the input was eliminated?
- Is there a way to eliminate the need for the input?
- Is there a better source for the input that is cheaper or higher quality or both?

Figure 5.31 shows a simple activity's interface with the process' suppliers. Because each activity within itself is both a customer and a supplier, the total interfaces are twice as complex. (See Figure 5.32.)

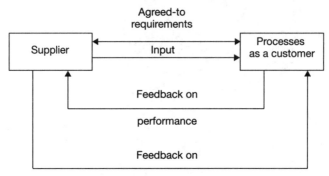

Figure 5.31 Interface between the process and the suppliers

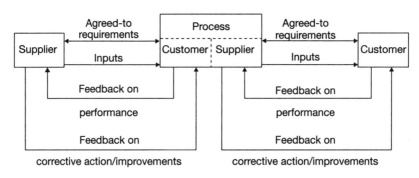

Figure 5.32 The cascading customer/supplier model

All activities within the process are highly dependent upon people outside of the activity that provide input in the form of materials, information, and ideas. Just as you as the provider of your process are a supplier of products or services to your customer, the people that provide input into your process or activity are your suppliers. In these supplier-customer relationships both parties have responsibilities. The PIT has the responsibility to provide the process' suppliers with documented input specifications that define the process' needs and expectations. The supplier should carefully review these specifications and agree that he or she can meet the requirements. If the supplier cannot, the PIT needs to work with the supplier to understand what can be supplied and to help the supplier develop a plan to upgrade his or her output if necessary. The customer should never ask for more than is needed and will be used. Remember, nothing is free; everything costs the organization that created it something. The customer may not pay for it directly, but it cost someone somewhere time and effort.

Task 8. Technology (Figure 5.33)

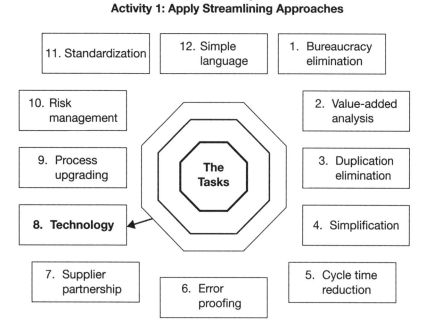

Phase III: Streamlining the Process
Activity 1: Apply Streamlining Approaches

- 11. Standardization
- 12. Simple language
- 1. Bureaucracy elimination
- 10. Risk management
- 2. Value-added analysis
- 9. Process upgrading
- The Tasks
- 3. Duplication elimination
- 8. Technology
- 4. Simplification
- 7. Supplier partnership
- 6. Error proofing
- 5. Cycle time reduction

Figure 5.33 Task 8. Technology

To begin this section we first want to define *technology*. We use it as an umbrella term that includes automation, mechanization, computerization, and information technology.

In 1991 for the first time ever, companies spent more money on computing and communications gear than the combined monies spent on industrial, mining, farm, and construction equipment. Over two-thirds of U.S. employees work in the service sector, and knowledge is our most important product. Now is the time in the streamlining process to make use of the money your organization has already invested in technology to speed up the process that is being improved and reduce the cost. The cost of computing power drops about 30 percent per year, and microchips are doubling in performance power every year and a half. The birthday card that plays "Happy Birthday" when it is opened has more computer power than existed in the entire world before 1950. Your wristwatch has more computer power than existed before 1961. The video camera you use to take home movies has more processing power than the IBM 360 system that was the product that started the mainframe computer age.

With all these rapid improvements in technology, there often is a better way to use technology in the process than is being used at the present time. The following list presents some of today's technology enablers:

- Parallel processing
- High-performance workstations
- Laptop and handheld computers
- Disk arrays
- CD-ROMs
- High-density storage
- Packet radios
- Wireless LANs
- Cellular voice
- ISDN
- VSAT
- LAN/WAN routing
- FDDI
- Frame relays and fast packets
- OSI
- APPC/APPN
- Middleware
- Electronic mail
- EDI
- Voice mail
- Information interchanges
- Architectures
- Operating system services

- Computer-to-PBX links
- Rapid application development
- Code generation
- Object-oriented programming
- Fourth-generation language (4GL)
- Repository
- Relational DBMS
- Object-oriented DBMS
- Distributed DBMS
- Expert systems
- Neural networks
- Windowing and graphical user interfaces
- Pen-based computing
- Voice recognition and speech synthesis
- Bar coding
- Scanning
- Optical character recognition
- Light pens
- Group decision support systems
- Calendaring

- Image processing
- Multimedia
- Compound documents
- Video conferencing

- Fax
- Desktop publishing
- Color
- ODA/ODIF

Table 5.12 provides a list of ways that IT can impact process design.

You may feel it is late in the SPI cycle to think about the use of IT and automation applications, as many of these applications could have been identified during any one of the preceding tasks. You are right. In streamlining the process you probably have already observed opportunities to apply automation, mechanization, and IT applications since most organizations already use computers for at least some business functions.

We recommend that as IT potential applications are identified, they are added to the parking list (a list of ideas that will be discussed later). This provides the PIT with an excellent starting point for Task #8. The cost of computerizing a poor process is immense, and all it does is allow the organization to produce poor output even faster.

Table 5.12 IT Capabilities and Their Organizational Impact

Capability	Organizational Impact/Benefit
Transactional	IT transforms unstructured processes into routine transactions.
Geographical	IT transfers information rapidly and easily across large distances, making process independent of geography.
Automation	IT replaces or reduces human labor in a process.
Analytical	IT brings complex analytical methods to bear on a process.
Sequential	IT enables changes in the sequence of tasks in a process, often allowing multiple tasks to be worked on simultaneously.
Knowledge management	IT allows capture and dissemination of knowledge and expertise to improve the process.
Tracking	IT allows detailed tracking of tasks' status, inputs, and outputs.
Disintermediation	IT connects two parties within a process that would otherwise communicate through an intermediary (internal or external).
Dematerialization	IT can eliminate a process by replacing physical objects with information management.

IT can produce at super-human speed either brilliant guidance or business garbage.

—H. James Harrington

You should never consider automating or computerizing your process until your process is streamlined. Time after time we have identified processes that can be simplified to the point that there is no need for expensive computerization.

In this task we address two very different types of applications:

- Movement of physical objects
- Movement and analysis of data

Now we can talk about turning data into information and turning information into wisdom and action.
    —Paulette Everhart, Corporate Controller, EDS (*CFO*, 1996)

Movement of physical objects is primarily directed at in-process and finished-goods inventory. To accomplish this, we look at our revised process to identify places where there are:

- Things picked up
- Movement of people
- Storage
- Product being moved
- Things that are being done by hand
- People who have to shift from doing one thing to another

It is the PIT's objective to automate repetitive jobs and activities. Typical automation activities are:

- Storage and pulling of stock
- Painting operations
- Welding operations
- Filling operations
- Continuous flow line
- Phone message systems
- E-mail reservation systems

- Cranes in construction application
- Container shipments
- Hydraulic lifts
- Computerized production equipment
- Packaging equipment

It doesn't have to be complex and costly; simply putting rollers on a skid can keep the operators from having to get up and find a forklift to move the skid into their work area.

Robotics has been a real breakthrough. Today robots can do almost every repetitive job that a human can do, and they do it better. This has eliminated many of the health and safety problems that organizations face and much of the fatigue in the individual worker's job.

In terms of movement and analysis of data, this is the area where IT shines. IT concepts were originated to handle data at speeds that are impossible for people to attain (literally processing billions of calculations in microseconds). Today we exist in a service economy in which our major products are not physical items. The Internet has opened the world to everyone. I can sit in my office in Dubai and talk to Marcos Bertin in Argentina while visually watching his reaction through Skype for free. We run our business relying on a whole set of acronyms to help us make decisions. These include things like CRM, ERP, SAP, and MRP2. More and more, the computer is replacing the human factor. Human beings and errors are being removed from our business and replaced by software projects.

Look for the following applications where IT can have a big impact on process performance:

- Processor capacity
- Processor portability
- Storage
- Portable networking
- Remote site networking
- LAN interconnecting
- Computer interoperability
- Network computing
- Network message services
- Applications portability

- Voice and data applications
- Application development technologies
- Data management
- Knowledge systems
- User interface
- Information entry
- Groupware
- Multimedia communications and processes

Unfortunately IT solutions may not give you the projected return on investment because your competition is implementing similar service software solutions at the same time. As a result, you get no competitive advantage; quite the contrary—not putting in these solutions puts you at a competitive disadvantage. This is forcing organizations to keep pace with the current state of software development. Savings only occur in reduced in-house cost and decreased error rate.

The effective computerization of operations requires teamwork by people throughout the organization, as many different organizations are usually affected. For example, when Ford installed at the receiving dock computer terminals capable of reading packing slips, the number of people required to issue payment to suppliers decreased by 75 percent. As an order arrives, the Ford employee using the computer reads the parts packing slip, confirming that the price on the slip is the one Ford agreed to pay. As soon as everything clears in the computer system, the check is written automatically by the machine and sent out. The success of this change depended on the cooperation among many people from purchasing, manufacturing, finance, information systems, personnel, and the union. Finance worried that the early payment to the suppliers would be more costly than the savings. The union worried about the loss of jobs. Each of these concerns needed to be addressed before the system could be implemented.

When a parts clerk at Honda needs a part, his or her transfer terminal looks at 10 different warehouses to define the status at each warehouse and determine which warehouse can get the part to the parts clerk the fastest. A similar network is used by Digital Equipment Corporation, slashing inventory cost by over half during a five-year period. Today we are combining telecommunication, local area networks, and data network systems to maximize the handling of data. Combining one or more technologies keeps people in touch with one another and provides them with the latest information.

American President Line (APL) has established a system that allows a customer to call APL to find the location of a ship on which he or she has merchandise. The caller is connected to a computer that goes through a space satellite and land-based communication links—all of this within 10 seconds—to generate a computer voice response that specifically addresses the customer's questions.

What Can IT Do for Your Process?

Often insufficient time is expended at the start of IT projects to set strategic targets and plan accordingly. The focus on achieving quick results by adopting IT-based solutions leads to the problems of lack of integration, employee resistance, insufficient training, and ultimately poor morale, particularly if the people perceive that the IT project is a smoke screen for downsizing through productivity improvements.

The following IT tools are most often used (Neubauer, 2009):

- ERP systems—52 percent
- Proprietary systems—57 percent
- WFM—45 percent
- CRM—44 percent
- Groupware—50 percent
- Portal solutions—29 percent
- SCM—15 percent
- EAI solutions—8 percent

The object of this task is to apply current IT, automation, and mechanization approaches to the processes being streamlined, not to create new IT requirements for a supplier. (*Note:* Process reengineering activities usually result in requiring new and more advanced software packages to be developed.)

We wanted our teams to design the best processes and then find the best applications to automate them.

—Harry Beeth, Assistant Controller, IBM Corporate
Headquarters (*CFO*, 1996)

As an example, through the use of IT technologies and other SPI-type approaches the labor required per transaction at ESD Corp.'s billing and budgeting processes has gone down 82 percent per transaction. According to Mark Andrews of EDS, "As we look at the billing process, we see that many organizations—Finance, Operations, legal and so on—have pieces of information about the customer. We have built a knowledge warehouse that EDS does business with."

Task 9. Process Upgrading (Figure 5.34)

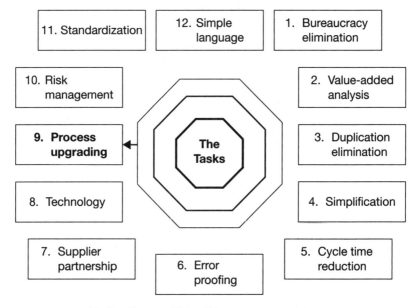

Phase III: Streamlining the Process
Activity 1: Apply Streamlining Approaches

Figure 5.34   Task 9. Process Upgrading

A well-designed work layout makes happy workers.

—H. James Harrington

At the very beginning of this activity I wrote about the evils of the seven types of waste as defined by Lean Six Sigma:

- Production
- Wait time
- Transportation

- Processing
- Inventory
- Motion
- Errors

In the previous eight tasks, we have attacked most of the types of waste, but now is the time to step back and be sure we have addressed all the opportunities. To do that, we will use some of the Lean methodology approaches that Henry Ford, Sr., used in the early 1900s. All the basic principles of Lean manufacturing appear in Ford's *My Life and Work* (1922), *Today and Tomorrow* (1926), and *Moving Forward* (1930). These books also describe all the quality and productivity improvement techniques that Japan made famous, including *Kaizen* (continuous improvement), *Poka Yoke* (error proofing), *Muda* (waste), and *Muri* (strain reduction and even elements of 5S). Lean and Just-in-Time manufacturing are Henry Ford's inventions, as he was the first industrialist to combine them into a mutually supporting comprehensive system. Ford stated that he didn't own a single warehouse. He noted, "We will not put into our establishment anything that is useless." That is a good definition of today's Lean approaches.

Lean is defined as the elimination of all non-value-added activities from the business. Lean enterprise extends this concept through the entire value stream or supply chain.

> *It is the little things that are hard to see—the awkward little methods of doing things that have grown up and which no one notices. And since manufacturing is solely a matter of detail, these little things develop, when added together, into very big things.*
>
> —Ford (1930)

Lean, as it is practiced today, covers many of the best approaches that we have already discussed and one or two that still need to be discussed:

- 5S
- Error proofing
- Reduced inventory (Just-in-Time)
- One-piece flow
- Quick changeover
- Theory of constraints
- Work flow diagrams

Even though we have addressed many of these approaches earlier in this book, it is good practice to look at the simulation model to be sure that all the possible waste creators have been minimized.

The PIT has now significantly improved the process. This is the time to look at the individual operations to see that they are optimized and then at the total process to see if the organization is in line with the process.

The 5S Workstation Layout

Everything that a person uses should be within his or her reach.
—H. James Harrington

We will start this analysis by looking at the layout within the work areas to minimize movement and storage. To do this, we will use many of the Lean tools. One of the most powerful tools is *5S*, sometimes called the *Five Pillars*. It is designed to organize the workplace.

Although parts of the 5S concept have been practiced in the United States and Europe since the early1940s, the idea of putting them all together in an approach called *5S* was originated in Japan by Hiroyuki Hirano. A translation of the original 5S terms from Japanese to English went like this:

- *Seiri*—Organization
- *Seiton*—Orderliness
- *Seiso*—Cleanliness
- *Seiketsu*—Standardized Cleanup
- *Shitsuke*—Discipline

In order to assist users of this tool to remember the elements, the original terminology has been retranslated to the following:

- Sort
- Set in Order
- Shine
- Standardize
- Sustain

In the original book, *5 Pillars of the Visual Workplace* (Hirano, 1990), the word *pillar* is used as a metaphor to mean "one of a group of structural elements that together support a structural system."

> *Some guys who were here when I started weren't too excited about 5S; they saw change as bad. But once they started seeing improvements, everybody got on board.*
> —Jason Bloy, Machinist, G&G Machine Inc.
> (Southwest Research Institute, 2010)

A Description of the Five Pillars
Now let's look at each of the five pillars, one at a time.

The first pillar—Sort. Removing all items from the workplace that are not needed for the current operation
As easy as this seems, it is often difficult to identify what is needed versus what is wanted.

Getting rid of items in the workplace can be stressful. People tend to hang onto parts, equipment, and tools, thinking that they may be needed for future orders or operations. This causes inventory and equipment to accumulate and get in the way of everyday production activities. Files grow and grow, filling up with unneeded and unused documents and slowing down the process of finding needed documents. If everyone does this, it can lead to a massive buildup of waste across the organization.

The following types of waste lead to errors, defects, and an unmanageable work space:

- Unneeded inventory creates extra costs, such as storage space and management.
- Unneeded transportation of parts requires extra pallets and carts.
- The larger the amount, the harder it is to sort out needed inventory from unneeded inventory.
- Large quantities of stocked items become obsolete due to engineering changes, limited shelf life, etc.
- Quality-related defects result from unneeded in-process inventory and machine breakdowns.
- Unneeded equipment poses a daily obstacle to production activities.

The presence of unneeded items makes designing equipment layout more difficult.

One word of caution: be careful about what you throw away. Sometimes you will need an unused item at a later date that you cannot go out and acquire. For example, I got rid of all the technical reports that were over 10 years old in 2005. It was not six months later that I needed a copy of a report I wrote in 1986 to prove a copyright problem, and I could not produce one. It was typed on an old software program and stored on a floppy disk that no one could read.

The second pillar—Set in Order. Arranging needed items so that they are easy to use and labeling them so that they are easy to find and put away
This activity should always be implemented with Sort. Once everything is sorted through, only what is necessary to the task remains. Next it should be made clear where these things belong so that anyone can immediately understand where to find them, as well as where to return them. For example, the outline of every tool can be painted on the surface where it should be stored.

The third pillar—Shine. Keeping the work space clean
The third pillar includes sweeping floors, emptying trash, wiping down machinery after use, cleaning up spills, etc. It also includes having a clean, clear deck at the end of the day. In a manufacturing organization and the support areas, this activity is closely related to the ability to produce quality outputs. Shine also includes saving labor by finding ways to prevent dirt, dust, and debris from piling up in the office and manufacturing and support areas. In the support areas, having a clean, neat desk when you leave at the end of the day is a best practice.

Shine should be designed into the preventive maintenance process to combine cleaning checkpoints with maintenance checkpoints.

The fourth pillar—Standardize. Doing it the same way each time
The Standardize activity differs from Sort, Set in Order, and Shine in that the first three pillars can be thought of as activities, as something we do. However, Standardize is the activity you use to maintain these first three pillars.

This activity is related to each of the first three pillars, but it relates most strongly to Shine. It results when we keep machines, desks, files, offices, and their surroundings free of debris, oil, and dirt. It is the condition that exists after we have practiced Shine for some time.

The fifth pillar—Sustain. Making a habit of properly maintaining correct policies and procedures
The first four pillars can be implemented without difficulty if the workplace is one where the employees commit to sustaining 5S conditions. Such a workplace is likely to have high productivity as well as high quality.

In many organizations much time and effort are spent in vain sorting and cleaning because the company lacks the discipline to maintain and continue 5S implementation on a daily basis. As with all continuous improvement tools, if the process does not have the Sustain pillar, the other pillars will not last long.

Benefits of 5S Implementation for You and Your Organization
Implementing 5S should have many benefits for you:

- It can give you an opportunity to provide input regarding how your workplace should be organized and laid out and how your work should be done.
- It can make the workplace more pleasant to work in.
- It can make the job more satisfying.
- It can remove some of the obstacles and frustrations related to the work.
- It can make it easier to communicate with everyone in the workplace.

Using 5S, G&G Machine Inc. threw out 150 tons of material it didn't need, and it found room to add a weld shop and install larger, more efficient machines in space it didn't know it had (Southwest Research Institute, 2010).

Your organization can also experience many benefits from implementing the five pillars. It can:

- Increase product diversity.
- Raise quality.
- Lower costs.
- Encourage reliable deliveries.

- Promote safety.
- Build customer confidence.
- Promote corporate growth.

Table 5.13 provides an example of a 5S checklist for a drill press.

The 5S method is a very effective and yet simple way to save money. For example, at Ceradyne, Inc., the cost savings from implementing 5S (plus safety—see the section below where we discuss safety as the sixth S) exceeded $900,000 annually. In the hot press department during the first

Table 5.13   5S Checklist for a Drill Press

Equipment Cleanliness Checklist	Yes	No	Comment
Are the gauges working and readable with no cracks in the glass?			
Are V-belts broken or loose?			
Is oil leaking from the equipment?			
Is there oil on the floor?			
Is the oil in the oil tanks murky?			
Are there oil air leaks from hydraulic and pneumatic devices?			
Are any nuts or bolts loose or missing?			
Are there chips on the floor?			
Is there abnormal vibration or noise?			
Are the motors abnormally hot?			
Has the total machine been cleaned in the last 24 hours?			
Are the tools hanging in their indicated location?			
Are the parts to be processed and the already processed parts in a location where dirt or oil cannot drop or be blown on them?			
Is the paperwork in oil-proof folders?			

Comments:

Checked by_____ Date _____ Time_____

three months of using 5S, Ceradyne realized a 25 percent increase in productivity. (California Manufacturing Technology Consulting, 2010).

For another example, St. Louis Community College (St. Louis Community College Center for Business, Industry & Labor, 2011) reports that organizations that implement 5S have realized savings such as:

- $300,000 in inventory cost at one facility
- $6,000 reduction in office supply expenses in the first month
- $1.2 million per year
- Cycle time reduced from 15 to 3 days
- Space reduced by 50 percent
- Manufacturing productivity up over 30 percent

We like to add a sixth S—it is safety. The other five Ss can reduce cycle time and save money, but you do not want to end up by creating an unsafe environment. So be sure you use all six Ss when you are streamlining your process.

We have found it helpful to use a four-step approach to get a 6S process started in an organization:

Step 1. Define the area where it will be applied and set up a 6S team. Provide all the team members with 6S training.

Step 2. Identify unnecessary or infrequently used equipment and red-tag it. Often red tags are used also to identify things that are out of place or inconvenient or a safety hazard. These red-tagged items are assigned a control number and are targets for corrective action.

Step 3. Straighten the area. The infrequently used items are removed from the files and work areas. Permanent and best-home locations are defined and labeled for the things that are often used. Everything is labeled and put in its place. Then everything in the place is scrubbed clean.

Step 4. Individuals are assigned to maintain the 6S advancements. An audit team is assigned to measure compliance to the 6S standards.

When the Aircraft Directorate at Ogden Air Logistics Center went through this cycle (Southwest Research Institute, 2010), it resulted in:

- $680,000 savings a year
- Decreased flow time from 15 to 4 days for the pylon rib process
- Reduced overtime from between 18 and 25 percent down to less than 5 percent

Upgrading the Office Areas

Management knows the importance of upgrading the equipment in the manufacturing operations. The same is true for the support areas. Old computers that run slow and don't interface well with each other can cause more problems than an old lathe in the machine shop. Look around the office. Is the copier up and running, or is it down half the time? How far does the engineer have to go to get a copy of a document? How hard is it to copy on both sides of a sheet of paper? Is the scanner good enough to scan a document, or do you have to retype it? Can you sign documents electronically, or do you need to process paper to get a signature? Is each computer backed up two or three times a day; or when there is a problem, do you lose weeks of information that may never be replaced? Do the people who use the phone a lot have a headset that allows them to free up a hand when talking on the phone? Do you microfilm the documents that need to be filed to reduce space and recovery time? Are you using bar coding on documents to keep track of where they are and how long they have been there? Are you using voice recorders on your phone to save time so individuals don't have to call back? (This often saves days of cycle time.) Do all your key people have pagers?

Have you designed the office to a so-called effective office design where the size and features throughout the office are the same? If you did, you probably have a very nice looking office that doesn't meet the needs of some, if not most, of your people. People are not all the same size. Some jobs require more work space than others. I need a bigger, wider chair; Mary needs a small one. A programmer with a lot of printouts on his desk needs a different desk than another engineer or salesperson might need. It may not look as neat, but customizing the office to the individual improves morale, effectiveness, and efficiency.

Lighting also is important. Does the light cast a shadow over the work area? Are you taking maximum advantage of the natural light? Does the light reflect on the computer screens? Is the light too bright or too dim?

Is the room laid out so that drafts are minimized, and does the layout ensure even, adequate cooling and heating throughout the entire work area? Does the color scheme reflect the mood you want to set in the office? The color of the walls and the furniture has a major impact on the attitude and productivity of your people.

The work environment itself can promote or hinder productivity. As early as the 1900s, both Frederick Winslow Taylor and Frank Bunker Gilbreth, Sr., recognized the importance of the environment and its influence upon productivity and job satisfaction. Ventilation, air-conditioning, heating, lighting, colors, and even music and entertainment can all influence productivity. ISO 9000 specifically requires that the work environment be suitable to the job.

Maintaining desired temperature in summer as well as winter by forcing into workrooms air that has been passed over heating or refrigeration coils has a great effect on the workman. Many factories, such as chocolate factories, have found that cooling the air for better results to the manufacturing also enables workers to produce more output—an output quite out of proportion to the cost of providing the cooling.

—Gilbreth (1911)

Good lighting, heating and ventilation pay. A factory manager by painting the walls cream-white toned up his whole working force. Hard to measure, he could "feel" the improvement brought about by this simple means.

—The System Company (1911)

The well-known Hawthorne study revealed that productivity went up as the light intensity was increased. Unfortunately, productivity went up also when the light intensity decreased. These production improvements were largely the result of the worker receiving attention related to the experiments. But further studies revealed that having the proper level of lighting is critical to productivity and quality of the outputs.

Gilbreth (1911) wrote:

The subject of lighting has, indirectly as well as directly, a great influence upon output and motion, as upon the comfort of the eye depends, to a large extent, the comfort of the total body. The arrangement of lighting in the average office, factory, or house is generally determined by putting in the least light necessary in order that the one who determined the location of the light may be able to see perfectly. This is wrong. The best light is the cheapest. By that is not meant which gives the brightest light.

In fact, the light itself is but a part of the question…A light to be right must pass five tests:

1. It must furnish the user sufficient light so he can see.
2. It must be so placed that it doesn't cause the user's eyes to change the size of diaphragm when ordinarily using the light.
3. It must be steady.
4. There should not be any polished surfaces in its vicinity that will reflect an unnecessary bright spot anywhere that can be seen by the eyes of the worker.
5. It must be protected so that it doesn't shine in the eyes of some other worker.

… For the work done on a flat surface, like the work of a book-keeper or a reader, the light should be placed where the glare will reflect the least in the worker's eyes … It is wholly a question of fatigue of the worker. The best lighting conditions will reduce the percentage of time required for rest for overcoming fatigue. The difference between the cost of the best lighting and the poorest is nothing compared with the saving in money due to decreased time for rest period due to less fatigued eyes.

I fly business class, and I do a lot of my writing while flying. One of my pet peeves is the location of the lights on the airplane. All too often they are located so the shadow of my hand (I'm right-handed) covers the areas I am writing on, making it impossible to work effectively. You would think by now that Boeing would know where to place the lights on a 747.

Fluorescent lights can also be a problem; they don't admit white light. White light is the kind that the human eye is designed to work with. White light has a continuous rainbow spectrum; fluorescent lights have several bands depending upon the kind of gas inside the tube.

The No-Value-Added Parts in Value-Added Activities

We evaluated each task in the process and defined it as no-value-added, business-value-added, or value-added. But this was not enough—we now need to take our microscope out and look within the value-added activities because few tasks are all value-added. Take, for example, the task of addressing and mailing an envelope:

1. Search the in-box to find the letter—1.0 minute
2. Read the letter to know whom it is going to—0.5 minute

3. Look for the right-size envelope—1.0 minutes
4. Go to the printer and put the envelope in the printer—2.0 minutes
5. Return to desk—2.0 minutes
6. Move the cursor to the address book—0.2 minute
7. Bring up the address book—0.5 minute
8. Find the name of the person the letter will be going to—0.2 minute
9. Send the name and address to the printer—0.1 minute
10. Go to the printer and pick up the envelope—2.0 minute
11. Return to desk—2.0 minute
12. Put the letter in the envelope—0.3 minute
13. Seal the envelope—0.2 minute
14. Find a stamp and put it on the envelope—3.0 minutes
15. Take the envelope to the mail drop—4.0 minutes
16. Stop on the way to talk to a friend or get a cup of coffee—5.0 minutes
17. Go back to desk—3.0 minutes

All these tasks took a total of 27.0 minutes.

Addressing and mailing the envelope was a value-added activity that took 27.0 minutes to accomplish. The real value-added-activities were only tasks 6, 7, 8, 9, 12, and 13 which took only 1.5 minute. The other tasks are no-value-added but are required to do the value-added task. Each of these tasks is a candidate for elimination or at least is a target for reducing the time it takes to do the tasks. For example, the task of looking for the right-size envelope would be eliminated if all letters went out in the same-size envelope. Or the time looking for a stamp could be reduced if the mail room put stamps on all outgoing mail. The time to go to the printer could be reduced if a personal printer was put on every desk. To take it a step further—question why it had to go out as a letter and could not have gone out as an e-mail.

Managing Process Flow

First, define what the output from the process per time interval needs to be, e.g., one every 15 minutes. Then look at each of the activities, as each should be equal to or less than the output requirements for that process. If any of the activities in the process is greater than the takt time, the workload at that activity needs to be adjusted. Takt time is the heartbeat of any process.

Theory of Constraints

The theory of constraints was highlighted in Dr. Elyahu M. Goldratt's book entitled *The Goal: A Process of Ongoing Improvement* (1993). The theory of constraints is based on the belief that any manageable system is limited to achieving its goals by a very small number of constraints. And there is always at least one constraint in every process.

The theory of constraints seeks to identify constraints within a process and restructure the rest of the organization around it. The theory of constraints and takt time have many things in common. They both focus on the limitations of the process, reductions in inventory, and production of the appropriate number of items as required by the external customer.

A constraint is any activity or step in a process that can't deliver as much output per time period as all the other activities or steps in that process. It limits the flow through the total process. For example, suppose the customer requirements are 100 units/day, or 12.5 units/hour average, and the process has five activities.

- Activity 1. Pull parts from stock—20 parts/hour.
- Activity 2. Weld part a and part b together—15/hour.
- Activity 3. Assemble items—6/hour.
- Activity 4. Test assembly—18/hour.
- Activity 5. Pack for delivery—20/hour.

In this case, Activity 3 is the constraint.

To give an example of a nonmanufacturing process, let's look at a sales process where the requirements from the company for the salesperson are 15 sales calls per week. It is made up of a six-activity process:

- Activity 1 (A1). Secretary sets up a meeting schedule—(1.3 activities per hr, or 10.4 activities per 8 hrs = 0.77/hr per activity).
- Activity 2 (A2). Assistant salesperson prepares sales package—(2.0 activities per hr, or 16 activities per 8 hrs = 0.5/hr per activity).
- Activity 3 (A3). Salesperson travels to meeting—(0.625 activities per hr, or 5.0 activities per 8 hrs = 1.6/hrs per activity)
- Activity 4 (A4). Salesperson meets with client—(1.0 activities per hr, or 8.0 activities per 8 hrs = 1.0/hrs per activity)

- Activity 5 (A5). Salesperson sends in order—(10.0 activities per hr, or 80 activities per 8 hrs = 0.1 hrs/per activity)
- Activity 6 (A6). Production specialist enters order into system—(10.0 activities per hr, or 80 activities per 8 hrs = 0.1hr/per activity)

Based upon this data, the total hours invested in an individual sales call is 3.3 hours. In this case, the constraint is the salesperson's time, as he or she is responsible for Activities 3, 4, and 5 (sales person hrs. per call = A3+A4+A5= 1.6+1.0+0.1= 2.7 hrs per sales call.) Assuming an 8-hour day, the maximum number of sales calls a salesperson can make is 3 per day. The next limiting activity is Activity 1 that can support 10 sales calls per day. This means that this process can support a total of 3 sales people with ease.

To increase throughput in the process, either we need to reduce the time it takes the salesperson to make a call, or we need to add an additional salesperson to the process.

The theory of constraints is based upon the assumption that organizations can be measured and controlled in three measurements: throughput, inventory, and operating expense. We will define the three measurements as follows:

- *Throughput (or money from sales)*. The measure of the marginal profit at each transaction, not the cost accounting value. It is the sales price minus the cost of raw materials. Of course, lead time plays a major role because it is the time between when the order is accepted and when the order is delivered. Henry Ford was able to have negative inventory turns because he received payments before he had to pay for the raw materials. Harley Davidson has accomplished this in the modern environment.
- *Inventory*. The money that the system must invest in the items it intends to sell.
- *Operating expense*. The money that the system expends to convert inventory into output.

The theory of constraints is based upon the assumption that only by increasing the efficiency (flow-through) of the constraint operation can overall output be increased. It makes use of a four-step approach to accomplish this that focuses on an existing or proposed future-state solution flowchart:

Step 1. Identify the constraint.

Step 2. Decide how to maximize throughput through the constraint.

Step 3. Design all other activities to support smooth flow through the activities.

Step 4. Evaluate the constraint to determine if increased capacity is required.

Note: If the constraint is removed from one operation, the constraint will move to another part of the process.

For additional improvement, refocus your effort back to Step 1, focusing on the new constraint area.

The theory of constraints applies both to constraints that are internal to the organization and to constraints that are external to the organization. Internal constraints exist when the market requires more from the system than it can deliver. External constraints occur when the external market is not capable of accepting everything that the process can produce.

Visual Office

Knowledge is power. Keeping the employees informed is one of the best ways to ensure that the process continues to flow smoothly. The *visual office* is a key part of keeping the employees focused on key measurements. The visual office makes use of quick feedback to the employee on how the natural workteam is doing. For example, a large display located where employees can see it provides call center personnel with the number of minutes the average caller is waiting for his or her call to be answered by a live person. This display is updated every three minutes. A second number on the screen shows the average for the day that callers have been waiting, and a third number on the screen shows the longest wait time for any single caller for the day. On the bulletin board in the area, the wait-time distribution for the previous day is posted every morning along with a statistical analysis of the wait time. The second monitor in the area shows the same information for the call processing time.

The key is to look for measurements that are important and reflect the activities that are going on right now in the area. In an assembly department it could be the number of units per hour that are completed, or maybe in an inspection station it might be the percentage of defective units. We have seen sales offices where the amount of sales for each salesperson is posted on a monitor when there is a quick turnover of sales or on a bulletin board when the sales cycle is longer.

The bulletin board is also part of the visual office. Often the work going on in the area does not lend itself to a minute-by-minute feedback situation. In these cases, the bulletin board provides the visual feedback to the employees. For example, we have seen banks where the customer-satisfaction level per person servicing a customer is measured on a daily basis and reported back to them on the following day. A histogram-type graph is posted each week on the bulletin board along with the name of the person who had the highest level of customer satisfaction. This allows each employee to understand how he or she is performing compared to the rest of the staff. The person with the highest customer-satisfaction level for the month is named the employee of the month, and the person's picture is posted on the bulletin board.

The key is to make a game out of work. Why is it that people will expend so much effort and energy in sports but don't want to put the same amount of dedication into their work? How popular do you think bowling would be if no one kept score or if you got your score once a month? People like to compete against other people, other teams, or even themselves. A well-designed visual office provides them with this opportunity. People compete in sports because there are set ground rules that everyone understands and the measurements of success or failure are readily available and well understood. You need to create the same conditions in the work environment.

Total Process Alignment and Organizational Restructuring

Now that the individual process steps have been addressed, it is time to look at the process as a whole. To start this task, we must evaluate the organization's structure. We often find that the old functional structure is no longer viable. Organizations that have been stand-alone need to be combined. Accounts payable becomes part of purchasing. Product engineering and manufacturing engineering are combined. Receiving inspection may become part of purchasing. Sales and marketing are combined. Often the new process defines the organization's structure: Sometimes all

the activities that are involved in the process are combined into one organization managed by the process owner. In other cases the individual
people who operate the process report to two managers—the process
owner and the functional organization's manager.

Measure the distance that the product travels and reduce it. Bring
together the key people in the process to minimize the travel the document or activity has to go through.

At Aetna, the Hartford-based health-care provider, the people
who performed the accounts payable function were moved out of the
accounting organization and into the purchasing group. Kathleen A.
Murray, chief operating officer at Aetna Business Resources, notes:
"And it is not just the megadeals ... There will be a lot of little deals
where we wouldn't be a player if we didn't have purchasing set up the
way we do" (*CFO*, 1996).

In addition, Aetna combined six purchasing organizations into one,
speeding up delivery time for purchased items by as much as 15 days,
cutting staff by 88 percent, and cutting net material acquisition cost per
dollar of items purchased $0.016 (or 1.6 cents).

> *We set goals for ourselves that seemed impossible, and to actually realize
> them is true reengineering.*
> —Kathleen A. Murray, Chief Operating Officer,
> Aetna Business Resources (*CFO*, 1996)

> *Dun & Bradstreet's retooling of accounts payable included merging the
> process with travel and entertainment expense reporting. The project
> resulted in cost reductions of 75%, headcount reduction of 66% to 25 full-
> time employees.*
> —*CFO*, 1996

IBM had more than 100 different groups around the world maintaining their own banking and insurance relationships. "We had no idea how
much duplication of effort there was and how little coordination," stated
Bob Captello, corporate treasury analyst for IBM. By combining these
together, the economy of scale resulted in a $62 million savings per year
for IBM. Before combining them, IBM bought insurance through 66 bro-
kers and 203 insurers. IBM reduced this number to 2 and 25, respectively,
a move that slashed millions of dollars in premium payments. IBM in two
years boosted treasury productivity by 45 percent.

IBM developed an integrated system and data warehouse to serve the company's information needs on a global basis. The result was a 50 percent staff reduction, a 48 percent gain in productivity, and a 35 percent decrease in cost (*CFO*, 1996).

Look at the process to determine if the organizational structure complements or detracts from the product flow. Why not locate people involved in the process in the same place under the same manager? Is it more important to keep a functional organizational structure, or should you have a process organizational structure? For example, if you are streamlining the product development process, it makes sense to transfer the mechanical engineers, electrical engineers, quality engineers, and some of the manufacturing people into the development laboratory reporting to a development manager, thereby reducing cost, cycle time, and communications. Don't freeze your organizational structure. Keep it fluid so that it can be easily adjusted to the changing customer and the process needs.

Task 10. Risk Management (Figure 5.35)

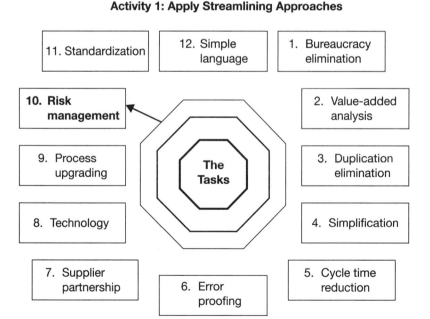

Phase III: Streamlining the Process
Activity 1: Apply Streamlining Approaches

Figure 5.35   Task 10. Risk Management

You will never have all the information you will need to make a decision—if you did, it would be a foregone conclusion, not a decision.
—David Mahoney (1988, p. 156)

Now is the time to step back and determine if you have removed too many non-value-added activities from the process. Ask yourself:

- Is the process protected against unethical behaviors and fraud?
- Are there still enough checks and balances designed into the process to provide the organization with adequate protection?
- What are the risks of the future-state process proposal being turned down?
- Who are the key people that will resist installing the new process?
- Is there any chance that the future-state solution process will have a negative impact upon the customer?
- Is there a risk that the goals set for the streamlining process will not be met?
- Is there a risk that the software packages proposed for the future-state solution will be obsolete before they provide a payback?
- Is there a risk that the proposed future-state solution is not in line with the organization's culture so it will be rejected by the users?

Often in the PIT's enthusiasm to remove bureaucracy and no-value-added and business-value-added activities from the process, the team overcorrects, thereby creating more risks of fraud and unethical behavior and producing unhappy customers. A limited amount of checks and balances is needed in most processes. I heard one customer state, "If management does not measure it, it is not important." The degree of checks and balances that should be part of the process will vary from organization to organization and from country to country. In some countries that I have worked in, it is common practice to pay an individual for favors he or she does for the organization, e.g., giving the organization a contract. In other countries, people would be fired for as much as accepting a pencil set from a supplier unless it was a promotional item with the supplier's name on it. One of my very dear friends at IBM was released from IBM because he went fishing with a contractor on the contractor's small 16-foot fishing boat.

If the process that the PIT is working on is a financial or procurement process, the process must be evaluated very closely to be sure that only acceptable risks remain in the future-state process. I have worked with companies when only one signature on the organization's checks was sufficient and in other organizations where a minimum of two was required due to the culture in the region.

As you identify a risk, analyze it to define how big the risk is and what is its probability of occurring. It is often better to live with some risk—for example, the risk of not being paid the full amount was addressed by EDS. EDS would check to see if the customer's check matched the invoice. When the amounts did not agree, EDS would classify the difference as a deviation and investigate what caused the discrepancy even if it was just a few cents (*CFO*, 1996).

Those risks with significant exposures need to be corrected by changing the process or finding another solution to mitigate the problem. For example, you could bond the person who is signing checks, or you could do internal audits of the process without increasing cycle time. The PIT needs to be creative when it adds non-value-added activities back into the process in order not to cause additional costs or delays.

I like to do a survey of the people who will be affected by the change to determine the implementation risk. The survey is called a *change-resistance scale*, and it is designed to aid in dealing with the human aspects of the adaptability of the specific change. It provides the PIT with insight to determine the overall resistance to an organizational change and its contribution to the risk of implementation failure. Each of the questions is evaluated on a 1-to-10 scale. Typical questions are:

- Do you believe that the change is really needed?
- How compatible is this change with existing organizational values?
- Do you believe the change will impact the way you relate to others in the organization that are important to you?

If your change management activities that were started in Phase I have been effective, there should be little resistance to the proposed new process, as the human aspects of the organization have been adequately informed, have been involved with, and have accepted the future-state solution.

I like to use a computer program to identify problems with the future-state solution that I am working with. The one I use is Anticipatory Failure Determination. It includes two software programs:

1. A failure analysis software program that performs a systematic procedure for identifying the root cause(s) of a failure or other undesirable phenomena in a system and for making corrections in a timely manner
2. A failure prediction software program that performs a systematic procedure for identifying beforehand and preventing all dangerous or harmful events that might be associated with the system

Task 11. Standardization (Figure 5.36)

Phase III: Streamlining the Process
Activity 1: Apply Streamlining Approaches

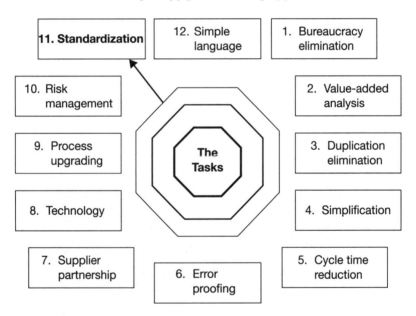

Figure 5.36   Task 11. Standardization

Standardization does not stop creativity; it just helps everyone benefit from it.

—H. James Harrington

Standardized work flow is finding the most effective way to carry out the present job and getting everyone to use it. The objective is to improve repeatability to reduce variation and proliferation. The correct procedure needs to be documented, and everyone has to be trained to use it so that everyone follows the same approach. Without it, processes cannot be improved. (See Figure 5.37.)

Why not just tell people what results you want and then get out of their way and let them do it any way they would like to? That is what many of the futuristic management consultants are advocating. Well, it sounds good, but, and this is big but, if you do not have a standard process, people will not learn from each other. Everyone can make the same mistake over and over and over again. Each time new employees are assigned to a job, they will start with a zero knowledge base. If many people are doing similar activities, the results will vary from person to person. If you have 10 people doing the job, you will have 10 different processes with 10 different sets of root causes. Process improvement is

Figure 5.37 Standardize—then improve

almost impossible without everyone doing the job the same way. Root causes cannot be identified and processes will not improve and be controlled without standardization. All the work the PIT has done to date is lost.

Standardization of work processes is important to be able to project what the process output will look like and how the process will perform. When each person is doing the activity differently, it is difficult, if not impossible, to make major improvements in the process. Standardization is one of the key steps in improving any process. This is accomplished by the use of procedures. Procedures tell management and the employee how the process functions and how to do the activities. These procedures should:

- Be realistic based upon careful analysis.
- Clearly define responsibilities.
- Establish limits of authority.
- Cover emergency situations.
- Be easy to interpret.
- Be easy to understand.
- Explain each document, its purpose, and the issues.
- Define training requirements.
- Define minimum performance standards.

> *And whenever the new method is found to be markedly superior to the old, it should be adopted as the standard for the whole establishment. The workman should be given the full credit for the improvement, and should be paid cash premium as a reward for his ingenuity.*
> —Taylor (1911, p. 67), emphasis is ours

Installing the procedures is not enough; certainly the employees have to be trained to use the procedures, and an audit system needs to be put in place to ensure that the employees adhere to the procedures over a long time period. The procedures should not be cast in stone. When a better concept or approach comes along, it should be adopted and documented. It should not be implemented throughout the process until it has been thoroughly checked out and the documented procedures have been changed.

Furthermore, all organizations should have an operating manual. A typical operating manual is made up of two sections. The first section contains executive policies and should include things like:

- Mission statements
- Vision
- Values
- Objectives
- Core competencies and capabilities
- Organization chart
- Roles and responsibilities of the organizational structure

The second part of the operating manual should be the operating procedures. Typically they are broken down into functional groupings. Typical functional groupings could be:

- General operating procedures
- Financial operating procedures
- Human relations operating procedures
- Sales and marketing operating procedures
- Quality and system assurance operating procedures
- Business operations procedures
- Production operating procedures

Operating procedures are used at the cross-functional process level. As we delve into the process to the individual activities and tasks, employees can use work instructions, check sheets, and job descriptions as guidance on how to perform the activities and tasks.

IBM simplified and standardized travel policies, levering technology and taking sufficient steps for getting remuneration back to the travelers. The benefit to IBM included $30 million a year in annual savings. One of the key breakthroughs was an electronic expense form that was filled out on the PC. According to IBM, it takes only 10 minutes to complete the electronic expense form and send it in. Also a tracking system was put in place that allowed the traveler to know the exact status of his or her expense account by telephone voice response. Other things that simplified the process were corporate charge cards for cash advances, paycheck distribution of travel expenses, and imaging of all receipts at central locations. "I submitted my T&E on Friday, and the money was in my bank account on Monday morning," reported a typical traveler. Quarterly quality surveys indicated nearly 90 percent satisfaction with the new system (*CFO*, 1996).

Task 12. Simple Language (Figure 5.38)

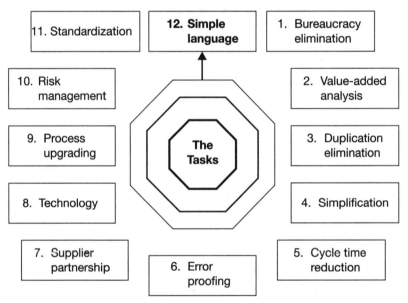

Phase III: Streamlining the Process
Activity 1: Apply Streamlining Approaches

Figure 5.38   Task 12. Simple Language

Keep it simple and it saves time.

—H. James Harrington

Ask yourself the question, Is all this documentation necessary? Managers spend 40 to 60 percent of their time reading and writing job-related materials. And 90 percent of the documents retained are never used. Clerks spend 60 percent of their time on checking, filing, and retrieving information (Harrington, 1991).

There are at least four good reasons to document the existing process:

- *To understand the current process.* The PIT will be streamlining the current process and working with it as it fits into the organization's culture today. Without a good understanding of the current process, it is impossible for the PIT to identify improvement opportunities.
- *To operate the new process.* The new process needs to be well documented so there is no doubt by any of the employees about what they need to do.
- *To understand customer values.* It is important that the PIT understand what the customer requirements are and what the major objectives are within the process. By understanding the current process, the PIT can identify added-value points from the customer's perspective.
- *To define current problems.* The organization must understand the problems it is having with the current process in order to get the support to implement the new process. The new process must be designed so that it eliminates these problems. Very often many of the problems go unrecognized until the entire process is put together and studied.

Too many people write to impress rather than to communicate. They write big, long documents that no one reads. They believe that management rates a report based on its weight, not its content. They don't consider that a big report takes longer to read and that it costs more to communicate the information. It may take more time to consolidate what you want to communicate, but in the long run it will save the organization money. Too many people use the longest words in the dictionary rather than short, more common words that everybody understands. I have seen procedures written in English for which I had to use a dictionary to understand. Too many procedures and reports are full of acronyms and abbreviation that many of the readers do not know or understand. Studies have proved that a procedure or report written at the tenth grade level compared with a report written at a college graduate level can be read in 30 percent less time with 34 percent better retention by a college graduate. In business, no letter or procedure should be written higher than a tenth grade level.

Procedures that are written by engineers often will be used by people that don't have a high school degree. As a rule of thumb, you should write procedures at two grade levels lower than the educational level of the least educated people that will be reading it.

If the language you are using is not the readers' native language, it should be written at least three grade levels lower than their educational level. Some simple ground rules are:

- Be familiar with your audience.
- Understand how familiar your audience is with the terms and abbreviations.
- For procedures that are more than four pages long, include a flowchart.
- Determine the reading and comprehension level of your audience; the document should be written so that all readers can easily comprehend the message.
- Use acronyms with care; don't force your reader to learn new acronyms unless they are used frequently throughout the report.
- Never use an acronym or abbreviation unless it is defined in the document.

There are many good documents out there that are very short but present a very powerful message. Let me give you some examples:

- The Lord's Prayer—57 words, very short
- Ten Commandments—71 words, no acronyms
- Gettysburg Address—266 words, easy to understand
- U.S. Declaration of Independence—300 words, to the point

And then there are examples of another kind:

- The U.S. government contractor, management system evaluation program—38,000 words (Would you believe it?)
- The GM repair manuals produced since 1980—they would take 56 years to read!

Evaluate your writing using a readability index. This can be calculated as follows:

- A = average number of words per sentence
- B = percentage of words with 3 or more syllables
- R = readability index = 0.4(A + B)

- 10 or less = good
- 10.1 to 16 = caution
- 16.1 to 22 = dangerous
- Above 22 = ridiculous

Figure 5.39 provides an easy way for you to determine your readability level. Many computers have a program built into them that will calculate your readability index. We recommend that you evaluate the readability of all the documents you prepare.

Forms are another area we do not give the proper thought to before we release them. We allow programmers to design computer input screens and forms that work well with their software package. However, little thought is given about the person that inputs the data to make it easy to implement all the data.

Designing forms is an art. The forms must be directed at saving time for the person who is recording the data and helping the person reduce input errors. They should not be directed at how it is best to enter the data into the computer. Forms should be designed for the user and should use the software to arrange the data so that the data can be used by the software package.

Does a good form make a difference? When the British government agencies focused their attention on form design, errors plummeted and productivity soared.

For example:

- The British Department of Defence revised its travel expense form. The new form reduced errors by 50 percent, the time required to fill it out by 10 percent, and processing time by 15 percent
- By redesigning the application form for legal aid, the British Department of Social Services saved more than 2 million hours per year in processing time.

The NASA Engineering and Safety Council had developed 30 procedures that were well above average in complexity from a benchmarking standpoint (Olson and Kelly, 2005). The agency wanted to shorten and make them more usable. As a result, NASA was able to cut the procedures by 60 percent without affecting technical content. Now the NASA procedures are not only short; they are more usable.

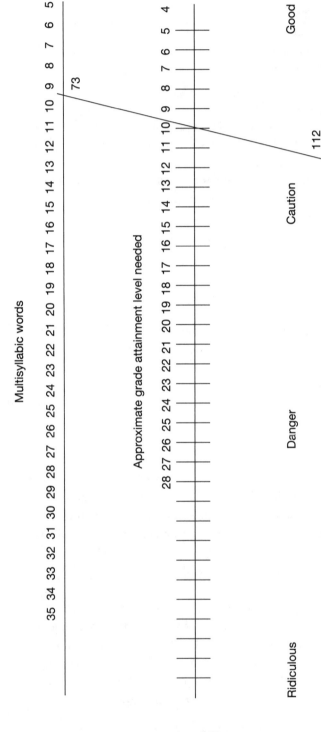

Figure 5.39 Readability index

NASA Ames ITSC Development located in Mountain View, California, documented its four key procedures in 19 pages. Similar procedures run over 100 pages.

Be aware of common mistakes when creating documents (Olson and Kelly, 2005):

- *Not enough pictures.* Most people prefer pictures to words. One picture is worth a 1,000 words, takes less space, and is quicker to analyze.
- *Too big.* Most documents are written to impress rather than to educate and train. Blaise Pascal stated, "I have made this letter longer than usual because I lack the time to make it shorter."
- *Unusable and one-size-fits-all.* Too often our procedures and descriptions are not designed with the customer and user in mind, making the material hard to use. Standardizing forms seems more important than making them easy to read.
- *Poorly designed documentation.* Principles such as grouping and consistency are often not followed. Good writing principles are often ignored.
- *Mixed information types.* Policies, procedures, processes, training, and standards are often mixed together, making the end product difficult to understand. Each of these document types needs to be used in a different scenario.
- *Written sequentially.* Process documentation is meant to be used non-linearly. It is not a novel and needs to be written in a manner where each piece stands alone. This allows readers to find the information they need quickly.
- *Information that can't be found quickly.* Documents that are hard to read are not used and often ignored.
- *Dust-catching documents.* Too many documents become dust catchers rather than useful documents. Having them online makes them easy to change and thus helps keep them up to date.

And keep in mind these guidelines for good documentation (Olson and Kelly, 2005):

- Tailor documentation and processes to the organization and each business unit.
- Write so the new person to the process will understand it; not just so the expert will understand it.

- Use chunking and sectionalizing to organize the document. Label the chunks so readers can quickly find what they are interested in.
- Use information mapping to quickly find specific parts of the document that the individual is interested in.
- Minimize abbreviations and acronyms.
- Do a process map that answers *where, why, what, when, who,* and *how.*

The Internet has sped up the distribution of information, but it has also caused a lot of needless information to be passed around. Too often we use distribution lists rather than selecting the individuals who need to read the information. This is very costly for people that don't need or even want the information.

> *Streamlining allows you to right-size, not downsize.*
> —H. James Harrington

> *Nothing is more dangerous than an idea when it's the only one you have.*
> — Emile Chartier

Often depending on the skills of the PIT, Activity 1 will be repeated one or two more times using different control parameters. For example, the first time, there are no restrictions on the team. The next time, the new design must be installed and operational within 90 days. The third time, the cost of installing the new process can't be more than 25 percent of the cost of the first proposed new process. This frequently leads to a fourth new process design that includes the best features of the other three designs. All too often a team defines a solution and does not look for other solutions that may be better. The team members spend all their time justifying the process they designed. This approach makes the PIT look at other solutions with an open mind.

> *Too often we have an idea and hold on to it without searching for a better solution.*
> —H. James Harrington

Activity 2: Conduct a Benchmarking Study

In Activity 2 of Phase II, the PIT may have conducted a benchmarking study to ensure that the goals set by the PIT were realistic and stringent enough. If the team did, during this study sometimes organizations that are performing better than your own organization are identified. In these cases the PIT may want to perform a benchmarking study to understand the details related to the activities within the other organization's process.

Benchmarking is a very popular tool that compares the present process with the best similar processes available in the world. It may or may not compare processes from the same industry. Benchmarking results in a reduction of cycle time, cost, and error rates between 10 and 60 percent. It takes between three and six months to develop a best-value future-state solution for the process that the PIT is working on to improve. For more details about benchmarking, read *The Complete Benchmarking Workbook* (Harrington, 1996) or *High Performance Benchmarking* (Harrington and Harrington, 1996).

Activity 3: Prepare an Improvement, Cost, and Risk Analysis

The PIT members have developed a new process that they believe is better than the old one. Now they need to analyze their solution to determine if the changes can be justified. This is a critical step and one that is often done poorly. Why? Because it is often hard to get the required information that the PIT needs and because a lot of the implementation costs are an estimate of the time required to do the job. To help in doing this job better, get purchasing to give you an estimate of the costs for the things you need to buy. Get your IT shop to estimate how much time it will need to set up the software and IT support. In other words, get the people who will need to install the change to estimate the costs of the change. Typically, for improvement you will compare the projected performance of the process with the present process for the following:

- Effectiveness
- Cycle time
- Processing time
- Cost
- Impact upon the customer
- Quality

In many cases you will set up a pilot run to collect the needed information. Be sure you use a control sample when you do design an experiment to collect the data.

That covers the benefits. Now you need to define the cost side. Typical costs are:

- The cost of the materials and consultants
- The length of time required to make the change
- The cost of training people
- The negative impact upon the output of the process during the cutover and learning cycle
- The cost of setting up the process layout
- Support department costs

> *SPI is a lot like the TV program Extreme Makeover; it takes an average person and transforms him or her into a raving beauty.*
> —H. James Harrington

Organizational change management of the new porcess becomes critical at this point. We first realized the problem people have in accepting a new process back in Phase I where we developed a change management plan. Now we have a chance to evaluate how effective these activities have been and to define how much the cultural change each individual solution will require. Hammer and Champy (2003) wrote in their book, *Reengineering the Corporation,* "Some 50 to 70% of the reengineering attempts fail to deliver the intended drastic results."

One of the primary causes for this high failure rate is the lack of good organizational change management structure to support the change activities. During Phase II the PIT should have developed a culture model of the current process and its related environment. It should have been based upon the following cultural enablers:

- Management style
- Organizational structure
- Performance management
- Compensation benefits and rewards
- Education and development

- Communication
- Behavioral models
- Environmental factors

The PIT will need to evaluate each of the solutions to define its impact on the present-state culture model developed in Phase II to determine:

- The risks related to the change
- The time required for it to be accepted
- The extent that the culture will have to change in order to meet the requirements of the change

Typical behavior changes that will need to be considered are:

- Trust in management
- Team orientation
- Communications
- Constraints
- Commitment
- Flexibility
- Respect
- Proactivity
- Responsibility
- Pride

The PIT will then compare the new culture model for each solution with the present-state model to define the gap between both (plus and minus). The greater the gap between the proposed change and the present process, the greater the risk of failure. This is not an easy job, and it is often done without proper analysis, leading to project failure. It is absolutely imperative that this risk analysis is done well and that an effective mitigation plan is prepared and executed.

Results of Different Future-State Solutions

> *Nothing is more dangerous than an idea when it is the only one you have.*
> —Emile Chartier

Table 5.14 is an example of a cost-benefit analysis. It shows the original performance and looks at the costs and benefits of two different solutions. Solution #1 had no restrictions on the future-state process, and Solution #2 required that all the changes needed to be functional within six months. Solution #1 seemed to be the best answer, saving over $10 million over a three-year time period. Solution #2 only saved $8.5 million. But when you consider that Solution #2 was up and running 12 months sooner than Solution #1 could have been implemented, it calculates out to be the correct solution, saving over $11.4 million.

When people are learning a new process, for a short time productivity drops off often below what it was on the old process. Productivity increases once the people involved in the new process have mastered it.
— H. James Harrington

Activity 4: Select a Preferred Process

The PIT should now schedule a meeting with the executive team to present its findings. If the PIT developed more than one recommendation, it should review each of them and explain why it selected the one it is recommending. Be sure to go over the change mitigation plans with the executive team in detail.

I like to meet with each of the executive team members first so that I know their concerns ahead of time, thereby assuring that I have addressed them during the presentation. I feel it makes this very important meeting run much smoother. It also often gets a number of people coming into the meeting already planning to support the change. I call these people "advocates."

The outcome from this meeting should be an approval to develop a preliminary implementation plan and implementation detailed budget.

Activity 5: Prepare a Preliminary Implementation Plan

Very often the members of the PIT will not be the people required to implement the future-state solution. As a result, the PIT members will need to add implementation specialists to the PIT in order to come up with a budget that is fully supported by the people who will need to do

Table 5.14   Example of a Cost-Benefit Analysis

Implementation Analysis of Two Future-State Solutions
Solution #1: No limits on it
Solution #2: Must be installed within 6 months
Quantity per year = 10,000 units
Cost per defect = $35
Competitor's price is $460 to $504
Number of employees is 120 @$32 per hour

	Current Process	Solution #1	Solution #2
Defect Rate	3/100	2/100,000	10/100,000
Defect Cost per Year	$3,500	$7	$35
Cycle Time	720 hours	35 hours	80 hours
Processing Time	15 hours	4 hours	6 hours
Cost per Unit	$480	$128	$192
Impact on External Customer	Can live with it	Excellent	Good
Total Cost for 3 Years	$14,403,500	$3,840,021	$5,760,105
Cost to Make the Change			
Cost of Materials and Labor		$200,000	$65,000
Time Required to Make the Change		18 months	6 months
Training Time Per Person		16 hours	4 hours
Training Cost		$61,440	$15,360
Negative Learning Curve*		$60,000	$30,000
Total Cost to Implement		$321,440	$110,360
3-Year Total Cost	$14,403,500	$4,161,461	$5,870,465
3-Year Savings Compared with the current process	0	$10,242,039	$8,533,035
Risk Related to Change	0	High	Medium

Note: Because Solution #2 is completed 12 months before Solution #1, it has another year's savings.

Solution #2 added savings: (480 − 192) × 10,000 = $2,880,000

Savings from Solution #2: $2,880,000 + $8,533,035 = $11,413,035

Results: Solution #2 Is the Best Solution

the work. This often includes people from purchasing who will get the commitment from the suppliers, IT who will implement the software solution, industrial engineering staff who will need to install the change process, etc. People from HR are also included so that they can make an analysis that compares the skills of the people who are presently involved in the process with the skills that are required by the new process. This type of analysis is necessary to develop the training and staffing requirements for this new process. You will also need to identify the change agents who are required to support the cultural change model.

When the preliminary budget is ready and the suggested implementation team is defined, the plan is submitted to the executive team for its approval.

Activity 6: Conduct Phase III Tollgate

At the end of Phase III it is an excellent time to do a complete review of the Phase III deliverables. The tollgate should be chaired by the project sponsor, and the total EIT should be invited to attend. During this tollgate the following questions should be addressed:

- Has the PIT developed a future-state solution that is practical and in line with the goals set in the project plan?
- Did the PIT look at other options and present them?
- Is the estimated cost to implement the solution realistic?
- Is the ROI great enough to justify going ahead and installing the solution?
- Is the future-state solution in keeping with the organization's culture and its long-range plan?

When these questions are answered in the affirmative, the project is ready to move into the implementation phase. You can't exit Phase III without an approved Phase IV plan and budget plus an assigned implementation team.

Summary

We now have an approved future-state solution, but that is only the first half of the project. The real proof of how good a job the PIT has done in developing the future-state solution and the change management activities will be measured by how much resistance there is to implementing the new design and how well it works after it is implemented.

> *Don't forget to reward the PIT if the members did a very good job at this point in the project.*

—H. James Harrington

Phase IV: Implementing the New Process and Phase V: Continuous Improvement

When you have an excellent future-state process design, the project is 30 percent complete.

—H. James Harrington

Introduction

We have tried to provide you with detailed information on how to develop a breakthrough future-state solution that has made this book already too long. As a result, we are going to just glance over Phases IV and V. If you would like more detail on these phases, we recommend you read Chapter 7, "Measurement, Feedback and Action," and Chapter 8, "Process Qualification," in *Business Process Improvement* (Harrington, 1991).

Phase IV: Implementing the New Process

Even if you're on the right track, you'll get run over if you just sit there.

—Will Rogers

During this phase, an implementation team is pulled together to install the selected process, measurement systems, and control systems. The new in-process measurement and control systems will be designed to ensure that there is immediate feedback to the employees, enabling them to contain the gains that have been made and to improve the process further. As Figure 6.1 shows, this phase consists of six activities:

- Activity 1: Prepare the Final Implementation Plan
- Activity 2: Implement the New Process
- Activity 3: Install In-Process Measurement Systems
- Activity 4: Install Feedback Data Systems
- Activity 5: Transfer the Project
- Activity 6: Conduct Phase IV Tollgate

> *We underestimated the amount of communication required.*
> —Harry Beeth, Assistant Controller,
> IBM Corporate Headquarters
> (*CFO*, 1996)

Phase IV: Activity 1: Prepare the Final Implementation Plan

It is extremely difficult to migrate from the current state to the future-state solution without a good understanding of the current state. By understanding the current state and comparing it with the future-state solution, the magnitude of the change can be identified, and proper change management activities can be put in place to break down resistance and to build support.

An implementation team is formed to prepare a detailed implementation plan and coordinate the changes. It may or may not include all the members of the original PIT. Often, Department Improvement Teams (DITs) become part of the implementation plan so that the teams within the functions that will be impacted by the change are part of the group that plans and implements the change.

Implementation is usually the most difficult part of the SPI process because the future-state solution is often a radical change from the way the process is presently organized. This means that the implementation team needs to very carefully consider these questions:

- How will the users of the process react during the transition period?
- How will the training be accomplished?

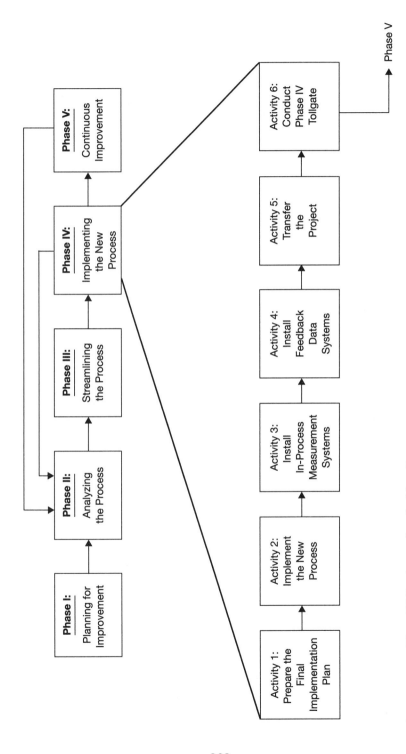

Figure 6.1 Phase IV: Implementing the New Process

- What infrastructure changes need to be made?
- How will the interruption to the process flow be minimized?
- Will productivity decrease during the transition period as it usually does, and how will this additional workload be handled?
- What will be done to involve the people that will own and control the process during implementation?
- How will the impact on the employees' morale and customer satisfaction be measured?
- Will the users have the required background and skills to effectively use the process?
- How will the surplus in materials and people be handled?
- What changes in technology, systems, and equipment will be needed in the process and supporting processes?
- What other activities are going on in the organization that will impact the process during the transition period?
- Are people available with the required skills to perform the transition?
- How will the social and psychological impact on the process users be handled?

Sometimes the implementation team is divided into subteams (*example:* information system teams). The implementation plan usually is divided into three parts (see Figure 6.2):

1. *Short-term changes.* Changes that can be done in 30 days
2. *Midterm changes.* Changes that can be done in 90 days
3. *Long-term changes.* Changes that require more than 90 days to implement

A very formal project plan should be prepared for Phase IV that includes an implementation plan and a measurement plan for each change. Also the change management plan needs to be updated to reflect the culture changes that the new process will require. Based upon the outputs from this new planning cycle, the project budget will be updated.

The implementation team should present the new plan and budget to the executive team members for their final approval. This is necessary to ensure that both the implementation team and the executive team are committed to the success of the project.

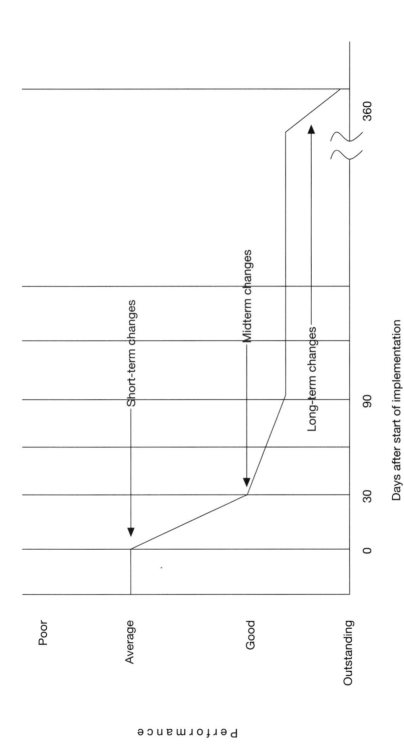

Figure 6.2 Future-state process implementation plan

305

Phase IV: Activity 2: Install the New Process

The implementation plan and the change management plan are now united to bring about an effective overall implementation of the new process. The implementation team will maintain close control over each change to be sure that it is implemented correctly. Often, complex changes will go through a series of modeling or prototyping cycles to prove out the concept and to ensure smooth implementation. After each change is installed, its impact is measured to ensure it accomplishes its intent and has a positive impact upon the total process. As the change is implemented, the simulation model is updated so that it always reflects the present process.

> *People truly understand the amount of communication required to get buy-in. Let people know what is going on and why. What the new world will look like and how they will fit into it.*
> —Paulette Everhart, EDS Corporate Controller (*CFO*, 1996)

Phase IV: Activity 3: Install In-Process Measurement Systems

> *The carpenter's rule is measure twice, cut once.*

Before you can design a measurement system, you need to define requirements. Each activity on the final flowchart should be analyzed to define what the customer requirements are and how compliance to these requirements can be effectively evaluated. You will note that up to this point the measurement system focused on the total process. Now the task is to develop measurements and controls for each major activity within the process. (See Figure 6.3.)

A good measurement and feedback system is one in which the measurements are made as close to the activity as possible. Self-measurement is best because there is no delay in corrective action. Often, however, self-measurements are not practical or possible.

Poor-Quality Cost

In his book *Applications of Quality Control in the Service Industry*, A. C. Rosander (1985) reported that 25 percent of a bank's total operating

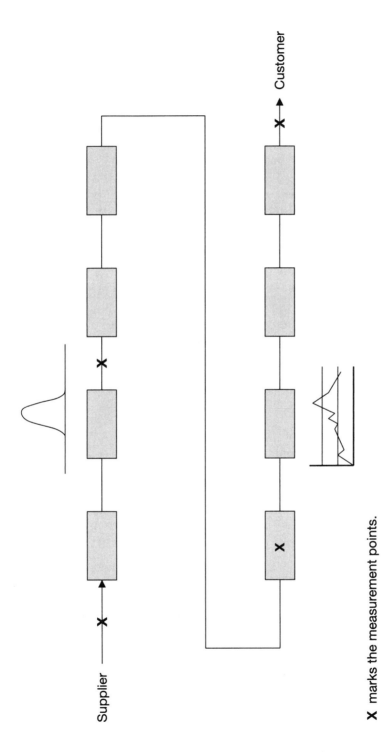

X marks the measurement points.

Figure 6.3 Putting the measurement points close to the activity that it is measuring

costs were devoted to poor-quality cost. He estimated that the opportunity is broken down in the banking industry as follows:

- Preventive savings—2 percent
- Appraisal savings—28 percent
- Internal error savings—41 percent
- External error savings—29 percent

Waste costs money. In many business processes, poor-quality costs run as high as 80 percent of the budget. Poor-quality costs of 50 percent or more are common in business processes before SPI is applied to them. For example, at IBM the accounts receivable poor-quality cost was running 63 percent of the budget before the process was streamlined. If that is cut by 50 percent through the use of SPI, the process is still wasting 40 percent of the organization's budget and is a gold mine for future continuous improvement.

There is a big difference between the quality cost and the poor-quality cost systems. The quality cost system was developed in the 1950s by Val Feigenbaum. It was divided into four elements:

- Prevention cost
- Appraisal cost
- Internal defect cost
- External defect cost

With the focus on what the organization was losing due to poor quality, this was an acceptable approach. But today our survival depends on how well we are servicing our customers. As a result, the poor-quality cost system was developed and used by IBM. It incorporated eight elements:

- Prevention cost
- Appraisal cost
- Internal error cost
- External error cost
- Customer incurred cost
- Customer dissatisfaction cost
- Loss-of-reputation cost
- Lost opportunity cost

The poor-quality cost for the customer is often greater than the organization's cost related to an error that the organization makes. It is therefore very important to include all the costs related to an error in order to define its importance. More information on the poor-quality cost system can be found in the book *Poor-Quality Cost* (Harrington, 1987).

Phase IV: Activity 4: Install Feedback Data Systems

Measurement without feedback to the person performing the task is just another no-value-added activity. Feedback always comes before improvement. (See Figure 6.4.) In most organizations, too much data are collected and too little are used. Employees need ongoing positive and negative feedback about their output.

Figure 6.5 is an example of the results we received when we started giving feedback to each individual on the number of errors he or she created weekly. You will note that after 15 weeks, 10 out of 13 people went a week without creating an error, and for 2 out of the other 3 people the error rate was cut in half.

Although we need ongoing feedback to the employees involved in the process, we also need summary reports for the same people and for management. The summary reports should be exception reports so that masses of data do not waste management's and the employee's time. Exception reporting allows everyone to focus in on where improvements can be made.

Phase IV: Activity 5: Transfer the Project

The PIT and the implementation team have been driving the process transformation to this point in the project. As we end Phase IV, the process needs to be developed to the point that it has a management and control system in place that is not part of the SPI project. This means that the organization's standard infrastructure has to be ready and budgeted to accept the responsibilities for sustaining the gains and continuously improving the total performance of the new process. All too often the implementation team does a good job of installing the new process, but the team considers its job done once the new process is put in place and the people are trained to use it. This is a terrible mistake.

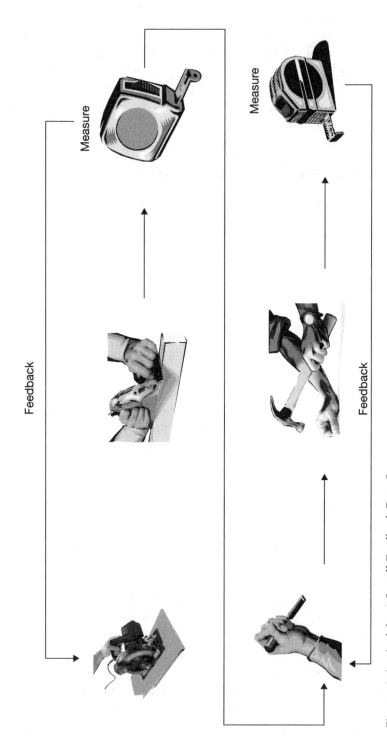

Measure

Feedback

Measure

Feedback

Figure 6.4 Activity 4: Install Feedback Data Systems

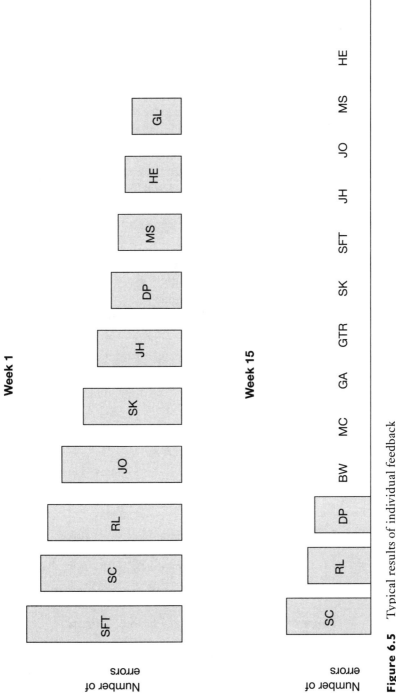

Figure 6.5   Typical results of individual feedback

This installation is not complete until the established infrastructure is in place to ensure the process will continue to improve. Questions like the following need to be answered, and the activities need to be staffed and budgeted.

- Who is responsible for the performance of the total process?
- Who will record the measurement data?
- Who will control the process?
- Who will generate the reports?
- How will new people be trained?
- Who will analyze the data and take action to correct problems?
- Who will update the process documentation?
- How will changes in customer requirements be understood and be reflected back into the process?
- How will suboptimization be controlled?
- What are the roles and responsibilities of the owners of the sub-processes that make up the total process?
- Who will audit the process, and how will it be audited?

These are typical questions that need to be addressed, and the answers need to be documented before the implementation is complete and the project implementation team can be disbanded.

> *All too often the new process performs well when it is getting special attention, but falls apart when the project team is reassigned.*
>
> —H. James Harrington

> *This is your process, so don't let them hand you a process that doesn't work. Get involved and make sure it does.*
>
> —Thomas Young, Dun & Bradstreet
> Corporate Controller (*CFO*, 1996)

Phase IV: Activity 6: Conduct Phase IV Tollgate

At the end of Phase IV it is an excellent time to do a complete review of the Phase IV deliverables. The tollgate should be chaired by the project sponsor, and the total EIT should be invited to attend. During this tollgate, the following questions should be addressed:

- Has the change met the goals set in the project plan?
- Was the cost to implement the change more or less what it was estimated to be?
- Did the change take more time to implement than projected?
- Is the ROI great enough to justify the change?
- Did the change management activities prepare the employees for the change?
- Is the future-state solution in keeping with the organization's culture and its long-range plan?
- Is the project transfer complete, and are the managers who are responsible for the process and the supporting processes during Phase V ready to take over total responsibility for their parts of the process?
- Are the budgets that are required to support the new process in place?

When these questions are answered in the affirmative, the project is ready to move into the continuous improvement phase. You can't exit Phase IV without an approved Phase V plan and budget plus an assigned implementation team.

Don't forget to reward the Implementation Team members if they did an excellent job.

—H. James Harrington

Phase V: Continuous Improvement

When you stop improving, you start slipping backwards.

—H. James Harrington

This phase consists of three activities (see Figure 6.6.):

- Activity 1: Maintain the Gains
- Activity 2: Implement Area Activity Analysis
- Activity 3: Qualify the Process

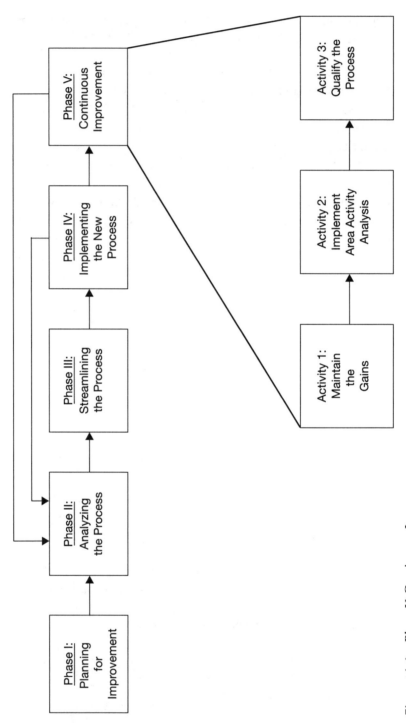

Figure 6.6 Phase V: Continuous Improvement

Figure 6.7 shows two processes that went through breakthrough improvement. One had continuous improvement after the break-through, while the other one didn't focus on continuous improvement.

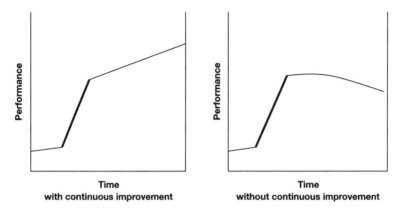

Figure 6.7   Two processes that have gone through breakthrough improvement—one with continuous improvement applied after the breakthrough and one without it

Phase V: Activity 1: Maintain the Gains

Organizations are typically organized in a *functional structure*. This places all the people who do the same kind of work in the same organizational structure. (For example, all the maintenance people are in the same function.)

Some organizations, however, have advanced to the point that they have a *process structure* where everyone in a major process is in the same organizational structure. (For example, the people that used to be in individual functions like production control, manufacturing, quality, manufacturing engineers, and production engineers for each major process are in the same organizational structure.) This is the ideal case for the streamlined process because the process owner has all the departments and natural work teams related to the process reporting to him or her.

Another type of organizational structure is called a *matrix structure.* In this case, the people working in the process have two managers—one because they are part of a functional-type organization and the other because they are part of the process. The process owner manages them from a total process standpoint, and the functional manager manages them from a technical standpoint. The matrix-type organization has become more and more popular.

Another approach to keeping the total process improving is to appoint a person as the process owner with the responsibility for measuring the total process and taking appropriate action if the process measurements aren't improving at an acceptable rate. No matter what the organizational structure is, I strongly recommend that someone be assigned to own the process throughout the continuous improvement activities. Without a process owner who is looking at the total process cycle "across the many smokestacks," suboptimization will slowly creep in, and the gains that were made will slowly disappear into thin air.

Phase V: Activity 2: Implement Area Activity Analysis

Now that the process has undergone a major breakthrough in performance, you cannot stop improving. This is not the end of the improvement activities; it is just the beginning. The process must continue to improve, usually at a much slower rate (10 to 20 percent per year), but it must continue to improve. The natural work teams (NWTs) now take over, working to improve their part of the process.

We recommend using Area Activity Analysis (AAA) to do this. Of course, there are other approaches like Six Sigma, TQM, and Quality Circles, but we have found that AAA does an outstanding job at driving the continuous improvement cycle. AAA is designed to cement the external and internal customer-supplier relationships.

With the AAA methodology the process is now subdivided into small parts that take place within each NWT. First, the NWT accepts its role as the supplier to the next NWT in the process. The team members then develop a set of customer requirements and meet with the receiver of their output to get their customer's documented agreement. At this meeting the receiving NWT (customer) defines how it will feed back information on the acceptability of the inputs it receives.

The next step is for the NWT to set up effectiveness standards for its part of the process. Based upon this agreement to output requirements, the NWT evaluates its process to be sure it is capable of meeting these requirements. Typically the NWT will flowchart in detail the activities and tasks of the process that it is involved in. Then for each activity in the flowchart and for the total flowchart, the acceptable processing, cycle time, and cost are defined. The efficiency measurement of the NWT's part of the process is documented and approved by the next-level manager and the other functions that approve and set standards for the NWT (for example, manufacturing, engineering, and finance). Typical standards would be 15 minutes to process an order, $12.25 to change a record, etc. This leads to the NWT defining the inputs that are needed in order for it to meet the output requirements.

Now the NWT puts on its "customer hat" and meets with its suppliers to obtain a documented agreement on what the supplier must produce in order to meet the NWT's input requirements. At the same time, the NWT develops a system that gives feedback to each supplier on the acceptability of the impact of the inputs the supplier provides. The NWT now makes use of the visual office concept by putting up a performance board. (See Figure 6.8.)

This is a very simplified explanation of AAA. For more information on AAA, read Harrington, Hoffherr, and Reid's (1998) book, *Area Activity Analysis.*

Phase V: Activity 3: Qualify the Process

You can't earn this week's paycheck with last week's press clippings.
—H. James Harrington

Process qualification is a way to create a data base that will provide the organization with a high degree of confidence that the output from the process will meet requirements over a long time period. It will also validate that the process will be able to produce the quantity of output that is planned for at the right cost.

Is Business Process Qualification Necessary?

Manufacturing process qualification guarantees that the process design provides customers with acceptable products. As manufacturers, we wish to demonstrate consistency and quality. Each new process puts our business reputation at risk. One bad process can destroy years of hard work. Customers remember the bitterness of poor performance long after the sweetness of outstanding service has faded.

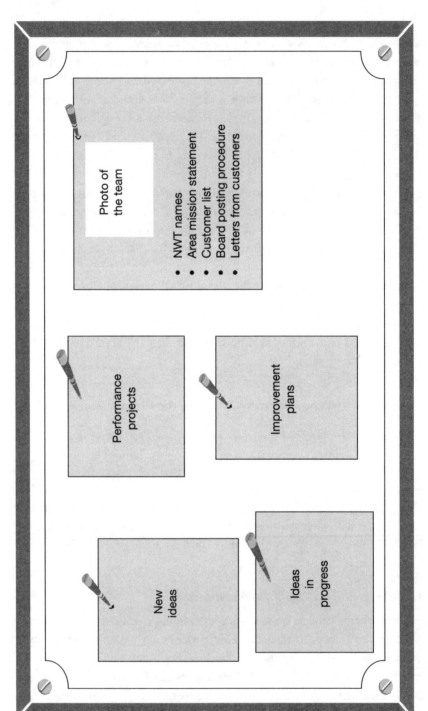

Figure 6.8 AAA performance board

Because business processes largely service internal customers, it is easy to lose sight of their importance to our overall business survival. This is where process qualification helps, by motivating us to take the first steps toward continuous improvement. Whether office professionals, clerical employees, or middle managers, people love to be recognized for their efforts and are stimulated by public acknowledgment. Process qualification provides a measurement system that instills a sense of pride within each team.

Process qualification supports the goals set forth in the beginning of the SPI effort. There is no better way of showing how serious we are than by installing a systematic business process qualification strategy.

Process qualification will motivate the process owner to keep the process improvement high on the priority list by measuring the process's progress. If you are not improving, if you are standing still, you are not holding your own. In fact, you are sliding backward, because your competition is improving. As noted above, you can't earn this week's paycheck with last week's press clippings. We use a process maturity grid to document progress and improvement. Qualifying a process typically includes these steps:

- The process is evaluated using the appropriate requirements list.
- The process owner reviews the process status.
- The process owner requests qualification-level change.
- The process owner prepares a process status report and sends it to the review committee. The EIT often serves as the review committee.
- The process owner presents the process change data to the review committee.
- The review committee chairperson issues the process qualification change letter.
- The review committee rewards the process team for its accomplishments.

Process Maturity Levels

A six-level process maturity grid can provide an effective structure and guide for the streamlining activities. (See Table 6.1.) These levels lead the process from an unknown process status to the ultimate best-of-breed classification.

Table 6.1   Six-Level Process Maturity Grid

Level	Status	Description
6	Unknown	Process status hasn't been determined.
5	Understood	Process design is understood and operates according to prescribed documentation.
4	Effective	Process is systematically measured, streamlining has started, and end-customer expectations are met.
3	Efficient	Process is streamlined and more efficient.
2	Error-free	Process is highly effective (i.e., error-free) and efficient.
1	World class	Process is world class and continues to improve.

Table 6.2   Process Maturity Grid

Item	6	5	4	3	2	1
Customer measurement						
Process measurement						
Supplier performance						
Documentation						
Training						
Benchmarking						
Adaptability						
Continuous improvement						

Note: The darker the shade, the better the performance.

Until the streamlining methodology has been applied, all business processes are considered to be at level 6. As the process improves, it progresses logically up to level 1. This enables the organization to evaluate the process's progress status. (See Table 6.2.)

A quick look at a business process overview chart provides the status of an organization's business processes. See Table 6.3, for example. In the case of accounts payable, the organization has decided that it does not need to be at error-free certification level 3. You will note that the accounts payable process is at certification level 4 and still needs to improve to level 3. In the case of order entry, the organization wants it to be highly effective and efficient but does not require it to be world class. In this case a level 2 is acceptable. These types of decisions are usually based on business factors and priorities. As business conditions and priorities change, the decision not to be the best in all critical business processes should be addressed.

Table 6.3   Business Process Overview Chart

Business Process	Level 6	Level 5	Level 4	Level 3	Level 2	Level 1
Order entry	X	X	X	X	X	NR
Accounts payable	X	X	X		NR	NR
Customer complaint handling	X	X	X	X		
Special product price request	X	X				
Engineering change release	X	X	X	X	X	
Customer-requested information	X	X	X	X	X	X
New product design	X	X	X	X		

All processes in all organizations may not need to progress through all six levels. Often there are considerable costs involved in becoming the best. In most cases, organizations have many business processes that need to be improved. Because of the magnitude of this job, it may be wise to bring some of the processes under control and then direct the limited resources to another critical business process. Once all the critical processes are under control, PITs can be assigned to bring the most critical processes up to level 1 (world class). Frequently the people using the process will make major improvements in the process as a result of their continuous improvement activities, while the PIT is working on another process. When the EIT decides that something less than a world-class performance level is acceptable, it should communicate this information to the PIT immediately.

Ideally this decision should be made prior to forming the PIT. When management decreases its expectations late in the process cycle, it can negatively impact the PIT's morale by being interpreted as management's loss of faith.

Differences among Business Process Levels

To determine whether the process has evolved to the next level, eight major change areas should be addressed:

- End-customer-related measurements
- Process measurements and performance
- Supplier partnerships
- Documentation
- Training
- Benchmarking
- Process adaptability
- Continuous improvement

The following definitions will help you understand the changing expectations that must be met to change qualification levels:

- *Requirements.* What the customer must be supplied with
- *Expectations.* What the customer would like to have to do his or her job the best; what the customer thinks can reasonably be provided or can be obtained from a competitor
- *Desires.* What is on the customer's wish list; what it would be nice to have but is not essential

To get the details related to the requirements for each of the levels, see Chapter 7 in *Business Process Improvement* (Harrington, 1991).

Does SPI Work?

You can bet on it. IBM Credit slashed its six-day turnaround cycle to four hours, decreasing the number of people required in the department while the number of deals increased over 100-fold. Not 100 percent, but 100 times.

Ford North America employed 500 people in its accounts payable department. By putting in computers to automate the process, Ford was able to cut that head count by 20 percent. Under this automated system, the Ford purchasing department sends a purchase order to the supplier with a copy to accounts payable. When the supplier ships the goods, they arrive on the back dock, at which time the back dock completes a form describing the goods and sends the form on to accounts payable. The supplier meanwhile sends accounts payable an invoice. To streamline the process, accounts payable clerks no longer match purchase orders with receiving documents, primarily because the new process eliminates the invoice entirely. The new process requires the buyer to issue the vendor a purchase order that is simultaneously entered into an online database. When the goods are received in receiving, the receiving clerk checks the computer to see whether the received shipment corresponds with the purchase order. He or she has only one choice—it does or it doesn't. If it does, the clerk accepts the goods by pushing the acceptance button. The results of the new system were drastic; instead of 500 people, Ford now just uses 125 people. In some parts of Ford, accounts payable is just 5 percent of its former size.

Does SPI work? Just ask any of the organizations that have tried it—Ford, Boeing, IBM, 3-M, Corning, Nutrasweet, McDonnell Douglas, Federal Mogul, and Aetna—and you will get a resounding yes. The following are some typical examples of results:

- McDonnell Douglas
  - 20–40 percent overhead reduction
  - 30–70 percent inventory reduction
  - 5–25 percent material cost reduction
  - 60–90 percent quality improvement
  - 20–40 percent administrative cost reduction
- Federal Mogul
  - Reduction in development process cycle time from 20 weeks to 20 business days, resulting in a 75 percent reduction in throughput time
- Aetna Life and Casualty Co.
  - Reduction in information technology workload by 750 employee-years per year
  - Consolidation of 65 property casualty claim offices to 23
  - Rise in net income of 50 percent to $207.2 million

After redesigning its warehouse processes, Ford Motor Company now distributes auto parts faster and with fewer errors while using fewer warehouses and a quarter of the people. Rank Xerox UK realized a 20 percent revenue growth, reduced noncustomer contact jobs by nearly 30 percent, and reduced order delivery time by 36 days to 6 days following a redesign of critical business processes.

Federal Mogul reduced its new product sample development from 20 weeks to 20 days through redesigning the process.

The streamlined process improvement methodology is like a GPS that will get anyone to the correct destination when you don't know how to get there.

—H. James Harrington

Summary

The process and the system that controls it represent the real problem facing business today, not the people who work within the boundaries set for them by management. Employees must work within the process, and management must work on the process to improve it. The improvement efforts and their supporting systems must be directed at the process and not at the individual. This means that all functions must work together to optimize the efficiency, effectiveness, and adaptability of the total process. This can best be accomplished when one person is held accountable for the performance of the total process and is given the authority to bring together members from all the individual functions involved within the process, with the objective of maximizing its total performance.

Now let's look at how different types of organizations feel about their business processes:

Losers

- The employees are the problem. They need to be motivated.
- If everyone does his or her job, things will get done.
- Employees and management cannot be trusted. There need to be a lot of checks and balances.

- Downsizing is equally distributed across all functions. That's the fair way to do it.
- Business processes, on an average, have 15 percent real-value-added content.

Survivors

- If each natural work team improves its part of the process, everything will be OK. It is the high number of errors that are the problem.
- Bureaucracy is something that everyone has to live with.
- Management decides to use either continuous improvement or breakthrough methodologies.
- Computerization of the business processes is used to decrease cycle time and costs.
- SPI activities are directed at reducing costs.
- Process changes that will reduce head count are kept confidential until the last minute.
- Business processes, on an average, have 30 percent real-value-added content.

Winners

- Any bureaucracy is bad.
- When downsizing is necessary, winning organizations remove the no-value-added activities from the processes. Unnecessary work is eliminated, and the associated resources are removed from the budgets.
- They never computerize until the process has been streamlined.
- They prioritize their investment in SPI activities based upon their business plan, competitive position, core competencies, and core capabilities.

When everything is perfect, remove something to upset the process and start the improvement cycle over.

—H. James Harrington

Typical Business Processes Where SPI Can Be Applied

Function	Process Name
Development	Acoustics Control Design
	Advanced Communication Development
	Cable Component Design
	Competitive Analysis
	Component Qualification
	Cost Target
	Design/Material Review
	Design Systems Support
	Design Test
	Development Process Control
	Document Review
	Electronic Development
	Engineering Change Management
	Engineering Operations
	High-Level Design Specification
	Industrial Design
	Information Development
	Interconnect Planning
	Interconnect Product Development
	Interdivisional Design
	Logic Design and Verification
	Phase 0/Requirements
	Physical Design Tools
	Power System Design
	Product Development

Product Management
Product Publication
Records Management
Release
Reliability Management
System-Level Product Design
System Reliability and Serviceability (RAS)
System Requirements
Systems Design
Tool Design
Tool Development
User/System Interface Design

Distribution
Disbursements
Field Services/Support
Inventory Management
Parts Expediting
Physical Inventory Management
Power Vehicles
Production Receipts
Receiving
Salvage
Shipping
Storage
Teleprocessing and Control
Transportation

Financial Accounting
Accounts Payable
Accounts Receivable
Accrual Accounting
Cash Control
Cost Accounting
Employee Expense Account
Financial Application
Financial Control
Fixed-Asset Control
Fixed Assets/Appropriation
Intercompany Accounting/Billing
Inventory Control
Labor Distribution
Ledger Accounting
Payroll
Procurement Support
Revenue Accounting

| | Taxes |
| | Transfer Pricing |

Financial Planning   Appropriation Control
                        Budget Control
                        Business Planning
                        Contract Management
                        Cost Estimating
                        Financial Outlook
                        Financial Planning
                        Inventory Control
                        Transfer Pricing

Information Systems   Applications Development Methodology
                        Service Level Assessment
                        Systems Management Controls

Personnel   Benefits
                        Compensation
                        Employee Relations
                        Employment
                        Equal Opportunity
                        Executive Resources
                        Management Development
                        Management Development/Research
                        Medical
                        Personnel Assessment
                        Personnel Programs
                        Personnel Research
                        Personnel Services
                        Placement
                        Records
                        Resource Management
                        Suggestions

Production Control   Allocation
                        Base Plan Commitment
                        Consignment Process
                        Customer Order Services Management
                        Early Manufacturing Involvement and
                        Product Release
                        Engineering Change (EC) Implementation
                        Field Parts Support
                        Inventory Projection

	Manufacturing Process Record
	New Product Planning
	Parts Planning and Ordering
	Planning and Scheduling Management
	Plant Business Volumes Performance
	Management
	Site Sensitive Parts
	Systems Work in Progress (WIP) Management
	WIP Accuracy
Programming	Distributed Systems Products
	Programming Center
	Software Development
	Software Engineering
	Software Manufacturing Products
Purchasing	Alteration/Cancellation
	Contracts
	Costs
	Delivery
	Expediting
	Invoice/Payment
	Laboratory Procurement
	Nonproduction Orders
	Process Interplant Transfer
	Production Orders
	Quality
	Supplier Payment
	Supplier Relations
	Supplier Selection
Quality	New Product Qualification
	Supplier Quality
Site Services	Facilities Change Request
Miscellaneous	Cost of Box Manufacturing Quality
	Service Cost Estimating
	Site Planning

Process Walk-Through Questionnaire

Date	
Organization	
Interviewee(s)	
Activity	
Flowchart No.	
1.0 INPUTS	
1.1 What inputs are required to do the activity?	
Input 1	
Input 2	
Input 3	
1.2 Who supplies these inputs?	
Input 1	
Input 2	
Input 3	

1.3 How good are they?	
Input 1	
Input 2	
Input 3	
1.4 Do the inputs arrive when you need them?	
Input 1	
Input 2	
Input 3	
1.5 How do the inputs get to you?	
Input 1	
Input 2	
Input 3	
1.6 How long do you have the inputs before you use them?	
Input 1	
Input 2	
Input 3	
1.7 Where do you store the inputs until you use them?	
Input 1	
Input 2	
Input 3	

1.8 Does lack of required inputs slow your job down?	
Input 1	
Input 2	
Input 3	
1.9 Are the inputs in the right format for you?	
Input 1	
Input 2	
Input 3	
1.10 Do you need them all?	If not, which can be removed or altered?
Input 1	
Input 2	
Input 3	
1.11 How do you measure the quality of the inputs you receive?	
Input 1	
Input 2	
Input 3	
1.12 What are the quality requirements for these inputs?	
Input 1	
Input 2	
Input 3	

1.13 How do you let your suppliers know how well they are performing?	
Input 1	
Input 2	
Input 3	
1.14 What would happen if each of your suppliers stopped providing you with input?	
Input 1	
Input 2	
Input 3	

2.0 ACTIVIY NAME AND NO.
2.1 What documents tell you how to do your job? Please show them to us.
2.2 Please explain to us what you do and how you do it.

TASK	ACTIVITY . TYPE NO	HOURS PER WEEK	PROCEDURE NO.	COMMENT

ACTIVITY TYPE NO.   PERSON INTERVIEWED

1. Appraisal/Inspector   Phone No.

2. Correcting/Repair

3. Review and/or Approval

4. Added Value/Generating New Output

2.3 Do you have any problem in performing these tasks?
If yes, explain.

| |
| |
| |
| |
| |
| 2.4 Are all the tasks necessary? |
| If no, explain. |
| |
| |
| 2.5 What has to change to eliminate the unnecessary ones? |
| |
| |
| |
| 2.6 What types of records do you keep, and are they used? |
| If you record data, who uses the data and how often? |
| |
| |

RECORD TYPE	YES	NO	USER	FREQUENCY

2.7 What keeps you from doing error-free work?

2.8 What can be done to make your tasks easier?

2.9 Do you have the equipment you need?

If not, what would help you do a better job?

2.10 Is your work area layout as good as it could be?

If not, how should it be changed?

2.11 Have you reviewed your job description?

If yes, does it really define what you do?

If no, how should it be changed?

2.12 What would you change in your job if you were the manager?

3.0 OUTPUTS	
3.1 What are your outputs?	
Output 1	
Output 2	
Output 3	
3.2 Who is the customer for each output?	
Output 1	
Output 2	
Output 3	
3.3 How do you know your output is good?	
Output 1	
Output 2	
Output 3	
3.4 Are your outputs satisfactory to your customers?	How do you know?
Output 1	
Output 2	
Output 3	

3.5 What measurements are made of your outputs by your customers?	
Output 1	
Output 2	
Output 3	
3.6 What feedback do you receive from your customers?	
Output 1	
Output 2	
Output 3	
3.7 What do you need in feedback to improve your performance?	
Output 1	
Output 2	
Output 3	
3.8 How are your outputs used?	
Output 1	
Output 2	
Output 3	
3.9 What would happen if you did not provide your outputs?	
Output 1	
Output 2	
Output 3	

3.10 Is there someone who is not receiving your output who should?	If yes, who and why?
Output 1	
Output 2	
Output 3	

4.0 TRAINING/JOB CONTENT	
4.1 What training did you receive?	
4.2 Was it adequate?	If not, how should it be improved?

5.0 MISCELLANEOUS	
5.1 What do you like most about your job?	

5.2 What do you like least about your job?	
5.3 Do you get rewarded for doing better work?	If yes, explain.
5.4 Do you get rewarded for putting out more work?.	If yes, explain
5.5 Do you have enough time to do a good job?	If not, why?

5.6 Is there anything else you would like to tell us about your job that will help make the process work better?

Some Process Simulation Tool Suppliers

Vendor	Tools	Web Address
CACI Products Company	SimProcess, MODSIM III	www.caciasl.com
Edge Software Inc.	Design/Analyst	www.workdraw.com
High Performance Systems	ithink	www.hps-inc.com
Imagine That Inc.	Extend	www.imaginethatinc.com
Micro Analysis & Design Inc.	MicroSaint	www.madboulder.com
MicroGrafx Inc.	OPTIMA	www.micrografx.com
PROMODEL Corporation	ProcessModel, ProModel	www.promodel.com
Scitor Inc.	ProcessCharter	www.scitor.com
Symix Inc.	AweSim	www.pritsker.com
Systems Modeling Corp.	BPSimulator, ARENA	www.sm.com

Definitions

5S

5S (Sort, Set in Order, Shine, Standardize, and Sustain) is a methodology for organizing, cleaning, developing, and sustaining a productive work environment. Improved ownership of work space, improved productivity, and improved maintenance are some of the benefits of a 5S program.

6S

6S takes the 5S methodology and adds safety to it making six words that start with S.

Adaptability Measurement

Adaptability measurement is the adaptability of a process to handle future, changing, customer expectation, and today's individual special customer requirements. It is managing the process to meet today's special needs and future requirements.

Benchmark

A *benchmark* is a specific number or point against which another measurement or point is compared.

Benchmarking

Benchmarking is a systematic way to identify, understand, and creatively evolve superior products, services, designs, equipment, processes, and practices to improve an organization's real performance by studying other organizations' items and adapting them to or adopting them into the organization.

Change

Change is a condition that disrupts the current state. Change activities disrupt the current state.

Effectiveness Measurement

Effectiveness measurement is the extent to which the output of a process or subprocess meets the needs and expectations of its customers. *Quality* is often thought of as a synonym for *effectiveness*, but effectiveness is a lot more.

Efficiency Measurement

Efficiency measurement is the extent to which a resource is minimized and waste is eliminated in the pursuit of effectiveness. Productivity is a measurement of efficiency.

Error Proofing (Poka Yoke)

Error proofing is a structured approach to ensure quality and an error-free manufacturing environment. Error proofing assures that defects will never be passed to the next operation.

Executive Improvement Team (EIT)

An *Executive Improvement Team* is a group of top managers that oversee the improvement efforts for the organization.

Future Reality Diagram

A *future reality diagram* is a sufficiency-based logic structure designed to reveal how changes to the status quo would affect reality—specifically to produce desired effects.

Future State

Future state is the point at which change initiatives are in place and integrated with the behavior patterns that are required by the change. The change goals and objectives have been achieved.

High-Impact Team (HIT)

The *high impact team approach* is a breakthrough strategy that focuses a group's attention on the processes that are going on within a specific area. It realigns the work area to minimize the movement of output between activities, resulting in decreasing stock and shorter cycle time. A typical HIT activity will last for two weeks, and between 70 and 80 percent of the future-state solution will be implemented within the two-week time period.

Inventory Turnover Rate

Inventory turnover rate is the number of times an inventory cycles or turns over during the year. A frequently used method to compute inventory turnover is to divide the average inventory level into annual cost of sales.

Just-in-Time (JIT)

Just-in-Time is a philosophy of manufacturing based on planned elimination of all waste and continuous improvement of productivity. It encompasses the successful execution of all manufacturing activities required to produce a final product.

Kaizen Blitz

Kaizen Blitz is the Japanese term for continuing improvement involving everyone—managers and workers. In manufacturing *Kaizen* relates to finding and eliminating waste in machinery, labor, or production methods.

Kanban

Kanban is a simple parts-movement system that depends on cards and boxes or containers to take parts from one workstation to another on a production line. The essence of the *Kanban* concept is that a supplier or the warehouse should only deliver components to the production line as and when they are needed, so that there is no storage in the production area.

Monte Carlo

Monte Carlo methods (or Monte Carlo experiments) are a class of computational algorithms that rely on repeated random sampling to compute their results. Monte Carlo methods are often used in simulating physical and mathematical systems. These methods are most suited to calculation by a computer. Monte Carlo methods are especially useful for simulating processes that have a lot of variation occurring randomly at many different parts of the process over time. They are used to model phenomena with significant uncertainty in inputs to the process and within the process that can result in changes in the process' performance and business risk. (from Wikipedia, 2011)

One-Piece Flow

One-piece flow, or continuous flow processing, is a concept that means that items are processed and moved directly from one processing step to the next, one piece at a time. One-piece flow helps to maximize utilization of resources, shorten lead times, identify problems, and improve communication between operations.

Organizational Change Management (OCM)

Organizational Change Management is a comprehensive set of structured procedures for the decision-making, planning, execution, and evaluation phases of the change process.

Overall Equipment Effectiveness (OEE)

Overall equipment effectiveness measures the availability, performance efficiency, and quality rate of equipment. It is especially important to calculate OEE for the constrained operations.

Present State

Present state, current state, as-is state, and *status quo* all refer to a state in which individual expectations are being fulfilled. It's a predictable state—the normal routine.

Problem

A *problem*, according to *Webster's Collegiate Dictionary* (11th edition), can be defined as a question proposed for a solution or as a state of difficulty that needs to be resolved. These two definitions suggest two important characteristics:

- Having a problem is by nature a state of affairs that is plagued by some difficulty or undesired condition.
- A problem presents a challenge that needs to be solved in order to establish more desirable conditions.

Process

A *process* is any activity or series of activities that takes an input, adds value to it, and provides an output to a customer.

Process Flow Animation

Process flow animation is a process model that pictorially shows the movement of transactions within the process and how variability and dynamics affect process performance.

Process Improvement Team (PIT)

A *Process Improvement Team* is a group of people who will be responsible to create a redesign process over a 2- to 3-month period. The team is usually made up of 6 to 10 people who represent the key departments involved in the process being redesigned and some key technical experts. The members of the PIT will typically devote about 50 percent of their time to redesigning the assigned process.

Process Owner

The *process owner* is the individual(s) responsible for process design and performance. The process owner is also responsible for sustaining the gains and identifying future improvement opportunities in the process.

Process Variation Analysis

Process variation analysis is a way of combining the variation that occurs at each task or activity in a process so that a realistic prediction of the total variation for the entire process can be made.

Quick Changeover (Single-Minute Exchange of Dies)

Quick changeover is a technique to analyze and reduce the resources needed for equipment setup, including exchange of tools and dies. Single-minute exchange of dies (SMED) is an approach to reduce output and quality losses due to changeovers.

Standard Rate of Work

Standard rate of work is the length of time that should be required to set up a given machine or operation and run one part, assembly, batch, or end product through that operation. This time is used in determining machine requirements and labor requirements.

Takt Time

Takt time is the time required between the completion of successive units of the end product. Takt time is used to pace lines in the production environments.

Theory of Constraints (TOC)

The *theory of constraints* is a management philosophy that can be viewed as three separate but interrelated areas—logistics, performance measurement, and logical thinking. TOC focuses the organization's scarce resources on improving the performance of the true constraint and therefore on improving the bottom line of the organization.

Tollgates

Tollgates are process checkpoints where deliverables are reviewed and measured and readiness to move forward is addressed.

Total Productive Maintenance (TPM)

Total Productive Maintenance is a maintenance program concept that brings maintenance into focus in order to minimize downtimes and maximize equipment usage. The goal of TPM is to avoid emergency repairs and keep unscheduled maintenance to a minimum.

Transition State

A *transition state* is the point in the change process at which people break away from the status quo. They no longer behave as they've done in the past, and yet they still haven't thoroughly established the "new way" of operating. The transition state begins when the solutions disrupt individuals' expectations and they must start to change the way they work.

Transition Tree

A *transition tree* is a cause-and-effect logic tree designed to provide step-by-step progress from initiation to completion of a course of action or change. It is an implementation tool.

Value Proposition

Value proposition is an analysis and quantified review of the benefits, costs, and value that an organization can deliver to customers and other constituent groups within and outside the organization. It is also a positioning of value, where value = benefits – cost (cost includes risk) (from Wikipedia, 2011).

Value Stream Costing

Value stream costing methodology simplifies the accounting process to give everyone real information in a basic, understandable format. By isolating all fixed costs along with direct labor, we can easily apply manufacturing resources as a value per square footage utilized by a particular cell or value stream. This methodology of factoring gives a true picture of cellular consumption to value-added throughput for each value stream companywide. Now you can easily focus improvement *Kaizen* events where actual problems exist for faster calculated benefits and sustainability.

Value Stream Mapping

Value stream mapping is a graphical tool that helps you to see and understand the flow of the material and information as a product makes its way through the value stream. It ties together Lean concepts and techniques.

Visual Management

Visual management is a set of techniques that makes operation standards visible so that workers can follow them more easily. These techniques expose waste so that it can be prevented and eliminated.

Work Flow Diagram

A *work flow diagram* shows the movement of material, identifying areas of waste. The diagram aids teams in planning future improvements, such as one-piece flow and work cells.

Work Flow Monitoring

Work flow monitoring is an online computer program that is used to track individual transactions as they move through the process to minimize process variation.

Other Simulation Symbols

 Batch. A batch activity combines a given quantity of entities into a single batch. An example of a batching activity is the accumulation of mail for delivery.

Branch. A branch activity allows for defining alternative routings for flow objects. Branching may be based on a probability or a condition. For example, the outcome of an inspection process may be modeled using probabilistic branching.

 Copy. A copy activity makes multiple copies of the original entity. For example, if a document that is being edited results in multiple copies of a file, this activity may be modeled using a copy activity.

 Delay. A delay activity defines value-added or non-value-added activity times. A delay activity with resource constraints provides queue statistics that can be used for analyzing wait times.

 Generate. A generate activity generates the arrival of entities into the model. Arrivals may be random, deterministic, or conditional. An example of a generate activity is the arrival of patients in a clinic. A generate activity may have values for arrival time, quantity, frequency, and occurrences.

Split. A split activity takes an incoming entity and creates clones of that entity as well as providing an output of the original entity. For example, clones of a purchase order may be created with a split activity and sent to accounts payable and shipping.

 Synchronize. A synchronize activity takes inputs that arrive at different times and outputs them in a synchronized fashion. For example, passengers and their baggage must be synchronized at a terminal.

 Transform. A transform activity converts an incoming entity into another entity. For example, a prospective buyer is transformed into a customer when an order is placed. This activity can be modeled using the transformation construct.

Typical Government Processes

I. Establish direction.

  a. Establish (national) policy.

    i. Assess current macroenvironment.

    ii. Establish (national) priorities.

    iii. Establish (national) strategies.

  b. Determine (agency) requirements.

    i. Evaluate current (agency) performance.

    ii. Develop regulations.

    iii. Structure the organization.

    iv. Establish resource requirements.

  c. Develop (agency) plans.

    i. Identify missions, goals, objectives.

    ii. Develop courses of action.

    iii. Develop detailed operational and emergency plans.

    iv. Deploy policy.

  d. Budget (agency) programs.

    i. Develop programs/budgets.

    ii. Consolidate and prioritize program requirements.

    iii. Balance programs/budgets.

II. Acquire resources.

    a. Manage acquisition.

        i. Develop (agency) acquisition guidance.

        ii. Define and justify program.

        iii. Administer acquisition program.

    b. Conduct research and development.

        i. Conduct research.

        ii. Design (agency) products and services.

        iii. Test and evaluate models and prototypes.

    c. Produce resources.

        i. Manufacture items.

        ii. Construct facilities.

        iii. Access labor.

        iv. Take delivery.

III. Provide capabilities.

    a. Manage resources and capabilities.

        i. Process requests for products and services.

        ii. Deliver products and services to customers.

        iii. Decide disposition of material assets.

        iv. Assign material assets.

    b. Support resources.

        i. Maintain resources.

        ii. Enhance/upgrade organizational capabilities.

        iii. Transport personnel and material.

        iv. Release personnel and assets from government control.

        v. Manage natural resources.

    c. Provide administrative support services.

        i. Inform and advise.

        ii. Provide electronic information systems.

        iii. Provide financial services.

        iv. Provide facility services.

        v. Provide community services.

        vi. Provide personnel services.

    d. Develop resource capabilities.

        i. Integrate physical and human resources.

        ii. Train personnel.

        iii. Assess performance readiness of resources.

        iv. Manage improvement and change.

IV. Execute the (agency's) mission.

    a. Designate the (agency) office of primary responsibility.

        i. Establish the operation's structure.

        ii. Assess adherence to laws, rules, plans, and orders.

        iii. Integrate resources.

    b. Provide operational information support.

        i. Collect operational information.

        ii. Aggregate and analyze operational information.

        iii. Provide situation assessments to decision makers.

    c. Conduct (agency) operations.

    d. Sustain field operations.

        i. Maintain material.

        ii. Sustain people.

        iii. Resupply operational assets.

APPENDIX

Nonmanufacturing Typical Processes Measurements

Nonmanufacturing measurements, which are sometimes difficult to establish, might include the following:

1. ACCOUNTING
   - Percentage of late reports.
   - Computer input incorrect.
   - Errors in specific reports as audited.
   - Percentage of significant errors in reports; total number of reports.
   - Percentage of late reports; total number of reports. Average reduction in time spans associated with important reports.
   - Pinpointing high-cost manufacturing elements for correction.
   - Pinpointing jobs yielding low or no profit for correction.
   - Providing various departments with the specific cost tools they need to manage their operations for lowest cost.

2. ADMINISTRATIVE
   - Success in maximizing discount opportunities through consolidated ordering.
   - Success in eliminating security violations.
   - Success in effecting pricing actions so as to preclude subsequent upward revisions.

- Success in estimating inventory requirements.
- Success in responses to customer inquiries so as to maximize customer satisfaction.

3. CLERICAL
- Accurate typing, spelling, hyphenation.
- Decimal points correctly placed.
- Correct calculations in bills, purchase orders, journal entries, payrolls, bills of lading, etc.
- Time spent in locating filed material.
- Percentage of correct punches.
- Paper used during a given period versus actual output in finished pages.

4. DATA PROCESSING
- Data input error rate.
- Computer downtime due to error.
- Rerun time.
- Promptness in output delivery.
- Effectiveness of scheduling.
- Depth of investigations of programmers.
- Program debugging time.
- KP efficiency.

5. ENGINEERING: DESIGN
- Adequacy of systems specifications.
- Accuracy of system block diagrams.
- Thoroughness of system concepts.
- Simulation results compared with original design or prediction.
- Success in creating engineering designs that do not require change in order to make them perform as intended.
- Success in developing engineering cost estimates versus actual accruals.
- Success in meeting self-imposed schedules.
- Success in reducing drafting errors.
- Success in maximizing capture rates on RFPs for which the company was a contender.
- Success in meeting engineering test objectives.
- Number of error-free designs.

- Correct readings of gauges and test devices.
- Accurate specifications and standards.
- Proper reporting and control of time schedules.
- Reduction of engineering design changes.
- Changes in tests or in illustrations of reports.
- Rework resulting from errors in computer program input.
- Advance material list accuracy.
- Design compliance to specifications.
- Customer acceptance of proposals.
- Meeting schedules.
- Thoroughness of systems concepts.
- Accuracy and thoroughness of reports.
- Adequacy of design reviews.
- Compliance to specifications.
- Accuracy of computations.
- Accuracy of drawings.
- Reduction in number of ECNs to correct errors.

6. ENGINEERING: MANUFACTURING

- Accuracy of manufacturing processes.
- Timely delivery of manufacturing processes to the shop.
- Accuracy of time study data.
- Accuracy of time estimates.
- Timely response to bid requests.
- Asset utilization.
- Accuracy and thoroughness of test processes.
- Adequacy and promptness of program facilitation.
- Application of work simplification criteria.
- Minimum tool and fixture authorization.
- Labor utilization index.
- Methods improvement (in hours or dollars).
- Contract cost.
- Lost business due to price.
- Process change notices due to error.
- Tool rework to correct design.
- Methods improvement.

7. ENGINEERING: PLANT

- Effectiveness of preventive maintenance program.
- Accuracy of estimates (dollars and details).
- Accuracy of layouts.
- Cost of building services.
- Completeness of plant engineering drawings.
- Adequacy of scheduling.
- Fixed versus variable portions of overhead.
- Maintenance cost versus floor space, manpower, etc.
- Lost time due to equipment failures.
- Janitorial service.
- Success in meeting or beating budgets.
- Instrument calibration errors.
- Fire equipment found defective.
- Lost time due to equipment failures.
- Purchase requisition errors.
- Schedule compliance.
- Timely response to bid requests.
- Adherence to contract specifications.
- Effectiveness of customer liaison.
- Effectiveness of cost negotiations.
- Status "ship not bill."
- Change orders due to errors.
- Drafting errors found by checkers.
- Late releases.
- Time lost due to equipment failure.
- Callbacks on repairs.

8. FINANCE

- Billing errors (check accounts receivable overdues).
- Accounts payable deductions missed.
- Vouchers prepared with no defects.
- Clock card or payroll transcription errors.
- Keypunch errors.
- Computer downtime.
- Timeliness of financial reports.

- Effectiveness of scheduling program "debugging" time.
- Rerun time.
- Accuracy of predicted budgets.
- Clerical errors on entries.
- Inventory objectives met.
- Payroll errors.
- Discounts missed.
- Amounts payable records.
- Billing errors.

9. FORECASTING
- Can departments function with maximum effectiveness with budgets set for them?
- Can the company buy needed capital equipment, keep inventories supplied, pay its bills?
- Do projects meet time schedules?
- Assistance to line organizations (scheduling, planning, and control functions).
- Methods for finance and cost control.
- Timeliness of financial reports.
- Assets control.
- Minimizing capital expenditures.
- Realistic budgets.
- Clear and concise operating policies.
- Timely submission of realistic cost proposals.
- Completeness of financial reports.
- Effectiveness of disposition of government property.
- Effectiveness of cost negotiations.

10. HOTEL FRONT DESK
- Guests taken to unmade rooms.
- Reservations not honored.

11. LEGAL
- Amount of paper used versus finished pages produced.
- Misdelivered mail.
- Misfiled documents.
- Delays in execution of documents.

- Patent claims omitted.
- Response time on request for legal opinion.

12. MANAGEMENT

- Management can be gauged by the output of staff elements, overall defects rates, budgets and schedule controls, and other factors that reflect on managerial effectiveness. In other words, the accomplishments of a manager are the sum total of those working under him or her.
- Success in developing estimates of costs versus actual accruals.
- Success in meeting schedules.
- Performance records of employees under the manager's supervision.
- Success in developing realistic estimates on a PERT or PERT/cost chart
- Success in minimizing use of overtime operations.
- All nonproduction departments can be measured.
- Each department should be measured against itself, using time comparisons, and preferably by itself.
- The best primary goals are those that measure cost performance, delivery performance, and quality performance of the department. Secondary goals can be derived from these primary goals.
- There should be a base against which quality, cost, or delivery performance can be measured as a percentage of improvement. Examples of such a base would be direct labor, the sales dollar, the materials dollar, or the budget dollar. A dollar base is more meaningful to management than a physical quantity of output.
- Pages of data compiled with no defects.
- Clarity and conciseness of operating procedures.
- Evaluations of capital investment.
- Errors in applying standards on process sheets.
- Accuracy of estimates; actual costs versus estimated costs.
- Effectiveness of work measurement programs.

13. MARKETING

- Success in reduction of defects through suggestion submittals.
- Success in capturing new business versus quotations.
- Responsiveness to customer inquiries.

- Accuracy of marketing forecasts.
- Response from news releases and advertisements.
- Effectiveness of cost and price negotiations.
- Success in response to customer inquiries (customer identification).
- Customer liaison.
- Effectiveness of market intelligence.
- Attainment of new order targets.
- Operation within budgets.
- Effectiveness of proposals.
- Exercise of selectivity.
- Control of cost of sales.
- Meeting proposal submittal dates.
- Timely preparation of priced spare parts lists.
- Aggressiveness.
- Effectiveness of G-2
- Utilization of field marketing services.
- Dissemination of customer information.
- Bookings budget met.
- Accuracy of predictions, planning, and selections.
- Accurate and well-managed contracts.
- Exploitation of business potential.
- Effectiveness of proposals.
- Control of printing costs.
- Application of standard proposal material.
- Standardization of proposals.
- Reduction of reproduction expense.
- Contract errors.
- Order description errors.
- Sales order errors.

14. MATERIALS
- Saving made.
- Late deliveries.
- Purchase order (PO) errors.
- Material received against no PO.

- Status of unplaced requisitions.
- Orders open to government agency for approval.
- Delays in processing material received.
- Damage or loss items received.
- Claims for products damaged after shipment from our plant.
- Delays in outbound shipments.
- Complaints about or improper packing in our shipments.
- Errors in travel arrangements.
- Accuracy of route and rate information on shipments.
- Success in meeting schedules, material shortages in production.
- Success in estimating inventory requirements.
- Clock card errors by employees.
- Damaged shipments.
- Stock shelf life exceeded.
- Items in surplus.
- Purchase requisition errors.
- Effectiveness of material order follow-up.
- Adequacy and effectiveness of planning and scheduling.
- Application of residual inventories to current needs.
- Inventory turnover.
- Manufacturing jobs without schedules.
- Timeliness of incorporating ECNs.
- Timely replacement of rejected parts.
- Adequacy of reject control plan.
- Effectiveness of packing operations.
- Floor shortages.
- Labor utilization index.
- Data processing rerun time on material programs.
- Bad requisitions.
- Value of termination stores and residual inventory.
- Manpower fluctuations around mean.
- Percentage of supplier materials (dollars) rejected and returned; total materials (dollars) purchased.
- Number of defective vendors (repetitive); total number of vendors.
- Number of single-source vendors; total number of vendors.

- Percentage of supplier materials (dollars) holding up production; total material (dollars).
- Number of late lots received (actually holding up production); total lots received.
- Percentage of purchased materials (actual); total materials bid or budgeted.
- Percentage of reductions in B/M effected through purchasing effort; total materials bid or budgeted.
- Correct quotations or rates.
- Customers called back as promised.
- Installation of exact equipment requested by customers.
- Appointments kept at the time promised to customers.
- Prompt handling of complaints.
- Accurate meter readings.
- Courteous treatment of customers.
- Right packages of goods ordered shipped.
- Number of telephone numbers correctly dialed.
- PMI rejects.
- Savings made.
- Material handling budget met.
- Travel expense against open shop orders.
- Orders to government disapproved, resubmitted, and open, not approved.

15. PERSONNEL
- Success in eliminating security violations.
- Hiring effectiveness.
- Thoroughness and speed of responding to suggestions.
- Employee participation in company-sponsored activities.
- Administration of insurance programs.
- Accident prevention record.
- Processing insurance claims.
- Provision of adequate food services.
- Personnel security clearance errors.
- External classified visit authorization errors.
- Speedy processing of visitors through lobbies records accuracy.
- Adequacy of training programs.

- Thoroughness and speed of investigating suggestions and grievances.
- Employment requisitions filled.
- Administration of insurance program.
- Acceptance of organization's development recommendations.
- Effectiveness of administration of merit increases.
- Overhead budget performance.

16. PRODUCT ASSURANCE

- Participation in design reviews.
- Customer liaison.
- Technical society participation.
- Accuracy of proposals and contracts.
- Application of program policies.
- Prevention of filed complaints.
- Effectiveness of reporting and recording.
- Customer rejects.
- Rejected material on the floor.
- Adequacy of vendor ratings.
- Effectiveness of field quality control.
- Rejects.
- Screening efficiency.
- Inspection documentation.
- Quality assurance audits.

17. PRODUCT CONTROL

- Success in developing realistic schedules.
- Success in developing realistic estimates.
- Success in identifying defective specifications.
- Process sheets written with no error.
- Transportation hours without damage to product.
- Parts shortages in production.
- Downtime due to shortages.

18. PRODUCTION

- Success in reducing the scrap, rework, and "use-as-is" categories.
- Success in maintaining perfect attendance records.
- Success in identifying defective manufacturing specifications.

- Success in meeting production schedules.
- Success in cost reduction through suggestion submittals.
- Success in improving first article acceptance.
- Performance against standard.
- Success in reducing required MRB action.
- Utilities improperly left running at close of shift.
- Application of higher learning curves.
- Floor parts shortages.
- Delays due to rework, material shortage, etc.
- Control of overtime (nonscheduled).
- Prevention of damage to work in process.
- Cleanliness of assigned areas.
- Conformance to estimates.
- Suggestions submitted.
- Labor utilization index.
- Defects.
- Asset utilization.
- Scrap.
- Utilization of correct materials, drawings, and procedures.
- Prevention of damage.
- Safety records.
- Inches of weld with no defects.
- Log book entries with no defects.
- Security violations.
- Compliance to schedules
- Accuracy of estimates.

19. PROGRAM MANAGEMENT

- Liaison with customers.
- Financial.
- Quality of proposals (technical approach, cost, time).
- Soundness of project plans.
- Coordination of support activities.
- Satisfactory field sell-off.
- Backlog.
- New business volume versus budgeted.

20. PUBLICATIONS
   - Compliance to specifications.
   - Errors corrected.
   - Thoroughness of coverage.
   - Usefulness of materials.
   - Quality of production.

21. PURCHASING
   - Purchase order changed due to error.
   - Late receipt of materials.
   - Rejections due to incomplete descriptions.

22. QUALITY CONTROL
   - Inspection errors.
   - Sampling program errors.
   - Timeliness of inspection reports.
   - Adequacy of vendor quality ratings.
   - Returned goods and field rework due to inspection oversight; customer rejects.
   - Quality assurance audits.
   - Inspection documentation.
   - Customer liaison.

23. RESEARCH AND DEVELOPMENT
   - Can it be applied?
   - Can it be developed?
   - Can it be manufactured?
   - Can it be marketed?

24. SECURITY
   - Personnel security clearance errors.
   - Timely and accurate processing.
   - External classified visit authorization errors.
   - Accurate processing of visitor identification.
   - Effectiveness of security program.
   - Guards, security checks, badges, passes.
   - Records accuracy.
   - Fire watch.

25. SERVICES: GENERAL
- Promptness in reply to requests.
- Quality of services rendered.
- Blueprint and drawing control, reproduction, distribution.
- Test equipment maintenance and calibration
- TRW communication.
- Reproduction facilities.

26. SUPERVISION

A supervisor's performance is measured by the overall effectiveness of his or her department; in other words, the supervisor is judged by the sum total of accomplishments of the people working for him or her. The worth of individual or group achievements should be evaluated against the following criteria:

- Impact of potential error (abort of mission, cost effect on schedules, etc.).
- Contributions of the individual or group to the prevention of error.
- Difficulty of the job and level of skill required.
- Work schedules and load impact on error potential.
- Ability of individuals to correct their own errors.
- Attitude of the individual toward work, project, or command mission.

HU Diagrams

HU Diagrams: A New Way to Tear Down the Walls of the Box

By

H. James Harrington,
CEO, Harrington Institute and 20/20 Innovation

Dr. Ron Fulbright
Chair, Department of Informatics, University of South Carolina
Upstate

and

Alla Zusman
Ideation, Inc.

Abstract

HU diagrams (harmful/useful diagrams) offer a new approach to defining how to correct problems and improve designs related to product and process. The HU approach also focuses on risk management to ensure the solution has minimized the potential risks related to the solution. Sometimes HU diagrams are called contradiction diagrams. They get better results than the old brainstorming approach.

HU Diagrams

To date, the tools used by performance improvement professionals have been mostly directed at process analysis tools, such as Ask Why Five Times. These tools have mostly been directed at defining and identifying root causes of problems. Now, at last, we have a problem-correcting tool called *HU diagrams* (harmful/useful diagrams), which are sometimes called *contradiction diagrams*. The HU approach is designed to guide the user to an effective resolution of a problem. It is a graphic presentation of the positive (useful) and negative (harmful) effects that are related to a situation, problem, or process. It is based upon Newton's Third Law: the force of two bodies on each other is always equal and directed in opposite direction, or to every action there is always an equal and opposite reaction.

HU diagrams are used to solve problems, to evaluate potential situations, and to evolve products and processes to a higher level of performance. This approach is designed to stimulate an individual or team into looking at a situation from a different point of view, helping them to come up with "out of the box" solutions. The team that might be assigned for this project is often referred to as a Performance Improvement Team (PIT). This is a group of people assigned to analyze and design an innovative solution to an assigned problem, situation, or product. It is typically a group of 6 to 10 people often from different functions. They may be assigned full or part-time to the project.

In today's environment we need to do more than just think outside of the box. We need to tear down all the walls of the many boxes that we compartmentalize ourselves in. See Figure H.1.

HU diagrams are designed around the concept that all systems have positive aspects (useful functions), and all systems have negative aspects (harmful functions). A function is defined as capturing some aspect of a system including function, activity, state, process, condition, and transformation. See Figure H.2.

HU diagrams only use two symbols: harmful functions (negative/undesirable features) and useful functions (positive/desirable features). The harmful functions in an HU diagram are represented by a rectangle with rounded corners. The useful functions are represented by a rectangle with sharp edges. Often, to make the two differences stand out, the background is a different color for each of the two types of

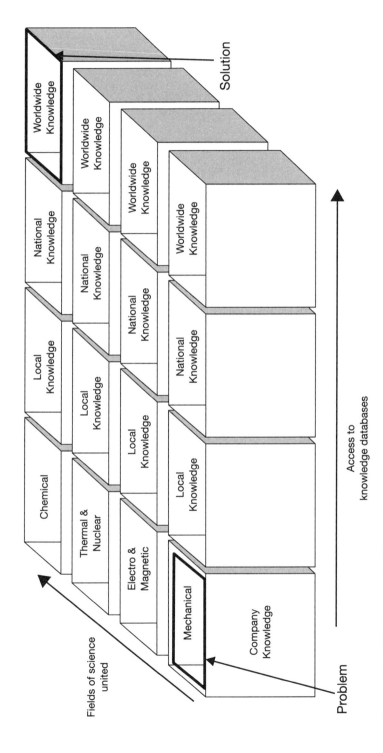

Figure H.1 The boxes we build around ourselves

Useful and Harmful Functions

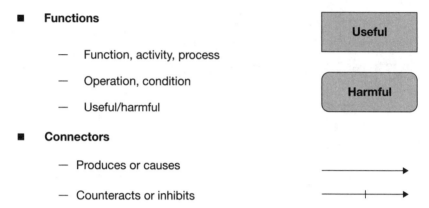

- **Functions**

  - — Function, activity, process

  - — Operation, condition

  - — Useful/harmful

- **Connectors**

  - — Produces or causes

  - — Counteracts or inhibits

Figure H.2 Useful and harmful symbols and the two types of connectors

functions. The arrows that connect them can be designated as one of two relationships as shown in Figure H.2.

The arrow from one symbol to the other symbol indicates that the first symbol established the relationship to the other symbol. The arrow without a vertical line through it indicates that the first symbol produced the other symbol or caused it to exist. The arrow with the vertical line through it indicates that the first symbol counteracts or inhibits the second symbol. Sometimes a useful function can cause another function that is desirable to occur. However, sometimes a useful function has undesirable side effects and causes something harmful to happen. On the other hand, a harmful function can cause a harmful function to occur, or it could cause a useful function to occur. See Figure H.3. An HU diagram is essentially a collection of cause-and-effect relationships describing various situations.

Contradictions

> **Definition:** A *contradiction* occurs when something useful has undesirable side effects and causes something harmful to happen. The term can also apply when something harmful has desirable side effects and causes something useful to happen.

The Useful-Harmful Interfaces

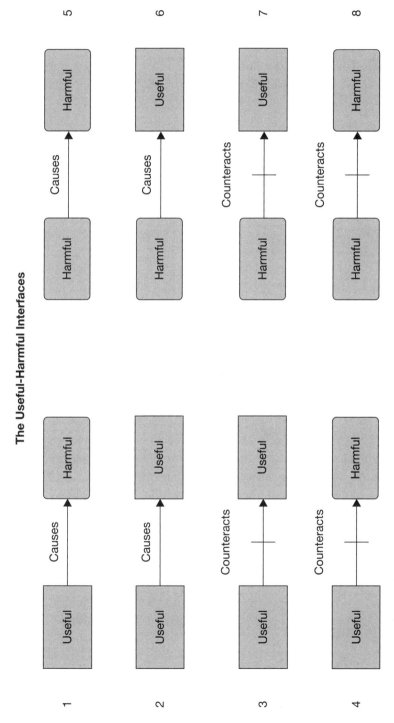

Figure H.3 The two functions can be related in eight different ways

Contradictions are the undesirable situations that fall into four categories. Relationships 1, 3, 6, and 7 in Figure H.3 are all contradictions, as they are two opposite functions connected together. Still, when two opposite functions are connected, they are not necessarily contradictions. Whether a relationship is a contradiction also depends on the time of the connector.

There are three types of contradictions:

- Type 1 is the contradiction that arises when a function produces a similar function but also produces an opposite function. For example, a useful function produces another useful function (desirable) but also produces a harmful function (undesirable). See Figure H.4.
- Type 2 is the contradiction that occurs when a function counteracts an opposite function but also produces another opposite function. For example, a useful function counteracts a harmful function (desirable) but produces a harmful function (undesirable). See Figure H.5.
- Type 3 is the contradiction that results when a function counteracts an opposite function but also counteracts a similar function. For example, a useful function counteracts a harmful function (desirable) but also counteracts another useful function (undesirable). See Figure H.5.

A process without contradictions would be the ideal process, but in reality, there is no such thing as a completely ideal process.

All processes have at least one contradiction. In fact, the reason for analyzing a process is to maximize the useful elements and minimize the harmful elements—in other words, to maximize the real-value-added content while minimizing the non-value-added content of the process.

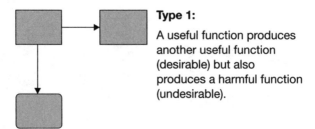

Type 1:

A useful function produces another useful function (desirable) but also produces a harmful function (undesirable).

Figure H.4 A useful function that produces another useful function and a harmful function (Type 1 relationship)

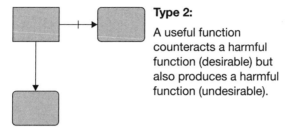

Type 2:

A useful function counteracts a harmful function (desirable) but also produces a harmful function (undesirable).

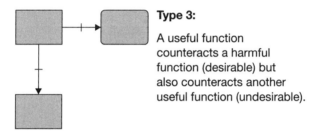

Type 3:

A useful function counteracts a harmful function (desirable) but also counteracts another useful function (undesirable).

Figure H.5 Example of useful functions that produce Type 2 and Type 3 relationships

Basically there are four ways to resolve contradictions:

- *Separation in space.* Find a space in which the harmful function doesn't occur.
- *Separation in time.* Perform the useful function at a time when the harmful effect doesn't occur.
- *Separation in structure.* Find a structural level at which the harmful function doesn't occur.
- *Separate in condition.* Find a condition under which the harmful function doesn't occur.

Let's look at one of the four options—separation in time. If you were to focus on separation in time, the following things should be considered:

- Separating opposite requirements in time
- Taking preliminary action
- Taking partial preliminary action

- Doing preliminary placement of an object
- Creating and using pauses
- Implementing staggered processing
- Dynamization
- Using post-processing time
- Concentrating energy
- Predestruction
- Reducing strength
- Preliminary stress
- Polysystem with shifted characteristics
- Decreasing stability
- Transitioning from stationary to mobile
- Dividing into mobile parts
- Applying physical effects
- Adding a mobile object
- Using interchangeable objects
- Using elements with dynamic features
- Using adjustable elements and links

To get a better understanding of the harmful and useful functions, let's consider a lawn mower. The primary function would be to cut grass, which is a useful function. To move that one step lower, think about what are the primary functions that allow it to cut grass. These would include blade rotates, blade has sharp edges, mower has wheels, etc. Each of these is a useful function. For each of these useful functions, we can expand by saying what causes a useful function to operate. For example, blade rotates as a result of an engine that turns the shaft; wheels move based upon a person pushing the lawn mower—each of these is a useful function, and each enlarges on the previous useful function. Continuing with this line of reasoning, what causes the engine to turn? What resources or raw materials are needed? In this case, internal combustion, gasoline, a gas tank, air, air intake, electric spark, spark plugs—each of these is a useful function or factor.

Now let's change our stream of thought to some of the negative things, for example:

- Turning blades throw objects.
- Turning blades cut feet and hands.

- Toxic exhaust is produced.
- Engine gives off heat.
- Gasoline costs money.
- Clippings clog motor.
- Motor produces noise.
- Pushing is tiring.

Each of these candidates is a harmful function. When you identify a function, ask yourself if there is any side effect or by-product. For example, the internal combustion side effects are heat, motion, component wear, noise, exhaust, etc. Whenever you identify a harmful function, ask yourself what caused it or what else has to function for it to happen. For example, for internal combustion you need:

- Air
- Kill switch closed
- Spark plugs
- Electricity

All of these could be useful or harmful functions depending on the situation. When you identify a function, ask yourself what inhibits this from happening. For example, for internal combustion we have:

- The ignition switch
- Dirt in gas
- Broken wire
- Water in air
- Clogged blade

We will now look at a problem related to an airplane's jet engine containment ring.

Figure H.6 is a simple HU diagram of a problem with the fan in a jet engine breaking and causing damage to the airplane. The fan rotates at high speeds (center useful symbol) causing a large quantity of air to move through the engine (useful symbol to the left of center). This is a useful function, as it causes the plane to move. The fan rotating at high speeds causes two detrimental or harmful things to occur—the centrifugal force applies high pressure to the impellers (blades) on the fan, and this high pressure can cause the impellers to burst. The particles

Jet Engine Fan Problem

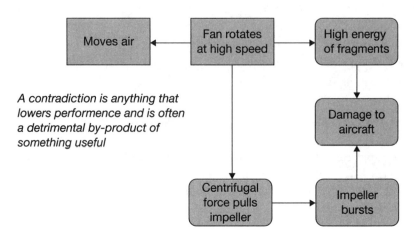

Figure H.6   Starting-point HU diagram of the jet engine problem

from the impellers can damage the airplane. At the same time, the high-speed rotation of the fan gives high energy to the fragments that are flying, which can cause damage to the airplane.

Figure H.7 is a more complete HU diagram of the problem of the fan in a jet engine breaking and causing damage to the plane. There are two boxes related to contradictions—fan rotates at high speed and ring is thick. In general, each box in the figure represents an opportunity to address the problem situation. The four circled areas in Figure H.8 indicate the areas that must be addressed first to offset the harmful parts of the diagram and bring into better balance the ratio of harmful and useful functions.

Definition: An *operator* is a little nugget of wisdom (recommendation, suggestion) that may be used to change the system design. Operators trigger you into thinking how to solve the problem or to improve the process under evaluation. Operators are drawn from successful results of previous action that resolve different technology problems and process problems. To date, approximately 1,000 operator principles have been defined. It is our experience that between 200 and 500 of these principles are all that are really needed to solve most problems a PIT will encounter.

The Containment Ring Model

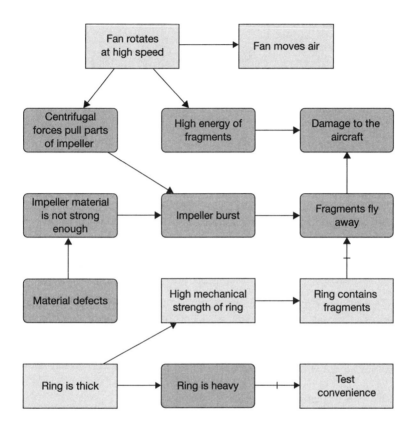

Figure H.7   Detailed HU diagram of a jet engine fan problem

The circled area that includes the useful symbol labeled "Test con-venience" and the harmful symbol labeled "Ring is heavy" is an area that presents improvement opportunities to reduce the weight of the containment ring. In this case, the PIT will use an operating principle called *uniformity*—changing an object's structure from uniform to nonuniform or changing an external environment (or external influ-ence) from uniform to nonuniform. Using this operator as a starting point, the PIT will adapt it to the conditions set up in the circled area. A typical idea that could come from this analysis would be to change the ring thickness (kind of like a two-liter soft drink bottle) over its

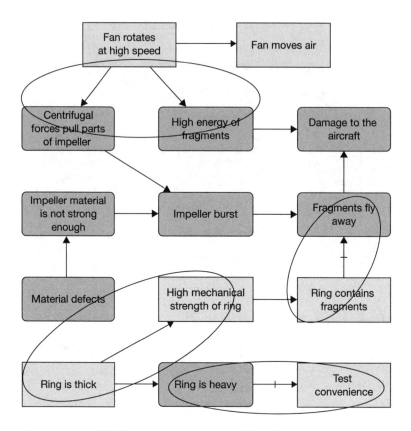

Figure H.8 HU diagram with four areas identified

length and over its width, making the ring denser and closer in to the blades and directly in line with the blades' motion but less dense everywhere else.

Another operator principle that could be applied is asymmetry—changing the shape of an object from symmetrical to asymmetrical. This leads the PIT to suggest that the side of the ring closest to the body of the airplane could be thicker to give maximum protection. There would be less damage if the fragments hit the side away from the body of the plane.

The circled area that includes the useful symbol labeled "Ring contains fragments" and the harmful symbol labeled "Fragments fly away" presents another opportunity for improvement. In this case the PIT will use an operating principle called *porous material*—making an object porous or adding porous elements (inserting insert, coatings, etc.). Using this principle, the PIT could suggest that a honeycomb structure would be more effective. The sharp edges of the structure would act like knives to shred the fragments.

The circled area that includes the harmful symbol labeled "High energy of fragments" and the harmful symbol labeled "Centrifugal forces pull parts of impeller" also presents an opportunity for improvement. In this case, the PIT will focus on reducing the energy of the fragments. To accomplish this, the PIT will use two operating principles—(1) making an object porous or adding porous elements (inserts, coatings, etc.) and composite materials and (2) changing from uniform to a nonuniform composite (multiple) materials. Based upon the use of the concepts in these two operators, the PIT could suggest using multiple lightweight rings. The first ring is thin and stiff but porous. This will shred the blade fragments but doesn't stop them. The second ring is made from carbon fiber, which is strong and lightweight and stops the fragments.

There is a fourth opportunity available even though it includes two useful symbols. It is the circled area that includes the symbol labeled "Ring is thick" and the useful symbol labeled "High mechanical strength of ring." In this case, the PIT could use an operating principle called *nested doll*—in which one object is placed inside another. Using this principle the PIT requires that object, in turn, is placed inside the other. By applying this operator to the situation, the PIT could come up with an idea of using two containment rings, one inside the other. The inside ring could be thicker than the outside one, but put together it will be lighter than one big ring.

The example we used was a design solution, but HU diagrams work equally well for process solutions. Figure H.9 is an HU diagram of the impact of change on an organization. Figure H.10 is an HU diagram of a mass-market problem highlighting two areas where additional actions need to be taken to offset the harmful effects.

Figure H.11 shows how a more in-depth study can be taken related to each of the two target areas using additional submaps of the HU diagram.

Figure H.12 is a typical HU diagram generated by a computer program along with the comments related to key elements on the diagram.

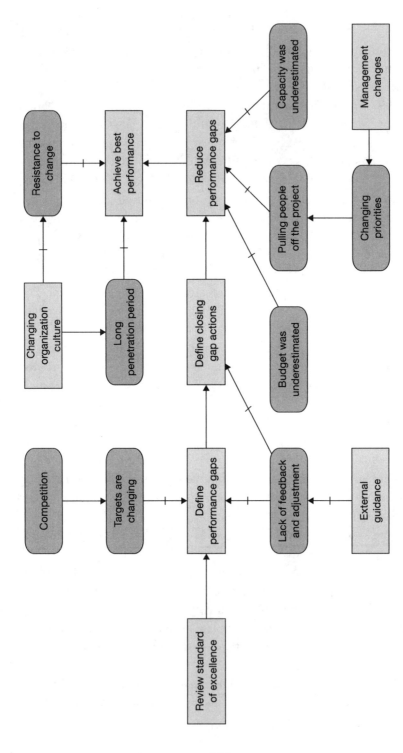

Figure H.9 HU diagram of the impact of change

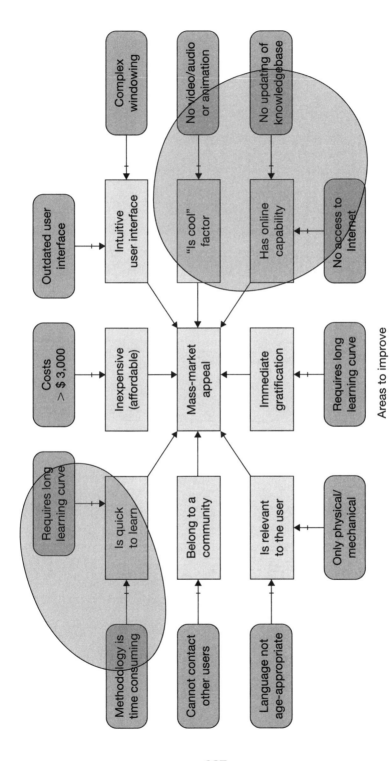

Complex windowing

No video/audio or animation

No updating of knowledgebase

Outdated user interface → Intuitive user interface

"Is cool" factor

Has online capability

No access to Internet

Costs > $ 3,000 → Inexpensive (affordable)

Mass-market appeal

Immediate gratification ← Requires long learning curve

Requires long learning curve → Is quick to learn

Methodology is time consuming

Belong to a community

Cannot contact other users

Is relevant to the user ← Only physical/mechanical

Language not age-appropriate

Areas to improve

Figure H.10 HU diagram of mass-market problem

387

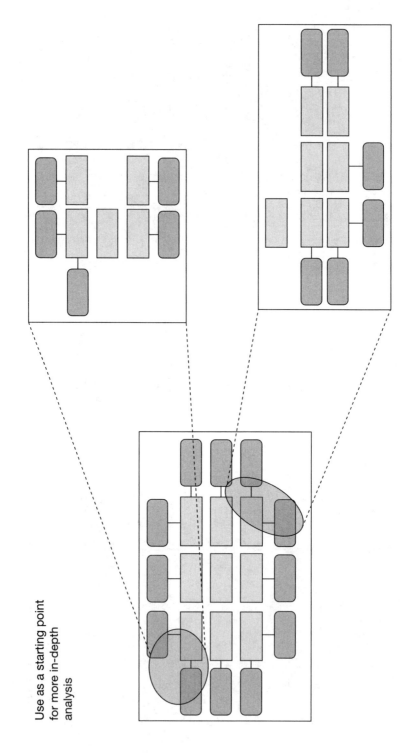

Use as a starting point
for more in-depth
analysis

Figure H.11 HU diagram of mass-market problem

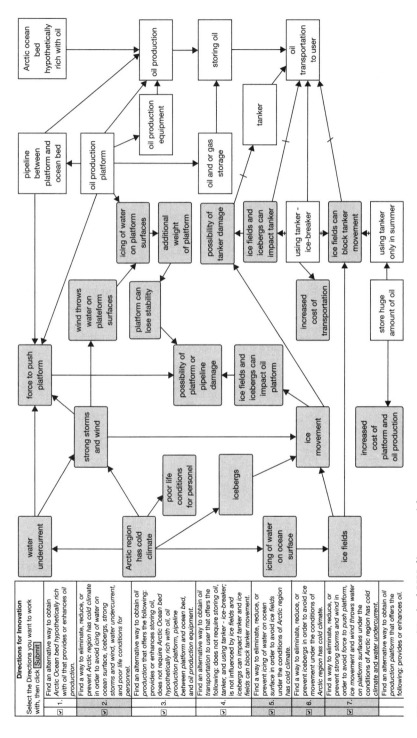

Figure H.12 Typical HU diagram with comments

Summary

We have found HU diagrams very effective in helping PITs generate highly innovative solutions, in particular when the diagrams are combined with a knowledge-based system like I-TRIZ. The I-TRIZ system contains a world of experience gleaned from problems that have been solved in the past and whose approaches continuously repeat themselves in being useful in solving future problems. It is an effective approach for defining the operator that relates to the problem the PIT is addressing, with practical examples of how to use each of the operators.

I-TRIZ or Operating System for Innovation is a software-supported system sold by 20–20 Innovation and Ideation Inc. It is made up of four software-supported packages. See Figure H.13.

I-TRIZ packages use HU diagrams as their analysis tool. It will construct the HU diagram using its computer program. We suggest that you start with the Inventive Problem Solving software package, although the Directed Evolution software package is a better but more complex methodology. Once the future-state solution is defined, we suggest you use the Failure Prediction software package to define the major risks related to the new process.

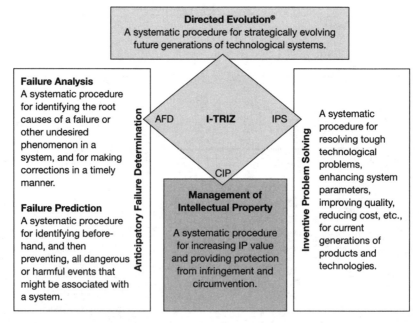

Figure H.13   The four software packages that make up I-TRIZ

References

Bittner, Kurt, and Ian Spence (2002), *Use Case Modeling,* Addison Wesley Professional, pp. 2–3.

California Manufacturing Technology Consulting (2010), "Aerospace & Defense Case Study: Ceradyne, Inc.," http://www.cmtc.com/success_stories/ad_ci.html, accessed February 2010.

CFO Magazine (1996, November), vol. 2, no. 11, pp. 28–52.

The Conference Board (2008, November), Department of Labor, Equilar, *Chief Executive Magazine,* p. 20.

Dusharme, Dirk (2006, March), "Federal Agency Requires Health Quality Reporting," *Quality Digest.*

Feigenbaum, A. V. (1991), *Total Quality Control,* 3rd ed. rev. (Fortieth Anniversary Edition), New York: McGraw-Hill.

Ford, Henry (1930), *Moving Forward,* Garden City, NY: Doubleday, Doran & Company.

Ford, Henry (1922), *My Life and Work,* Garden City, NY: Garden City Publishing Co.

Ford, Henry (1926), *Today and Tomorrow,* Garden City, NY: Doubleday, Page & Company.

Fran, David (1974), *Value-Analysis: A Way to Better Products and Profits,* New York: AMACOM.

Gilbreth, F. B. (1911), *Motion Study: A Method for Increasing the Efficiency of Workmen,* New York: Van Nostrand.

Goldratt, Elyahu M. (1993), *The Goal: A Process of Ongoing Improvement,* New York: Gower.

Hammer, Michael, and James Champy (2003), *Reengineering the Corporation*, New York: Harper Business.

Harrington, H. James (1987), *Poor-Quality Cost*, New York: Marcel Dekker.

Harrington, H. J. (1991), *Business Process Improvement*, New York: McGraw-Hill.

Harrington, H. James (1996), *The Complete Benchmarking Implementation Guide: Total Benchmarking Management*, New York: McGraw-Hill.

Harrington, H. James (1995), *Total Improvement Management*, New York: McGraw-Hill.

Harrington, H. James (2006), *Change Management Excellence: The Art of Excelling in Change Management*, Chico, CA: Paton Press.

Harrington, H. J., Erik K. C. Esseling, and Harm Van Nimwegen (1997), *Business Process Improvement Workbook: Documentation, Analysis, Design, and Management of Business Process Improvement*, New York: McGraw-Hill.

Harrington, H. James, and James S. Harrington (1996), *High Performance Benchmarking: 20 Steps to Success*, New York: McGraw-Hill.

Harrington, H. James, Glen D. Hoffherr, and Robert P. Reid, Jr. (1998), *Area Activity Analysis*, New York: McGraw-Hill.

Harrington, H. James, and Kerim Tumay (1999), *Simulation Modeling Methods to Reduce Risks and Increase Performance*, New York: McGraw-Hill.

Henkoff, Ronald (1991, February 25), "Making Your Office More Productive," *Fortune* magazine, p. 123.

Hiroyuki, Hirano (1990), *5 Pillars of the Visual Workplace: The Sourcebook for 5S Implementation*, Tokyo: JIT Management Laboratory Company.

Mahoney, David (1988), *Confessions of a Street-Smart Manager*, New York: Simon & Schuster, p. 156.

Mansar, S. Liman, and H. A. Reijers (2007), "Best Practices in Business Process Redesign: Use and Impact," *Business Process Management Journal*, vol. 13, no. 2, pp. 193–213.

Neubauer, Thomas (2009), "An Empirical Study about the Status of Business Process Management," *Business Process Management Journal*, vol. 15, no. 2, pp 166–183.

O'Hara, Margaret T., Richard T. Watson, and C. Bruce Kavan (1999), "Managing the Three Levels of Change," *IS Management*, vol. 16, no. 3, pp. 63–70.

Olson, Tim, and John C. Kelly (2005, May), "Developing Best in Class Processes at NASA," *Quality Progress*, pp. 58–65.

Rosander, A. C. (1985), *Applications of Quality Control in the Service Industry*, Orlando, FL: CRC Press.

Southwest Research Institute (2010, February), "Lean Manufacturing," www.swri.org/4org/d10/autoeng/leanmanu/stories.htm, accessed February 24, 2010; www.ggmachinewi.com/improvement.html entitled "Continuous Improvement Journey," accessed February 24, 2010.

St. Louis Community College Center for Business, Industry & Labor (2011, January 10), "5S System Success Stories," www.cbil.org/lean_enterprise_success.htm, accessed February 24, 2010.

The System Company (1911), *How Scientific Management Is Applied*, London: A. W. Shaw Company, p. 77.

Tennant, Charles, and Yi-Chieh Wu (2005), "The Application of Business Process Reengineering in the UK," *The TQM Magazine*, no. 17, pp. 537–545.

Tomasko, Robert M. (1993, June), "Intelligent Resizing: View from the Bottom Up (Part 2)," *Management Review*, p. 18.

Uno, Gordon (1999), *Handbook on Teaching Undergraduate Science Courses: A Survival Training Manual*, Philadelphia: Saunders College Publishing.

Wikipedia (2011), "Value Proposition," en.wikipedia.org/wiki/Value_proposition, accessed May 13, 2010.

Bibliography

Bridges, William (2003), *Managing Transitions*, New York: Perseus Book Group.

Feigenbaum, A. V. (1991), *Total Quality Control*, 3rd ed. rev. (Fortieth Anniversary Edition), New York: McGraw-Hill.

Goldratt, Elyahu M. (1993), *The Goal: A Process of Ongoing Improvement*, New York: Gower.

Hammer, Michael, and James Champy (2003), *Reengineering the Corporation*, New York: Harper Business.

Harrington, H. James (1987), *Poor-Quality Cost*, New York: Marcel Dekker.

Harrington, H. James (1995), *Total Improvement Management*, New York: McGraw-Hill.

Harrington, H. James (1996), *The Complete Benchmarking Implementation Guide: Total Benchmarking Management*, New York: McGraw-Hill.

Harrington, H. James (1996), *The Complete Benchmarking Workbook*, New York: McGraw-Hill.

Harrington, H. James, E. K. Esseling, and H. Van Nimwegen (1997), *Business Process Improvement Workbook: Documentation, Analysis, Design, and Management of Business Process Improvement*, New York: McGraw-Hill.

Harrington, H. James, and James S. Harrington (1996), *High Performance Benchmarking: 20 Steps to Success*, New York: McGraw-Hill.

Harrington, H. James, Glen D. Hoffherr, and Robert P. Reid, Jr. (1998), *Area Activity Analysis*, New York: McGraw-Hill.

Harrington, H. James, and Kerim Tumay (1999), *Simulation Modeling Methods to Reduce Risks and Increase Performance*, New York: McGraw-Hill.

Mahoney, David (1988), *Confessions of a Street-Smart Manager*, New York: Simon & Schuster.

Rosander, A. C. (1985), *Applications of Quality Control in the Service Industry*, Orlando, FL: CRC Press.

Index

About the Author

 Dr. H. James Harrington is one of the world's quality system gurus with more than 60 years of experience. He has been involved in developing quality management systems in Europe, South America, North America, the Middle East, Africa, and Asia. It has been said about him, "He writes the books that other consultants use."

In the book *Tech Trending*, Dr. Harrington was referred to as "the quintessential tech trender." The *New York Times* referred to him as having a "knack for synthesis and an open mind about packaging his knowledge and experience in new ways—characteristics that may matter more as prerequisites for new-economy success than technical wizardry …"

The author Tom Peters stated, "I fervently hope that Harrington's readers will not only benefit from the thoroughness of his effort but will also 'smell' the fundamental nature of the challenge for change that he mounts."

William Clinton, past president of the United States., appointed Dr. Harrington to serve as an Ambassador of Good Will.

The leading Japanese author on quality, Professor Yoshio Kondo, stated: "Business Process Improvement (methodology) investigated and established by Dr. H. James Harrington and his group is some of the new strategies which bring revolutionary improvement not only in quality of products and services, but also in the business processes which yield the excellent quality of the output."

The father of "Total Quality Control," Dr. Armand V. Feigenbaum stated: "Harrington is one of those very rare business leaders who combines outstanding inherent ability, effective management skills, broad technology background and great effectiveness in producing results. His record of accomplishment is a very long, broad and deep one that is highly and favorably recognized."

He was featured in the TV program "Heartbeat of America." The host, William Shatner, stated: "You [Dr. Harrington] manage an entrepreneurial company that moves America forward. You are obviously successful."

Present Responsibilities

Dr. H. James Harrington now serves as the chief executive officer for the Harrington Institute. He also serves as the chairman of the board for a number of businesses and as the U.S. Chairman of Technologies for Project Management at the University of Quebec in Montreal. Dr. Harrington is recognized as one of the world leaders in applying performance improvement methodologies to business processes.

Previous Experience

In February 2002 Dr. Harrington retired as the COO of Systemcorp A.L.G., the leading supplier of knowledge management and project management software solutions. Prior to this, he served as a principal and one of the leaders in the Process Innovation Group at Ernst & Young. Dr. Harrington was with IBM for 40 years as a senior engineer and project manager.

Dr. Harrington is past chairman and past president of the prestigious International Academy for Quality and of the American Society for Quality. He is also an active member of the Global Knowledge Economics Council.

Credentials

The Harrington/Ishikawa Medal presented yearly by the Asian-Pacific Quality Organization was named after Dr. Harrington to recognize his many contributions to the region. In 1997, the Quebec Society for Qualite named its Quality Award "The Harrington/Neron Medal," honoring Dr. Harrington for his many contributions to the Quality Movement in Canada. In 2000 the Sri Lanka national quality award was named after him. The Middle East and Europe Best Quality Thesis Award was named "The Harrington Best TQM Thesis Award." The University of Sudan has established a "Harrington Excellence Chair" to study methodologies to improve organizational performance. The Chinese government presented him with the Magnolia Award for his major contribution to improving the quality of Chinese products. In 2006 Dr. Harrington accepted the honorary chairman position of Quality Technology Park of Iran. In 2008 Dr. Harrington was awarded the Sheikh Khalifa Excellence Award (UAE) in recognition of his superior performance as an original Quality and Excellence Guru who helped shape modern quality thinking. In 2009 Harrington was selected as the Professional of the Year (2009). Also in 2009 he received the Hamdan Bin Mohammed e-University Medal. In 2010 the Asian Pacific Quality Organization (APQO) awarded Harrington the APQO President's Award for his "exemplary leadership." The Australian Organization of Quality NSW's Board recognized Harrington as the "Global Leader in Performance Improvement Initiatives" in 2010.

Dr. Harrington's contributions to performance improvement around the world have brought him many honors and awards, including the Edwards Medal, the Lancaster Medal, ASQ's Distinguished Service Medal, and many others. He was appointed the honorary advisor to the China Quality Control Association, and he was elected to the Singapore Productivity Hall of Fame in 1990. He has been named lifetime honorary president of the Asia Pacific Quality Organization and honorary director of the Asociacion Chilena de Control de Calidad.

Dr. Harrington has been elected a fellow of the British Quality Control Organization and the American Society for Quality Control. He was also elected an honorary member of the quality societies in Taiwan, Argentina, Brazil, Colombia, and Singapore. He is also listed in *Who's Who Worldwide* and *Men of Distinction Worldwide."* He has presented hundreds of papers on performance improvement and organizational management structure at the local, state, national, and international levels.

Dr. Harrington is a very prolific author, publishing hundreds of technical reports and magazine articles. He has authored 35 books and 10 software packages. His e-mail address is hjh@harrington-institute.com.